Tennessee Whitetails

Jay T. Langston

Stoeger Publishing Company, Accokeek, Maryland

Stoeger Publishing.
Great Outdoor Books & More Since 1924

STOEGER PUBLISHING COMPANY
is a division of Benelli U.S.A.

BENELLI U.S.A.
Vice President and General Manager:
Stephen Otway
Vice President of Marketing and Communications:
Stephen McKelvain

STOEGER PUBLISHING COMPANY
President: Jeffrey Reh
Publisher: Jay Langston
Managing Editor: Harris J. Andrews
Design & Production Director:
Cynthia T. Richardson
Photography Director: Alex Bowers
Imaging Specialist: William Graves
National Sales Manager: Jennifer Thomas
Special Accounts Manager: Julie Brownlee
Publishing Assistant: Christine Lawton
Administrative Assistant: Shannon McWilliams

Published by Stoeger Publishing Company
17603 Indian Head Highway, Suite 200
Accokeek, Maryland 20607

BK0424
ISBN: 0-88317-306-9
Library of Congress Control Number:
2004104796

Manufactured in
the United States of America.

Distributed to the book trade and
to the sporting goods trade by:
Stoeger Industries
17603 Indian Head Highway, Suite 200
Accokeek, Maryland 20607
301-283-6300 Fax: 301-283-6986
www.stoegerindustries.com

Contents

Acknowledgement

This book would not have been possible without the dedication of a few hard working Tennesseans. Tennessee Wildlife Resources Agency biologists like Joe Farrar, Jack Murrey, Larry Markham, Greg Wathen and many others spent countless hours trapping deer from lonely, out-of-the-way places and then trucking them to their new habitats. The backbreaking, dangerous work involved in catching and releasing large wild animals has to be experienced to be truly appreciated. Others, including TWRA game wardens who protected our growing resources and the county judges who enforced game laws, are owed a debt of gratitude as well. Every deer hunter in Tennessee today owes every hour they spend in the woods to these men.

An extra thank you goes to Larry Markham, now TWRA's chief of game, for the tremendous amount of time he spent compiling historical data about the Volunteer State's deer restoration program.

Foreword

I am not, nor have I ever been, a resident of the "Volunteer State," but when it comes to deer hunting I am a real Tennessee fan. Back in the 1950s as a teenager living in Alabama my dream hunt was to go hunt whitetails in the mountains near Tellico Plains, Tennessee. In those days Alabama had few deer and the mountains of East Tennessee were the subjects of many hunting articles in outdoor magazines. Thanks to an older friend I made many hunts to the Tellico Plains and Ocoee Wildlife Management Areas. They were grand hunts that helped me decide to make a career of wildlife management and writing.

Since those early days I, along with hundreds of other hunters, have enjoyed hunting the deer woods of Tennessee, from its high mountains in the east, through the rolling hills of its mid section, to the delta swamps to the west. It is truly a great state for deer hunting and the source of many stories about white-tailed deer management and the resulting big bucks.

Now these stories have been carefully crafted into a book that is both fun to read and accurately compiled. You are lucky; you hold this book in your hand. Whether your interest is in Tennessee as a future state in which to hunt a trophy buck, the history of deer management in the "Volunteer State" or just enjoyable reading about big bucks that have been taken in the state, well known author Jay Langston brings it all to you.

Jay has the advantage of being a native son and has a lifetime of experiencing and researching the history of whitetails in his home state. Having had the opportunity of seeing many mornings come alive on some wooded ridge with Jay, I know his ability to read the woods and his passion for the lore of the white-tailed deer. Also, having had Jay as my boss as the editor for a magazine for which I wrote, and as the publisher of several of my books, I know his professional goals of accurate research and good writing. He is the writer's writer. You will see, and enjoy, this in this book.

So get a fresh cup of coffee and settle into your favorite chair, for you are about to enter into the world of the white-tailed deer in the great state of Tennessee. Due to Jay's talent as a researcher and writer you are going to enjoy the trip. If you are a native of Tennessee you will come away planning for next season's opening morning and if you, like me, are a non-resident you will be thinking about Tennessee as a future destination. This book is a must for any whitetail hunter's library.

—J. Wayne Fears
Editor, *Progressive Farmer/Rural Sportsman*

Introduction

A hard day's drive was nearing its conclusion as I wound along the last few miles of western Kentucky's Highway 91 in Crittenden County. Cresting the Ohio River bluff, I could see the Cave In Rock ferry lights as it churned its way toward the east bank. After boarding the ferry for its last ride of the evening, I parked and walked to the rail to watch the dying day's last light, fading from burnt orange to shades of purple and blue. The familiar smell of diesel fumes and roar of the tugboat's big engines took me back 25 years to a time before the interstate highways crossed northwest from Nashville to Southern Illinois.

My thoughts shifted from those of a 4-year-old lad held up in his father's arms to see over the rail, to those surrounding the focal point of the trip—a November hunt for whitetails on our family's farm tucked in the midst of the Shawnee National Forest.

As I stared into the churning, coffee colored water, I pondered the day's travel: It started as a rush-hour struggle to escape Atlanta's hellish traffic. When I passed through Chattanooga and crested Monteagle, I began to relax, seeing familiar sites, and feeling welcomed back to my adopted home state. Stopping in Nashville for lunch, I munched on a Wendy's hamburger and wondered if the Dairy Queen was still in business on Broadway. The noon-time fare paled in comparison to Dairy Queen's little 11¢ burgers I devoured as a small child.

Crossing the Kentucky state line, my Chevy truck began running hot, so I limped it into Cadiz and seized the opportunity to visit with Harold Knight and David Hale while my truck's thermostat was replaced. David scurried about, working on his latest project while Harold and I kicked back and swapped a few deer hunting stories.

The trance was broken when the tug's deckhand began banging his mooring chains on the west-bank landing dock. The day's trip would have been quicker if I had stuck to the interstate highways, but that wasn't my intention. Traveling those two-lane tracks, I chose a slower, less complicated path, rekindling fond childhood memories of day's spent fishing and hunting with my father on my grandparent's farm.

Making memories is a big part of why I hunt, and later, their remembrance soothes my soul when meeting deadlines and paying the mortgage weighs heavy. I hunt deer and other game for the revival of spirit it brings. Hunting is a part of me, and I am a part of it. Killing is the logical and natural conclusion of hunting. The pursuit and killing

Author Jay Langston enjoys pursuing whitetails throughout North America, but feels most at home hunting his Henderson County farm.

of game—hunting—is a paradox. It is a dramatic portrayal of the circle of life, as it was set in motion at creation. Life begets death, which in turn begets life. The Indians that inhabited the hills and plains of Tennessee understood this simple truth.

Former Commissioner of Mental Health for the State of Tennessee, Nat T. Winston, M.D., spoke to the ideals of hunting. "It has been my observation that in 25 years of active practice I have never treated an avid hunter with a major mental illness," he said. "Possibly that is purely coincidental, but on the other hand, there may be some reasons for this. Spending one's spare time from childhood forward in the woods keeps one, particularly as a child, away from the pool halls and the 19th holes of our nation. The use of marijuana, drugs and alcohol in the field is not conducive to long life. Long hours in the field teaches one survival and a sense or responsible behavior and, paradoxically perhaps, it teaches respect for life. The implication is that those who prefer outdoor life to other activities might be less prone to severe mental illness. None the less, whether accurate or totally a statistical fluke, my observation remains. As a group, hunters are the finest folks I know. As long as we have reasonable and sane men existing on the earth we will have hunting."

I kill without shame, but at the same time feel a deep, quiet reverence mixed with joy when I take the life of a game animal. The burden of responsibility weighs heavy, but the load is a welcome one. In this time when having a "choice" is a prime concern of our society, I choose to hunt, to be an active participant in life's real drama, rather than just an observer.

To accommodate today's need for feeding a throng of people that stress the land's carrying capacity a mechanized system of mass production has been put in place that necessitates middlemen — and distances the majority from process of food procurement. Ranchers raise cattle, farmers raise wheat, truckers haul these to market, and who in unison transform the living into life-giving food. Distanced from the resource, the search for food has been reduced for most to bargain hunting at the local supermarket.

Certain religions hold forth that sexual activity is immoral — for a married couple — unless its participation is for procreation only. This man-ordained theology makes about as much sense as an animal-rights cultist screaming that all killing is wrong, and that eating meat is wrong as well. We're all free to eat the meat of animals, whether we buy it in the grocery store or go afield in its pursuit. The animal-rights cultist's stance that hunters are wrong is about as fair as saying that vegetarians are Nazis, just because Hitler was a vegetarian. God gave us the right to choose our own way, but not the right to judge.

Hunting dates back to the very beginning of man. At one time labeled the sport of kings, it has served as the provider for the poor. Hunting knows no sex, racial or cultural boundaries, and the camaraderie it fosters among like-minded folk is truly unique.

I have always been most fascinated with white-tailed deer, especially big, mature bucks. More than a decade ago I set out to write a book that celebrates the return of whitetails to Tennessee. I was motivated to begin writing after a chance meeting in the woods. I was hunting a farm in Henderson County owned by one of my teachers at Freed-Hardeman University and met a fellow hunter who had just bagged a nice 4-pointer. As luck would have it, the bearded gentleman was none other than Joe Farrar, the man who played a huge role in restoring deer to the woods we hunted. After visiting with Joe so many years ago, I enlisted his help and that of others to compile the historical data of where the Volunteer State's deer came from and where they were stocked. I was amazed to learn that many of the state's deer herd originated from far away places like Wisconsin, Michigan and South Texas, which are well known for producing large-antlered bucks.

Over the years, I have had the pleasure of visiting with hundreds of successful Tennessee deer hunters. I have been honored to meet some the state's legendary deer hunters, and from those visits I have compiled what I consider to be the Tennessee Whitetail Hall of Fame. This Hall of Fame is purely opinion and not a strict accounting of the largest bucks ever killed in the state... they're just some of my favorite stories.

Any Tennessee deer hunter who likes big bucks will be interested in the Tennessee Deer Registry, the "record book" of whitetails taken from this grand state. After studying the TDR patterns begin to form that tell where the biggest buck spent their lives. Add this information to the historical stocking data and you will see that genetics has a lot to do with why so many good bucks have come from the Volunteer State.

Along with the historical perspective, the reader will find specific information about life cycles and habits of deer in our state to help better understand these fascinating creatures. Put this information to use and it might just help you bag the buck of a lifetime next season.

Good hunting,
Jay Langston

Section I

Tennessee
Whitetail
Hall of Fame

Chapter 1

Gun Typicals

SONNY FOSTER BUCK
SCORE: 186⅛

A Tennessee deer hunting tradition has spanned five decades and four generations for William A. "Sonny" Foster's Cumberland County clan. Hunting with his father and father-in-law Allen Ables, Sonny downed his first Tennessee buck at the age of 15 in 1953, and his love for the sport has grown ever since. "Back in the '50s, the November deer season lasted less than a week," Sonny recalled. "The deer were hard to get to, and it took a four-wheel drive to get back into the places we liked to hunt." On many occasions Sonny and a half dozen or more family and friends would pile into his father-in-law's 1947 Willys Jeep and drive deep into the remote reaches of the Cumberland Plateau.

Favorite deer hunting spots for the Foster family were Chuck Swan Wildlife Management Area (WMA), known then as Central Peninsula; the Crab Orchard Mountains west of Rockwood; and Hatfield Mountain in Cumberland County.

As the November 1959 season approached, Sonny put his experiences to use and began scouting in earnest. "Before deer season each year, we'd always scout a place at least a month in advance," Sonny said in an article written by Duncan Dobie, which appeared in an October 1983 issue of North American Whitetail.

In 1959 Cumberland County native Sonny Foster killed the largest buck in Tennessee history. The buck's live weight was estimated at more than 375 pounds.

"We'd take my father-in-law's Jeep into places no one else would dare go. The buck sign was unbelievable. You'd see trees two to three inches in diameter just torn right out of the ground, and rubs on five-inch cedars were common. One time, I found a torn-up place with blood all over the ground where two large bucks had been fighting. I could tell from their tracks that they were really huge. The hills of East Tennessee grew some awfully big deer."

Without a single buck hanging from their meat pole, the deer season opener was a disappointment for the Foster clan. The next day, the weather turned bitterly cold. The temperature fell to 25 degrees. The Fosters returned to Hatfield Mountain, a secluded area just south of what is now Catoosa WMA. They had discovered the sign from several big bucks in the area and decided to spread out and form a picket line along a hardwood ridge to intercept the ridge-running bucks. "It happened pretty fast," Sonny said. "We all knew a big buck was using that ridge, so we all sort of scattered out in hopes that somebody might see him."

Just after sunrise on that frosty November morning, Sonny said, "Jackie Byrd, a friend who was hunting with us, fired three shots from his stand about a quarter mile down the ridge from me. I didn't know it then, but he had missed a huge buck. A few seconds later, this giant buck with the most unbelievable set of horns I had ever seen came running by me about 75 or 80 yards out."

It was a simple matter for him to raise his

Winchester lever-action .30-30, pick a spot behind the
11-pointer's shoulder and fire. At the shot, the buck
fell. Trying to settle his nerves, Sonny crept toward the
fallen monarch. "He was just lying there like he was
bedded down," Sonny said. "When I got fairly close to
him, he jumped up and started running. I fired two
quick shots from about 50 yards. The second shot hit
him in the neck, and he went down for good."

At that moment, Foster, now 65 and a veteran of
many seasons, earned the distinction of having killed
the largest buck in Tennessee history. The Foster buck
was a giant in all regards; its live weight was estimated
over 375 pounds, and its verified field-dressed weight
tipped the scales at 312 pounds.

Dave Murrian, a TWRA biologist and official scorer
for the Boone and Crockett Club, was called upon to
measure the enormous buck soon after it arrived at Zack
Woody's taxidermy shop in Knoxville. Sonny's buck was
judged by biologists to be 5½ years old.

The magnificent 11-point buck has a symmetrical
"basic" 10-point frame, with right and left main beams
measuring 25⅛ and 26⅝ inches, respectively. Its inside
spread spans 20⅛ inches, and its greatest width is 22⅛
inches. The rack's right and left basal circumferences
measure 4⅝ and 4⅞ inches respectively. The only
abnormal point is located on the right G-2, or first
fighting tine, and measures 3 inches. Grossing well
over 190, the Foster buck scores a net 186⅛ points on
the Boone & Crockett Club scale. It ranked among the
top 20 typicals in the world at the time it was killed. It

would be more than two decades before another Volunteer State buck would fall to a hunter's bullet that would even come close to challenging its score.

On a final note, Sonny remembers seeing several bucks that were killed during the 1950s in the remote places he hunted that would best his state record. "He wasn't anything special," Sonny recalled. "He was a good 11-pointer, but people thought more about his body size than his antlers. Most of the local hunters were used to seeing large deer come out of those mountains. In fact, that same year, a friend of mine killed a huge 10-pointer that was almost as large as my deer. To me of course, he was the largest buck I had ever killed, and I was awfully proud."

Maybe someday, one of those giant racks Foster remembers will surface, and a new state record will be realized.

BENNY JOHNSON
SCORE: 184⅝

They were the largest deer tracks Benny Johnson, of Collierville, Tennessee, had ever seen in his seven years hunting whitetails near the LaGrange community in southeast Fayette County.

"I knew a big deer was there," Johnson reminisced. "I hunted that deer from the opening day in November, but I never saw him. I always found his tracks with three or four sets of smaller tracks — probably does. I knew he was a big-bodied deer from

the size of his tracks. His rubs and scrapes were every-
where on the property I was hunting."

Stymied, Johnson decided to switch hunting locations to the edge of a small, freshly-cut soybean field
about 400 yards from where he had concentrated his
hunting activity during the first segment of the

*Viewed in profile, this magnificent 12-point white-tailed buck was killed in
December, 1979. It is the second largest buck ever taken in Tennessee*

Benny Johnson, seen here with his Boone & Crockett top-100 whitetail, found the 12-pointer's location by spotting the 200-pound-plus buck's enormous tracks.

firearms season. On Christmas Eve 1979, Johnson, then 31, spotted a small buck and two does in the field. Knowing a big buck haunted the area, Johnson held fire, hoping the owner of the a snuff-can sized tracks would step into view. His chance at the world-class buck would have to wait.

Every deer hunter's ultimate Christmas present came a day late for the West Tennessee deer hunter. Before sunrise on December 26, Johnson slipped through the thick timber surrounding the little bean field and eased into a honeysuckle thicket he would use for a blind. His wait was a short one, when at 7 a.m. the big 12-pointer stepped into the field at 60 yards. Deftly, he raised his Remington Model 742 Woodmaster semi-automatic .30-06 and found the buck's shoulder in the crosshairs of his Redfield 2x-7x scope. At the shot the monster buck jumped straight up in the air, then charged toward the opposite field edge. Quickly, Johnson fired another snap shot at the fleeing buck.

Rising from his hiding spot, Johnson slogged through the muddy bean field to the spot where the buck was standing when he shot the first time. Finding blood, he decided to wait the customary 30 minutes before beginning his search.

Following the buck's spoor was easy in the soft ground, and the good blood trail leading into the woods led Johnson another 75 yards to his prize. The 180-grain Remington Core-Loc had taken the buck through the heart, and death was quick — probably about 10 to 15 seconds, judging by the short distance the buck traveled.

"I like to never got the deer out of the woods he was so big," Johnson said. "I didn't have a three-wheeler and that bean field was real muddy." The buck was

The Scott County hills have produced their share of bragging bucks, but Charles Smith's 10-pointer was one of the best.

never actually weighed, but Johnson remarked that the checking station manager where he checked his deer estimated that the long-bodied buck would easily weigh over 200 pounds, field dressed.

Johnson didn't immediately realize he had killed the second largest buck in Tennessee history, but after driving to Jackson and having the buck's rack measured by Tommy Grimsley, a TWRA biologist and official Boone & Crockett Club scorer, he learned that his big 12-pointer was indeed special, ranking in the top 100 of the Boone & Crockett records at the time. The tale of the tape revealed that the Johnson buck had an inside spread of 17 inches, and an outside spread of 19⅞ inches. The first circumference, taken at the midpoint between the burr and the first point, measures 4⅞ inches for both the left and right beam. The right beam is 27 inches long, and the left beam measures 26⅞.

CHARLES H. SMITH
SCORE: 178⅝

Charles H. Smith killed a fine 10-point buck in late 1978, in Scott County. The buck's net score of 178⅝ was attained through sheer mass, tremendously long main beams and a wide spread. Its right beam tapes 27 inches, and the other 26⅞. Circumference measurements at the antler bases are the largest among the top Tennessee bucks listed in the Boone & Crockett records, measuring 5⅜ inches each. Its spread is also the widest, spanning 21⅛ inches inside and 23 inches outside.

JOHN J. HEIRIGS BUCK
SCORE: 173⅝ TYPICAL

When 9:30 a.m. approached on November 3, 1962, John Heirigs was ready for a break from the cold drizzle that soaked Ensley Bottoms, a lush Mississippi River hardwood bottom on the doorstep of Memphis. He had sat on a ladder stand since daylight and had only seen eight does during his vigil.

Sitting in the cab of his pickup, Heirigs and his host, Johnny Galina of Memphis, watched a brushy field through the rain-spattered windshield while munching on sandwiches. Suddenly a big whitetail rack loomed into view 400 yards across the field. Jumping from the truck, Heirigs fired four shots from his .300 Savage Model 99 lever-action, missing the buck cleanly each time. He had misjudged the range, believing the buck to be 200 yards from where he stood. He was heart sick at missing the big buck and thought, "It looked just like the elk on the Hartford Insurance ads."

Wishing for another chance at the massive whitetail, Heirigs decided to return to his stand. "I ran all the way back to my stand hoping the deer would follow the does I had seen earlier." He got into position on the ladder stand, and just 10 seconds later the buck arrived. "Out stepped the creature of my dreams, a gigantic whitetail buck, only 35 yards from my stand."

He propped his left arm on a branch of the tree supporting the stand and fired, missing the buck once again. "I couldn't believe I had missed. The deer ran to

Shelby County hunter John Heirigs poses with the record-class typical he shot in the Ensley Bottoms along the Mississippi River in 1962.

my right, so I swung around the tree and fired a second shot. When I shot I lost my balance and fell out of the stand."

Luckily, the stand was only nine feet high, and the ground was soft and muddy, cushioning the luckless hunter's fall. Picking himself up out of the mud, he was in a state of panic, fearing that he had bungled the chance at a once-in-a-lifetime trophy. Walking 15 yards to the gravel road that ran behind his stand to get a

John Heirigs' trophy collection was stolen from his Memphis office in 1989.

better look at the surrounding woods, Heirigs spied his buck lying dead 75 yards from his stand.

"I was so excited that I ran all the way to the buck," Heirigs recalled. "When I looked down at him, I couldn't believe what I saw." What lay before him was a giant 12-pointer that weighed approximately 300 pounds. Upon inspection, Heirigs found that his first shot from the stand was the lethal shot, and the second shot almost took the buck's hoof off. Later it was aged by TWRA biologists at five-and-a-half. Wanting a expert taxidermy job for his world-class whitetail, Heirigs sent his prize to Jim Gay in Laramie, Wyoming. The taxidermist was also an official Boone and Crockett scorer, and subsequently measured the buck—twice by mistake. He sent in both score sheets, with scores of 173⅝ and 173⅛, but recorded the buck as having been killed in both 1962 and 1963.

When Boone & Crockett published their record book a year later, Heirigs' buck was listed twice. Boone and Crockett finally caught the mistake, correcting it with a final score of 173⅝.

On a sad note, in 1989, Heirigs had several of his big-game trophies stolen from his office in Memphis. Among the prize possessions taken was his 12-point whitetail. Hopefully some day the criminals will be caught and his trophy returned.

Chapter 2

Gun Non-Typicals

LUTHER FULLER BUCK
SCORE 223 ⅛

*L*uther Fuller's hunt for the world-class buck that ranked as the largest non-typical in Tennessee history began in 1983. On the Friday before the November 1983 gun season closed, Luke, as his friends call him, was hunting on a private farm where Wayne Byington had killed a state-record non-typical buck scoring 207⅞ points the year before. Fuller had found sign that a large buck was using the area from the presence of tracks "the size of a cow's," and several large rubs.

As light was fading, the Kingsport hunter sat perched in a permanent stand built in the forks of a large tree. He glanced to his right and spied a nice 16-inch wide 8-pointer's head and shoulders sticking out of a thicket. Fuller decided to shoot the deer, and was preparing to shift his rifle around for a left-handed shot when the buck bolted and ran in a half circle

The palmated antlers of Luther Fuller's world-class non-typical whitetail buck tallied a B&C score of 223⅜ inches.

around him. Snapping his rifle up, the veteran of 19 deer seasons followed the buck in his scope and fired. The buck kept running and Luke fired twice more before it went out of sight. With three mortal wounds the buck soon crashed in a nearby thicket.

Looking back to his right, Fuller caught a glimpse of a huge buck running straight away. "I got enough of a look at him to tell that he was twice the size in body and antlers of the buck I had just shot," Luther said.

He came back and hunted for the buck during the last two days of the season, but the buck had limited his activities to nocturnal travel after his encounter with Fuller. Throughout the next few months Fuller spent several days scouting for the big buck.

After rifle season opened on November 21, 1984, Fuller returned to the area where he had seen a couple of old scrapes to scout for fresh rutting sign. Following a well-used deer trail that meandered through a dense thicket, the hunter spied a scrape "the size of a car hood." Soon he found another massive scrape and a huge set of deer tracks. Fuller applied some Tink's doe scent to the scrapes and immediately left the area.

The following day Fuller took his son, Luther, Jr., on a juvenile hunt in another area. Friday, November 23, Fuller returned with long-time friend Gary Rader of nearby Bluff City to the property where he had located the big buck. Taking a stand in a tree 60 yards down-wind of the buck's scrape line, Fuller awaited the frosty dawn in hopes of intercepting the mature deer as he worked his scrapes. The temperature was in the upper teens, and skies were clear with only a hint of breeze.

At 8 a.m., Fuller saw four does and a small buck moving down the trail. "Up to that day I had passed up six bucks because I was hunting that big deer," Fuller said. "I let some bucks slide that anybody else would have shot. At 8:15 I was looking down the steep incline at the area the buck would have to cross to check his scrapes, which were out of my sight."

Fuller saw a deer move through the thick brush to the right he immediately brought his gun up. "He was walking with his head down and rack back testing the wind," Fuller remembered. "I had a split second to decide if it was the buck I was after. He was moving at a fast trot, like a Tennessee walking horse."

Not having enough time to examine the buck's rack as it sped by, Fuller relied on his instincts, which told him it was the buck he was after. Finding the buck in his crosshairs, Fuller swung with the moving target until he found a two-foot wide opening and squeezed off a shot from his .270 Model 70 Featherweight Winchester bolt-action rifle. "I had the crosshairs on the top of his shoulders, and when I shot nothing happened, he didn't even flinch," he said.

The buck kept up his pace and Fuller caught a glimpse of the deer's hindquarters and sent a second 130-grain bullet on its way. The buck made two bounds and turned 90 degrees from his course of travel and faltered. The buck stopped and was facing straight away when Fuller found a small hole in the brush over the buck's exposed neck. A third shot to the spine put the buck down for good.

"After he was on the ground, I went flying down there, and when I walked up on him and saw how big his rack was, I couldn't believe it," Fuller reminisced. "I grinned and said to myself 'Son, you've done it now! This one's big enough to get mounted.' I felt very lucky. I had all happened so fast, but everything just sort of fell into place."

Fuller enlisted Rader's help and the two men worked for several hours to drag the monster buck from the woods. The huge, 30-point non-typical was taken to a local salvage yard and weighed. The scales settled at 218 pounds.

It was 3:30 p.m. when Fuller finally arrived at Wildlife Taxidermy in Kingsport, with his trophy riding in the back of his pickup truck. The studio was owned and operated by his cousin, Richard Hurd.

Luther had a running joke with his cousin about killing a buck big enough to mount. Fuller had killed several nice bucks, and each time Richard would ask if Luther would have it mounted. "When I get one wide enough I can sit down inside the spread, I'll have it mounted," Luther told his cousin. When Richard went outside to look at Fuller's prize, he asked, "Well, is this one big enough to have mounted?" "Yeah," Luther said, "I think this one in finally big enough!"

After the required 60-day drying period, Fuller took his buck to be measured by John Baker, a Virginia Department of Game and Inland Fisheries biologist and official Boone & Crockett scorer. The final tally was calculated to be 223⅝ points. The inside spread measures 23⅝ inches, with a greatest outside spread of 27⅞ inches. The unusual rack was scored as a "basic" 10-pointer with 20 non-typical points.

When Fuller's buck was originally scored in early 1985, Boone & Crockett penalized racks that had a wide inside spread, if it was greater than the longest main beam measurement. The Fuller buck's spread measures 23⅝ inches, but the longest main beam only tapes 23⅜. The original score tallied 223⅜, but was raised ⅛ inch in 1990, when B&C altered their rules removing the penalty for the difference in measurements.

Interestingly, Fuller's buck, which was killed on the same property as Wayne Byington's buck two years before, is very similar in appearance to the Byington buck, and they clearly appear to be of the same bloodlines. Until Fuller bagged his buck, Byington's buck was the largest non-typical to come from Tennessee. Two bucks of world-class proportions coming so close together from the same property is truly amazing.

JOHNNY WAYNE BYINGTON BUCK
SCORE: 209⅞

In November 1982, Johnny Wayne Byington of Church Hill bagged a Hawkins County buck that scored higher than any other Tennessee non-typical. This magnificent buck's rack sports 13 points on the right and 11 on the left, and gets high marks for 66⅛ inches of non-typical antler. Its right main beam is 20⅝ inches, and

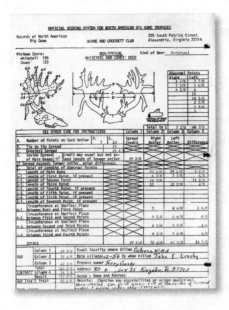

John Crosby's original score sheet, at left, was certified by John Baker, a Virginia Department of Game and Inland Fisheries biologist and official Boone & Crockett scorer.

the left tapes 19⅞ inches. The inside spread spans 19⅝ inches, with the greatest spread measuring 26⅜ inches. The basal circumferences are 4⅜ inches for both sides. Its all-time rank in the 1991 edition of Boone & Crockett's Records of North American Whitetail Deer places it as the 288th largest non-typical on record.

At this time, Wayne Byington's buck is not listed in the Tennessee Deer Registry.

JOHN CROSBY BUCK
SCORE: 204⅝

Nearly two decades after it was killed, a giant Tennessee whitetail was brought to the attention of TWRA personnel in 1985. The late John E. Crosby of Spring City, Tennessee, harvested a non-typical buck November 12, 1956, in the Pine Orchard section, now known as the Bicolor area of Catoosa WMA. John's son, Terry E. Crosby of Kingston, Tennessee, was hunting with his father that fateful day. "My father put me on stand one ridge over from where he was hunting that morning," Terry said. "He took his stand near an

John Crosby's massive non-typical buck, seen draped across the hood of his car in 1956, was taken with an Army surplus .30-06 M-1 Garand service rifle.

old farm site that had an old apple orchard nearby."

About 10:30 a.m., the trophy buck sauntered into a clearing in the apple orchard. When the buck reached for a bite, John raised his Army surplus M1 Garand .30-06 and fired, hitting the buck behind the shoulder. The buck ran a few yards and piled up.

"We had a signal worked out between us to let the other one know if we killed a deer," Terry said. "I heard him shoot once when he killed the deer, then three quick shots followed by another single shot. When I heard the signal, I jumped up and ran to where dad was hunting.

"That buck was really heavy. We field dressed him and finally got him to our old 1950 Ford pickup truck.

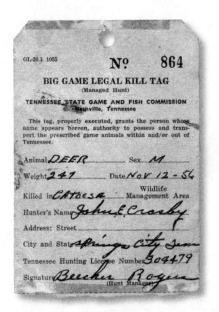

John Crosby's original game tag record's his non-typical buck at 247 pounds dressed weight. He harvested the whitetail in the Pine Orchard section of the Catoosa Wildlife Management Area.

The road was so steep that the tires just spun on the gravel. I had to get an old fence rail and jacked the truck up the mountain to get it to the checking station. When we got there, they didn't have enough counter weights to weigh the buck on their scales. They had to go to town to get more weights before we could weigh him. That buck weighed 247 pounds field-dressed, and was estimated to weigh about 340 pounds live."

Ten years after John Crosby died in 1975, Terry contacted Boone & Crockett Club to find an official scorer for his father's deer. He was put in contact with Clarence Coffey, who works as the Information and Education officer for the TWRA's Region III office in Crossville. Coffey, an official Boone & Crockett scorer, measured the buck and determined that it scored 204⅝ as a non-typical. The rack carries seven points on the right and 10 points on the left beam. The inside spread is 19⅜ inches, and the main beams are 27⅜ and 25⅜ inches, for right and left antlers, respectively. The rack is a basic seven pointer, four points on the right and three on the left. It has a total of 11 abnormal points totaling 55⅝ inches. An 18⅛- and a 13-inch abnormal

point add tremendously to the buck's overall non-typical score. Circumferences also add a lot to this big
whitetail's score. Its right circumference at the smallest
place between the burr and the first point is 7 inches,
and the left is 8⅜ inches. The smallest circumference is
4⅜ inches. The buck is very unusual in that it carries a
third antler that protrudes from the middle of the skull
between the other main beams. According to the
Records of North American Big Game Committee of
the Boone & Crockett Club, John Crosby's buck is considered to be a three-antlered deer, and does not qualify

*Because John Cosby's buck has an unusual third antler growing from the middle
of its skull, it is ineligible for inclusion in the Boone & Crockett record books.*

either for the typical or non-typical categories. The small spike that protrudes from the middle of the buck's skull was not treated as a non-typical point, nor was it entered into the final score. Although it will always rank as one of the best bucks in the Tennessee Deer Registry, John Crosby's buck will not be included in Boone & Crockett Club's listings of record whitetails unless a change in rules are made.

JAMES COBB BUCK
SCORE: 203⅝

Nearly two centuries ago earthquakes ripped the Mississippi River Valley wrecking havoc and sending shock waves as far as New York City. Reelfoot Lake, an elongated sunken mass of land, was born on February 7, 1812, when the mighty Mississippi River was forced to flow backwards and subsequently filled the new crevice. Over 177 years later as the morning of November 5, 1988, unfolded in Tennessee's northwest corner, Jimmy Cobb, a Volunteer State deer hunter from Jackson, Tennessee, was about to make some tremors of his own. The tremors took the form of conversations held between deer hunters. News quickly spread about the killing of the state's biggest buck of the season and Tennessee's third largest non-typical on record.

The first lesson that every successful deer hunter learns is that whitetails are creatures of habit. The converse of this basic axiom is also true. Trophy bucks learn that people are creatures of habit too. Acceptance

of this fact enables a yearling buck with good genetics
and nutrition the ability to avoid hunters and sometimes become a record book contender. Cobb, 37 when
he bagged his record-class buck, capitalized on these
two truths about people and deer, and was able to out-
wit one of the largest whitetails ever taken in the
Volunteer State.

The fact that this buck was taken on the Reelfoot
National Wildlife Refuge during an either-sex quota

*Jimmy Cobb of Jackson killed Tennessee's third largest non-typical buck in 1988
in the Reelfoot National Wildlife Refuge with a Marlin .30-30 lever-action rifle.*

hunt was a feat in itself. What really made this hunt special was that Cobb not only ignored all of the other hunter's tactics; he did just the opposite to bag a once-in-a-lifetime buck.

Cobb and his hunting partner Rex Smith, also from Jackson, spent the day before the quota hunt scouting for deer sign on Reelfoot's Long Point Unit. Lightning, rain, hail and wind hampered their search for the buck sign they knew should be present.

In between showers that day, Jimmy scouted the swampy area near the end of the lake looking for rubs. He knew rubs would be the only physical sign of a buck's presence likely to be left due the to heavy rains. Russell Cobb, Jimmy's younger brother, had bowhunted this unit at Reelfoot the season before. Russell reported his findings of several large scrapes and a well-defined rub line.

Not finding evidence that a large buck was working the same area Russell hunted the year before, Jimmy decided a drastic change in hunting tactics would be his only chance to down a big-racked whitetail.

That night, Cobb and Smith spent the early part of the evening doing their homework. They pored over topographic and aerial maps of the Reelfoot NWR trying to find the natural funnels deer would likely use to escape the wave of hunters the next morning.

Smith opted to stick with his regular routine of climbing a suitable tree to wait for the deer to be pushed by his stand. On the other hand, Cobb elected to do the opposite of what he predicted the other hunters, like Smith, would do. Purposefully choosing not to hunt from a tree stand would be a first for Jimmy. A change in hunting methods had not been warranted before. Over the previous 23 seasons Cobb had killed 63 deer while he was perched in a tree; 40 of those deer he had killed were bucks.

Like other Tennessee deer hunters, Cobb was frustrated with the unpredictability of the weather and the decrease of deer movement in general. This problem combined with the deer on the refuge being programmed to expect danger from above, he felt he

A TWRA crew prepare to release a whitetail on state land. Tennessee's trophy bucks are the legacy of a sixty-year deer restoration program.

would be most successful if he still hunted the over-grown fields and switch willow thickets away from the masses of other hunters.

Cobb, also an ardent bowhunter with 32 bow kills to his credit, had experienced a problem patterning deer movement the month before. The unusually heavy mast crop across the Mid-South meant deer were moving less during daylight hours in search of early-season food sources.

"It was really hard to pattern deer that year," Jimmy said. "One day (October 1988) I had 19 does bed down under and around me on a ridge. The acorns were so thick they would just reach out and pick one up and eat it without having to even get out of bed. The hunting was hit and miss, they just would-n't stick to the trails they used the season before."

Dawn the day of the fated hunt found Cobb hunting a narrow strip of woods that joined a larger woodlot occupied by several other hunters. His place of ambush was bordered on both sides by a newly planted field of two-inch high winter wheat. His plan of action was to sit tight for a couple of hours. The hunters deeper in the refuge would likely push the deer out of the woods, hopefully into the thicket where he was hiding.

At 9:30 a.m. Cobb worked his way to the edge of the field. It was time to put his plan into action.

Easing along the field's edge, he began jumping does at close range. The next field he came to had several felled trees lying along one side. The curious hunter searched each brush pile trying to jump deer, much as a rabbit hunter would do. At one point a large doe crashed out of its hiding place in a fallen pin oak's tangled limbs while Cobb was standing on the tree's trunk. Just as he predicted, the deer were holed up in the fields and brush piles.

Using the wind to his advantage, Cobb kept to the down-wind side of thick cover letting his scent drift out over the fields. He could spot deer hiding in the thick stuff, or any deer bedded in the adjacent field would flee when his scent drifted past. Either option would call for quick shooting on Cobb's part as he later would see.

Crossing the gravel road near the Refuge's checking station, Cobb found a 20-foot ditch covered with a lush growth of honeysuckle and young trees. Venturing into the thicket, he found a scrape "as big as a dinner table." He searched for more sign believing the theory that big bucks make big scrapes. Within 10 yards he located a "tree as big as your wrist all ripped up." In the buck's rut-crazed frenzy it had actually twisted the tree so badly its top was lying on the ground.

Now finding what he had been searching for the day before, Cobb stayed in the confines of the thicket to find the monster responsible for defoliating the tree. Fortunately he found the going too tough even for his 5-foot 4-inch size. Free of the clinging vines and low branches, Jimmy entered the field once again. With a renewed vigor, he carried his gun ready to shoot quickly. Jimmy said "I was stopping for a minute every couple of yards to make the deer holding tight nervous so they would show themselves. It worked because another doe got up in front of me at 15 yards and trotted off. I walked to where she got up and a 4-pointer jumped up out of the grass and headed for the ditch." Jimmy held fire passing up the small forkhorn. It wasn't the deer he was after.

As fate would have it, Cobb's favorite deer rifle, a Model 700 Remington .30-06 was at the repair shop. Instead, he had elected to hunt with a Marlin .30-30 lever-action topped with see-through mounts and a 2.5 power scope. The gun's quick handling capabilities would prove to be an asset for quick reflex shooting.

Adrenaline pumping through his veins, Cobb walked the next 30 yards with his thumb on the hammer ready to shoot.

Suddenly, "The big boy jumped out of the waist high broom sedge at 12 yards. When it jumped up, all I saw was antlers and fur. I just raised up and took a snap shot. Didn't aim or use the see-throughs. It was just like shooting quail."

Needless to say, the crafty buck had learned how to elude hunters before. It had chosen for its hiding place the edge of a 6-foot ravine adjoining the larger ditch. One bound and the buck was out of sight.

At the shot, Cobb ran to the edge while working the rifle's action, hoping for another shot. What lay before him was a sight that deer hunters dream about.

"The buck stumbled to the bottom of the ravine and fell with its belly facing me. The buck was trying to stand up. I couldn't see any blood or sign that he'd been hit. He was really carrying on. I shot him in the

Twice his weight, Cobb needed help dragging this bruiser buck from where he killed it on Reelfoot NWR.

heart and he finally lay still."

Cobb slid down the embankment to his prize, an enormous non-typical. The excited hunter ran his hand over the rack trying to count the numerous points. The rack sports 10 very even typical points with six sticker points over an inch long. These sticker points combined with a 9⅜-inch drop tine and 19⅞ inches of inside spread would place this buck in the "book."

Further inspection revealed that Cobb's first shot had entered high on the buck's left side. The .30-caliber slug had smashed the spine paralyzing the buck's hindquarters.

Cobb soon realized he had a major problem. The buck's size at 227 pounds was too much to drag for a hunter who weighed barely half as much as the deer itself. He was also concerned with loosing the once-in-a-lifetime buck to an unscrupulous hunter if he left it unattended.

"I looked around and didn't see anybody, so I cut a slot on the inside of the hide on the buck's back leg and slid the tag with my name on it under the skin," he said. "Then I ran 200 yards to the highway and jogged a mile back to the checking station."

Cobb arrived at the checking station out of breath. He struggled to give his story to Reelfoot's Refuge Manager Glen Stanley. Parking Stanley's truck as close as possible, the two men fought through the brush to Jimmy's buck. A shot rang out within 50 yards and another lucky hunter bagged the 4-point buck Jimmy had jumped only minutes before.

Back at the checking station the big non-typical was weighed before and after field dressing. Its final field-dressed weight tipped the scales at 178 pounds.

Next, Stanley studied the buck's jaw bone to determine its age. Checking four times to be sure, Stanley announced the buck was an surprising three-and-a-half years old. It is almost unheard of for a buck to grow such large antlers at such an early age.

Though Reelfoot's manager said the Cobb buck was the largest taken on Reelfoot so far, several other trophy animals had been killed during the past three seasons. Stanley added, "The Reelfoot deer herd has a good gene pool, and we have great agricultural diversity. That coupled with very restricted hunts lets some of the bucks get old enough to grow the big racks."

Indeed, the Cobb rack is a large one for the Volunteer State. After the 60-day drying period, the rack was officially scored by Tom Grimsley of the TWRA, scorer for Boone & Crockett. The official score was 203⅞ points, good enough for a Number 3 ranking in the Tennessee Deer Registry at the time. Cobb's buck was mounted by Buddy Hudson, a taxidermist from Gibson Wells, Tennessee.

One sticker point was broken off of the back of the longest tine on the buck's right antler. It was a fresh break with bark matching the destroyed sapling Jimmy had found earlier. It was possibly broken when the buck was sparring with the tree. If that broken point was still in place it might have boosted the buck's score past John Crosby's buck taken at the Catoosa WMA in 1956. It is interesting to note that four of Tennessee's top Boone & Crockett non-typicals were taken on public hunting areas.

An additional note on the Cobb Buck: The Tennessee/Kentucky border bisects Reelfoot NWR, and Cobb's buck was killed so close to the state line that both states claim the monstrous buck in their record books.

The Cobb buck's many sticker points and long drop tine add up to push its score above 203 Boone & Crockett points.

CLARENCE McELHANEY BUCK
SCORE: 198⅜ NON-TYPICAL

Seventeen-year-old Clarence McElhaney was just hoping for a shot at any legal buck on Fort Campbell's Area 6, but lady luck smiled and granted him a chance at one of the best whitetails in Tennessee history.

The military base allowed an early, slug-only hunt

Fort Campbell produced the McElhaney buck, and has been the source of several record-class whitetails over the years.

The MeElhaney buck's antler conformation is indicative of the South Texas whitetails stocked on Fort Campbell five decades ago.

for deer, so Clarence, his father, Roy McElhaney, and brother-in-law Tony Brown found themselves driving the thickets for bucks on October 22, 1978. The trio split up and walked parallel to each other, hoping to drive a deer out of the briar and honeysuckle tangles. Alerted to the sound of breaking brush close at hand, Clarence stopped just in time to see a large-racked buck crash out of the thicket just 10 feet from where he stood. The young hunter snapped his Remington 870 pump shotgun to his shoulder and fired three quick shots, one slug catching the fleeing buck squarely behind the shoulder. The three hunters quickly followed the buck's spoor, and found him about 150 yards from where he was shot. They tried to drag the 230-pound buck back to their vehicle, but were forced to drive to the downed animal instead, owing to its large size. Later at the fort's checking station it tipped the scales at 193 pounds, field dressed. While the three men waited for the base's wildlife personnel to gather data on the buck, they learned that it was four-and-a-half years old, and in prime condition.

A few months later Clarence had his trophy buck measured by a TWRA official Boone & Crockett scorer. The tale of the tape revealed that the 18-pointer had an inside spread of 17⅝ inches, 26⅞-inch right and 26⅛-inch left main beams, and bases measuring 4⅞ inches in circumference. The McElhaney buck's typical measurements coupled with 30⅞ inches of abnormal points nets the deer an impressive 198⅞ final score, ranking it as the fourth largest buck in Tennessee history.

CHARLES FORD BUCK
SCORE: 197 NON-TYPICAL

When Catoosa WMA opened for deer hunting in 1956, it was a banner year for producing monster bucks for several lucky hunters. One such woodsman was Charles A. Ford of Seymour, Tennessee.

On Tuesday, November 15, just four days after John Crosby killed his 204⅝ non-typical, Ford and four friends he worked with at Alcoa went to the mountainous WMA to bring back some venison. The Blair brothers, Luther, Theodore and James, and Johnny Keys formed the rest of the five-man party.

At daylight the five men struck out in different directions in search of game. On that fateful day, Charles parked his 1951 Ford sedan on the side of a dirt track

Charles A. Ford, 74 years old when photographed in 1992, shot this 19-point 325-pound whitetail in 1956. "Took four of us to drag him out," Ford recalled.

that climbed its way through Compartment 11 on the WMA. A heavy frost blanketed the grown-up pastures as Charlie stalked in search of game. Passing through three big pastures and climbing several hills tested the hunter's endurance. He decided time had come for a rest.

"I'd just clim outta this big gorge and was outta breath," Charlie told outdoors columnist Sam Venable for the January 25, 1985, issue of the Knoxville News Sentinel. "I leaned up agin' a dogwood tree and was smokin' a cigarette when I seen him comin'. Somebody musta jumped him down below me. He was comin' at sorta of a trot."

"When I saw him pass by I said, 'uh oh,' I want that there, and when he passed by I let him have it," he told

Seymour, Tennessee, resident Charles A. Ford harvested this 197 B & C whitetail buck in the Catoosa Wildlife Management Area. Ford made his shot at 150 yards with a .30-30 Winchester lever-action rifle.

the author. As the 325-pound whitetail cantered past at 150 yards Ford raised his .30-30 lever-action rifle and fired, hitting the animal in the neck. When he approached the buck, "He started to raise back up and I shot him behind his foreleg agin to keep 'im from getting up on me. But he wasn't a goin' ta go anywhere. I was shocked when I saw him up close," Ford said. What lay before him was a magnificent 19-pointer.

Ford had forgotten his skinning knife in the car

that morning, so he field dressed the buck with the only tool available — a small pen knife. To complete his job, he split the buck's pelvis bone by chipping away at it with a rock.

Afraid to leave his prize unattended, Charlie waited for his friends to arrive to help him drag the deer from the woods. "Took four of us to drag him out," said the 74-year-old hunter. "One fellar had t` walk along and guide the antlers around branches."

At the checking station the buck weighed 253 pounds, field-dressed.

Three decades passed before the Ford buck was measured for the record books. Steve Nifong, a TWRA biologist, determined the buck had nine typical points, four on the right and five on the left beam. The rack sports five non-typical points sprouting from the right base. On the left side, two points originate from the antler base, with a sticker point protruding just past the left brow tine. The third left tine (G-3) has a 4-inch fork, and a drop point comes off the left beam tip. The final net non-typical score comes to 197 Boone & Crockett points.

Chapter 3

Archery Typicals

ALAN ALTIZER BUCK
SCORE: 173

Over the past four decades, Tennessee has yielded big bucks that rival almost any other state in the United States To go along with a plenitude of outstanding whitetails, the Volunteer State has also earned the bragging rights to some of the best deer hunters anywhere. Among all the state's top deer hunters, Alan Altizer, a native of Kingsport, surely ranks at the very top of an elite crowd of successful trophy deer hunters.

Altizer, an archer by choice, began hunting with a bow at the tender age of four. Two decades later, in 1984, he reached a lofty pinnacle by arrowing the largest bow-killed buck in Tennessee history. The young hunter's skills were honed by several years following whitetails in neighboring counties. By the time he turned 14, Alan had bagged his first deer with a bow. Over the next few years, he went on to bag deer

Kingsport native Alan Altizer poses proudly with his 1984 Boone & Crockett trophy. Scoring 173, Altizer's prize was the largest recorded buck killed with a bow in Tennessee.

in North Carolina, West Virginia and Virginia, as well as his home state of Tennessee. "Some years I killed five or six deer with my bow," Alan recalled. "In Tennessee, I've killed my limit every year since I started deer hunting." By the mid 1980s, Alan had over 30 bucks to his credit, and all were taken with archery tackle. Alan's story began in the spring of 1984, when he saw a giant buck prior to turkey season in a remote section of the Cherokee National Forest in Sullivan County. "I had deer hunted all over those mountains," Alan said in an October 1985, article written by Duncan Dobie for *North American Whitetail.* "I was looking for turkey sign when I found a huge set of fresh deer tracks. They were the largest tracks I had ever seen, and they were so massive I couldn't get them out of my mind. I started following in the general direction the tracks were headed, and pretty soon I crossed a little mountain creek. On that particular day, I had a younger boy with me from the children's home in Kingsport, as well as a dog. We had been sneaking along, trying to make every effort to be quiet, but as soon as we got across the creek, the dog perked up his ears and made sort of a muffled bark, like he knew something was directly ahead. All at once, a massive buck stood up from his bed in some thick brush on the side of a small hill less than 30 yards away. He wasn't really alarmed, and I don't think he knew it was a dog that had made the sound, but he definitely had heard something. He stood up to see what was going on. He never saw us, and after a few minutes, he faded off into the brush. After that, I made a thorough check of the area. I found a number of fresh beds and numerous piles of old droppings on the top of the small knoll where he had been bedded."

Altizer didn't know it at the time, but he had walked right into the buck's main bedding area, and even though it apparently ranged a wide area, the buck always seemed to come back to this central spot.

Realizing he had found the buck of a lifetime, Alan scouted the area to learn more of the buck's habits. "One day in late June, I walked into the area early in the afternoon and climbed a tree with my portable stand on top of the knoll," the hunter said. "I had been sitting there for a long time, when suddenly, a terrific storm blew in. It began hailing, the wind was blowing something fierce, and I was getting cold and wet. All at

A heavy-bodied whitetail buck cautiously edges across a field. The state of Tennessee has yielded big bucks that match those taken in any other region.

once, the buck stood up from his bed, about halfway down the knoll. He didn't know I was there, and I had been there all that time without knowing he was bedded only a few yards away. He was in full velvet, and it was an awesome sight. I knew he would easily make Pope and Young, and I had a strong feeling that he would make Boone & Crockett as well. I watched him as he moved off—into the wind—and disappeared. On another scouting trip about a month later, I walked up on him as he was feeding on the same ridge. During the span of an hour, he moved in and out of my view three different times, but he never saw me."

Opting to hunt the buck during the pre-rut stage, when bucks are concerned more with food than sex,

Alan planned to set up a portable stand and wait for the buck to amble by on his way from his bedding area. "It was Monday, October 1, the third day of archery season," Alan recalled. "I had not been able to hunt the first two days because of school, but on this particular Monday, I got out of school early and was in the woods by 2 p.m. I took me about an hour and a half of careful stalking to reach the knoll where I planned to hunt, and just as I was slowly covering the final 200 yards, the wind shifted, ruining my plans. Because of this shift in the wind, I had to back up and circle all the way around the knoll, with the intention of approaching from the opposite side. I had to go through some extremely thick cover in the process, and that took a lot of time. Finally, I reached a little creek and a stand of tall hemlocks just below the knoll."

It was almost sundown, so Alan chose the cover of the hemlocks to hunt the creek bottom until dark. "There was a well-used deer trail leading down the ridge alongside the knoll, and I was facing that direction," he said. "Suddenly, I saw something flicker. It was a deer, walking down the trail. The deer took five or six steps in my direction, then stepped into some thick brush near the trail. I could see antlers, but at first I thought it was a spike. Then a group of five does and fawns came down the trail. As I was watching them, a 6-pointer came out of the woods between my position and the does, and bolted out across the open creek bottom in front of me. Suddenly, he snorted and leaped over to the hill where the other buck was stand-

From the mountains of Middle and East Tennessee to the swamps along the Mississippi River, Tennessee produces record-class bucks each season.

ing. I just knew the other buck was going to spook and run off, but he never showed the least sign of alarm."

"By now, he was about 40 yards away, still standing in the thick brush. I could see his hindquarters, and I knew he had an awfully large body to be a spike. All at once, he shifted his head and started scratching on his hindquarters. The minute he turned his head, a huge set of antlers loomed into view, and I knew he was my buck. The does were getting closer, and it was only a matter of time before they would see me. There was a small hole in the brush where I had a clear shot at the buck's front shoulder, and since I knew he wasn't going to stand there all day and that he might be gone any instant, I decided to take the shot while I could."

Quietly drawing his Jennings Shooting Star bow, Alan picked a spot on the buck's side and released. "I had been practicing shooting through thick brush like this quite a bit, and now my practice really paid off," he said. "The arrow made a good, solid hit, and the buck vanished."

Pacing off 39 yards from his hiding place to where the buck had stood, Alan found a good blood trail, but decided to wait until morning to track in better light. Back at first light, Alan enlisted the help of another bowhunter he had met on the way out of the mountains the evening before. A short tracking job found the buck lying dead from a deftly placed double-lung shot. It took quite a while for the men to wrestle the deer from the woods, owing to its large size. It was later weighed and aged. The buck's field-dressed weight tipped the scales at

226 pounds, and it was determined by biologist to be four-and-a-half years old.

Alan's trophy had 10 long, symmetrical points. Its inside spread is 19⅞ inches, with an outside span of 21⅛ inches. The right main beam measures 25⅝ inches, and the left 25⅛ inches. Its basal circumferences are 4⅝ inches, right; and 4⅝ inches, left. Its final net score is 173, which ranks it as the largest bow kill and the number 10 buck in the overall Tennessee Deer Registry listing for 1992.

An interesting note: Alan is close friends with Luther Fuller, and the two men have spent many days together afield in search of whitetails. It's an incredible story that these two close friends were able to locate and kill state record deer in the same year.

Chapter 4

Archery Non-Typicals

MARK PHILLIPS BUCK
SCORE 186⅞

Controlled access is a key element in producing trophy whitetails, and that's just what Holston Army Ammunition Plant in Kingsport has provided for its resident deer herd for many years. Seventeen-year-old Mark Phillips of nearby Mt. Carmel, Tennessee, was lucky enough to be drawn for the second day of a two-day archery hunt on November 13, 1984, and was able to take a state-record buck.

"I couldn't do any pre-scouting," Phillips said. "The regulations specified that we could only be on the area the day of the hunt for which we were drawn." With his Baker portable tree stand and bow in hand, the young hunter headed to his assigned area and began scouting at daylight. When he reached Area B near Igloo No. 63 across the Holston River at the foot of Bays Mountain, Phillips said, "I found several heavily used trails and followed them. I located a scrape line that had several small scrapes and one monster scrape. There were several horned bushes close by, so I decided this would be the best place to hunt. There were two little finger ridges with trails coming down into a hollow. I hung my stand where I could watch both of them."

After locating a series of well-used scrapes bowhunter Mark Phillips bagged this awesome buck on Holston Army Ammunition Plant property in 1984.

The temperature hovered around the freezing Phillips as a light snow fell. At 9:30 a.m. Phillips watched a doe approach downwind of his stand. He was using a cover scent that mimicked a skunk's foul smell, and the doe fed close to his stand without picking up his scent and becoming alarmed.

"The doe fed for about 15 minutes," Phillips remembered, "and all of a sudden she jerked her head up and started stomping on the ground. I thought she had caught my scent, but she was staring back up the ridge. A few seconds later I saw my buck come trotting down the ridge toward the doe."

When the buck trotted into range the young hunter tensed as he drew the 77-pound pull Jennings Arrow Star compound's string past the let-off point, anchored, and waited. Only a few seconds passed as the buck kept up his juggernaut pace toward the "hot" doe. When the big non-typical reached an opening 20 yards from Philllips' stand, a carefully aimed 2213 XX75 Easton shaft sliced through the air toward the buck's vitals. Upon impact, the buck sprang up and bucked his back legs into the air, turned and ran straight away from Phillips' stand. Watching the reaction of the buck after it had been struck, Phillips realized his shot had been a good one. His Satellite tipped arrow shaft had passed completely through both lungs, producing a quick, painless death for the monster-racked whitetail.

"After I shot the buck the doe was still not alarmed," Phillips said. "I came down the tree two

The rack on Mark Phillips' 10-point, non-typical buck bears two imposing drop tines and two additional non-typical points.

notches before she turned and trotted off."

Following a good blood trail, Phillips came upon his prize after a short 50 yards. "When the buck died he buried his antlers in a rotten tree stump," he said. "I had to grab him by the back feet and pull him out before I could count his points."

Later that morning when Phillips got his buck to the checking station he learned that his deer weighed 155 pounds, field-dressed. Two biologists at the checking station differed in their opinions as to the buck's age; one said it was five-and-a-half, while the other felt it was six-and-a-half years of age.

When Phillips got his prize home and began the skinning chore, what he found led him to believe his buck wasn't the only big buck on the area. "When I skinned the deer I found a hole in his side where he had been gored by another buck," Phillips said. "The back of his neck was scarred, his ear was torn and he had a puncture Phillips under his chin.

Several months later when Phillips got his buck back from the taxidermist, he got a good idea of how big his trophy really was. The taxidermist had to use a mule deer form to mount the big animal, which had a bullish neck that measured 23 inches just behind his ears. Even though Phillips took his buck-of-a-lifetime under "fair chase" conditions, there existed a point of controversy when he tried to enter it in the Pope & Young Club's records book, the long-standing organization in charge of keeping North American big game archery records. There was some question as to whether the buck was confined in a "deer proof" enclosure, preventing it from being entered in the Pope & Young records, according to their guidelines. It was presented to the Pope & Young record committee. It was a close vote, with Jim Dougherty, of Oklahoma, and Bob McGuire, a new resident of Kingsport at the time, casting the deciding "no" votes.

"I went to Bob McGuire's house and asked him about the decision," Phillips said. "Bob told me he voted 'no' because the buck had been killed in a fenced area. The trouble was that Bob never had actually gone to Holston to check it out."

Phillips maintained that Holston Army Ammunition Plant is not completely enclosed by a deer-proof fence. He added that the fence along the plant's boundary stopped at the river and allowed any deer that chose to swim the Holston River and come and go as it pleased. He also said that the back side of the Holston Plant lies at the base of Bay's Mountain and has no fence in this area. It would thus be a relatively easy matter for any deer on the area to climb Bay's Mountain and leave the area.

Officials at the TWRA realized that the Holston Army Ammunition Plant offers a fair-chase hunting opportunity and subsequently scored the Phillips buck. Several years have passed since Phillips attempted to enter the Pope & Young records with his trophy Tennessee ridge runner. He plans to try to have his buck entered in this prestigious archery organization's records again in the near future. Scored as a non-typical 10-pointer, Phillips' buck tallies an impressive 186% points, also enough to make the Boone & Crockett Club's three-year awards record book. The Phillips buck sports two impressive drop tines, as well as two other non-typical points, which place his buck as the best bow-kill in Tennessee history. Even though Phillips was stymied by the Pope & Young decision, he put the matter behind him and took great satisfaction in his accomplishment. "I was really lucky to find that trail and the deer sign I was looking for—everything just came together."

RODNEY MAYNARD BUCK
SCORE: 160⅞

If a deer hunter wanted a crack at a big whitetail, a wise choice might be some of the tightly controlled wildlife management areas spread throughout Tennessee. A glance at the Tennessee Deer Registry reveals that several of the bucks listed in the TDR came from WMAs. Coincidentally, just many of all gun-killed non-typicals listed in the TDR also come from WMAs.

Since 1985, when the Oak Ridge WMA first allowed deer hunting to control its skyrocketing deer population, this area has put more TDR bucks in the records than any other WMA in the state. Wanting a chance at a big buck, Rodney Maynard from McMinnville decided to give Oak Ridge a try during the 1986 season. He applied for one of the area's archery quota hunts and was drawn for a tag. He hunted the first day of the hunt, but only saw a lone deer just out of range. It began to rain and that seemingly brought deer movement to a halt. The next morning, damp conditions gave Maynard a chance to walk quietly to the area he wanted to hunt on Sunday, October 12. Arriving at his chosen spot, after a 30 minute hike from Park City Road, he climbed a tree with his Baker stand overlooking a well-worn deer trail.

At 8 a.m., he heard the unmistakable sound of a deer running down the trail toward his stand. "I think the buck had been spooked by a hunter near the road," Maynard said. "He came down the trail around by the

This non-typical buck is indicative of many of the trophy-class bucks that have been produced by the Oak Ridge WMA in East Tennessee.

river and stopped under my tree."

Unwisely, Maynard had relieved himself near his stand and the buck immediately picked up the foreign odor. Spooked, the buck took three bounds and stopped to check his surroundings. Already at full draw, Maynard placed his 20-yard sight pin low on the buck's chest as it stood broadside 18 yards from his stand. The 70-pound draw PSE compound launched a XX75 Easton shaft tipped with a three-blade Wasp broad-head. Mortally hit, the buck ran three or four seconds and piled up 60 yards from where it had been shot.

The excited hunter could only wait 20 minutes before climbing down to look for his deer. A short blood trail led Maynard to where his handsome 16-pointer lay.

Back at the checking station, Maynard waited anxiously as area biologists checked the buck for dangerous levels of radiation, which the deer might have picked up from exposure to waste products disposed of on the atomic site. The buck checked out okay, much to Maynard's relief. It tipped the scales at 136 pounds, field-dressed, and was aged at four-and-a-half years.

Maynard's hunting strategy was simple, "I got away from the crowds," he said. "I found several rubs near the road, but decided that other hunters in the area would move deer toward me when they began walking around."

When the Maynard buck was measured for Pope & Young, it was scored as a "basic" 8-pointer with eight additional abnormal points. Adding the tine lengths, circumferences and inside spread yielded a net "typical" score of 137⅝ points. Adding the eight non-typicals totaling 23⅜ inches boosted the buck's score to a total of 160⅞ points, which now ranks it as the seventh largest archery non-typical buck in the TDR.

Tennessee Whitetails Make a Comeback

Chapter 5

The Whitetail in Colonial Times

*F*our hundred years ago life was less complicated for the earliest inhabitants of the land we now know as Tennessee. If one desired shelter, he sought the raw materials and built it with his own hands. If one was cold, he fashioned clothing from the skins of large woodland creatures. If he hungered, he, like the cougar and bear, killed and ate. If he hunted wisely and often, he lived. This simplistic way of life had been held in delicate balance for thousands of years, with man at the top of the food chain.

At the zenith of Indian culture in North America, it is estimated that about 32,000 native Americans inhabited the lands of Tennessee when the Pilgrims landed on Plymouth Rock. Before Europeans crossed the Blue Ridge Mountains in their westward expansion, the white-tailed deer *(Odocolieus virginianus virginianus)* was a principal source of survival for native Americans. European-influenced expansion and settlement would reduce whitetail numbers from approximately 40 million to about 300,000 by the late 1800s.

Before the dawn of the 17th century, Ernest Thompson Seton estimated the whitetail population to be 20 deer per square mile in the 2 million square-mile area ranging from the Mississippi River Valley eastward.[1] A few simple calculations would place some 826,360 deer within the boundaries of modern day Tennessee's 41,318 square miles. At the same time, possibly as many as 32,000 Indians inhabited the lands of Tennessee. Using estimates from biologists Richard E.

Early records show that the Cherokees, Creeks, Yuchis, Chickasaws and Shawnees depended on whitetail deer for meat and used their hides for clothing.

and Thomas R. McCabe, the Indians in Canada and the United States may have harvested 4.6 to 6.4 million whitetails for food annually in pre-colonial times.[2]

Further citing the McCabes' research, calculating that the average deer weighs 100 to 140 pounds live, and produced an edible yield of 66.8 - 93.6 pounds per deer, they suggested that each Indian ate 181 pounds of venison per year. This might place the Indians' harvest of whitetails in Tennessee somewhere between 62,000 and 87,000 deer per year.

Further establishing the Tennessee Indian's dependence on whitetails are the accounts of Hernando de Soto's travels. De Soto's army explored the lands of southern Tennessee, during his trek from 1539 to 1542, and his men found venison and white-tailed deer hides to be the primary source of meat, clothing and shelter for the area's Indians.[3]

MORE THAN MEAT

Whitetails were used for much more than food in early Indian culture. The Chickasaws, Cherokees and Yuchi tribes that inhabited or hunted deer in Tennessee tanned deer hides and sewed them into clothing, coverings for their homes and quivers. Whole hides, including the heads and antlers of bucks, were worn as camouflage and decoys while hunting. Bones and antlers were fashioned into tools, weapons, and clothing adornments. Hooves and antler tips were boiled and the resulting paste provided glue that was used for

Indian hunters in Tennessee used all parts of a whitetail deer including antlers as tools and sinew as thread to stitch deer hide clothing and assemble weapons.

fastening feathers and points to arrows. Sinew and gut were twisted into string for sewing and for bow strings. Antler tines were carved into beads. They were also used as tools for chipping stone tools, as a source of fishhooks, and for arrow, spear and blowgun projectile tips. Cords were also made from the strong material provided by deer leather and sinews. No part of the deer was wasted; the brains were used in tanning leather, and the stomach contents were sometimes the only food that could be retained by a starving man.[4]

Although it is not commonly known, the Indian

Studies indicate that Native American hunters, dependent to a considerable degree upon whitetails for survival, killed deer of any age, sex or condition.

was an opportunistic hunter, killing for food whenever he had the chance. Some have the mistaken impression that Indians killed only the very old or the very young or the larger animals, or that he killed the weak or sickened ones. In spite of his inefficient equipment, the Indian was a crafty and successful hunter. But, faced with the problems of finding enough food for survival, he undoubtedly killed game regardless of age, sex or condition. Research conducted by Burd McGinnes and John Reeves in the mid 1950s in Virginia indicated that deer of all age classes were commonly killed by Indians. Using a deer-aging process that takes into account tooth wear and replacement, these two men set out to determine the ages from 19 whitetail jaw bones taken from Conner's Midden in Halifax County, Virginia, and the Parcell site in Giles County, Virginia. The jaws taken from these middens, or Indian trash dumps, were aged and found to be evenly distributed between all age classes. Also interesting was the fact that eight of the 19 jaws examined were from deer between five and seven years old — certainly the prime of life for whitetails.[5]

HOW THEY HUNTED

The bow and arrow were the principal devices employed by Tennessee's Indians to take deer. Early accounts noted that the Chickasaws in northeast Mississippi and southwest Tennessee primarily stalked deer and also wore the entire hide of a whitetail as a disguise to fool their quarry. The Cherokees who inhabited the area along the Smoky Mountains also stalked deer, but they employed the use of brush fires to drive fleeing whitetails to their waiting bows and arrows. The Yuchi tribe of eastern Tennessee and western North Carolina was the most versatile of the early hunters. Not only did they stalk and drive deer with fire, they also tracked them with dogs. Most interesting was the Yuchi's use of deer calls fashioned from a hollowed horn with a wooden mouth piece. These early calls emitted the bleats of distressed fawns, which in turn easily lured does to them.[6]

EARLY WILDLIFE MANAGEMENT

The use of wildfire to drive deer to waiting hunters led to the demise of countless whitetails in the centuries before settlement by white men. But the aftermath of wildfire had a profound positive effect on the whitetail herd carrying capacity of burned areas. This early use of fire had the same effect utilized by wildlife managers today—to set back plant succession—providing lush, green forage preferred by white-tailed deer.

Until Europeans invaded North America, the Indian lived in harmony and balance with the continent's wild creatures. They took no more than they needed to have a comfortable existence. Influenced by greed, they were responsible, as were the new country's settlers, for driving practically all game species to the verge of extinction in a short time.

A huge buck hurtles through the Tennessee woodlands. Indian hunters made extensive use of fires to drive deer during communal hunts.

PIONEER UTILIZATION AND
WHITETAILS IN DECLINE

During the 18th and 19th centuries, white settlers and Indians alike capitalized on the world's need for cheap leather. The white-tailed deer was one the chief sources of this highly sought after product. Deer meat was also highly prized by early settlers. Enticed by trinkets and trade goods, Indians began in earnest to kill increasingly more whitetails for barter.

Whitetail numbers then began a sharp decline. At the outset of the 19th century, whitetail populations had fallen to one-third their pre-colonial size. For a few decades their numbers increased slightly, until the advent of the railroad system made it profitable to harvest untold numbers of deer for consumption in the larger cities of the nation. The Christmas 1879 menu for the Maxwell House in Nashville, Tennessee, had for one of its main courses "Saddle of Minnesota Venison, with Red Currant Jelly" along with several other wild game dishes. Incessant market hunting drove for all practical purposes Tennessee's deer population out of existence by the late 1800s, requiring its importation from areas that still had game.[7]

To give an example of how extensive the trade for deer hides was: Between 1698 and 1715, the trade center of Virginia exported an average of 13,755 deer hides per year. During the same period, the Carolinas averaged 50,250 deer hides per year. Between 1715 and 1735, South Carolina ports averaged 75,000 hides per year. Between 1739 and 1765, Charleston, SC, exported an average of 151,000 hides per year.[8]

WHITETAILS ON
THE WAY BACK

Approximately 300,000 whitetails remained in the United States in 1890, according to T.S. Palmer of the U.S. Bureau of Biological Survey, the forerunner of today's U.S. Fish and Wildlife Service.[9] The passage of the federal Lacey Act of 1900 brought the era of market hunting to a close. It prohibited the interstate traffic of game taken in violation of any state's game laws. In 1911, Tennessee outlawed any hunting for deer in the state.

Chapter 6

Deer Restoration Prior to 1940

*A*t the dawn of the 20th Century, the United States still bore scars from the strife and turmoil of a great civil war. Three decades had done much to heal a wounded Volunteer State, its people and its land. Time had not been as kind to Tennessee's wildlife, silent victims of habitat destruction and unregulated hunting. Swarms of passenger pigeons no longer migrated along the Tennessee River Valley, their fate sealed by market hunters armed with clubs and guns. As in most states east of the Mississippi River, the Virginia white-tailed deer native to Tennessee was practically wiped out by the turn of the century.

The only deer that remained in Tennessee were small remnant herds of native deer on the wilder parts of the Cumberland Plateau, according to Rhoades.[1] More specifically, Ganier said remnant herds of white-tailed deer remained in Cheatham and Perry counties, "from which a few roam into parts of Wayne and Humphreys counties," and also the Great Smoky and Unaka mountains of East Tennessee.[2] Komarek and Komarek also reported that around the turn of the century a few deer were present in Blount and Cocke counties, and in the Great Smoky Mountains National Park.[3]

Many have experienced the pleasure and privilege of watching a whitetail trot past while sitting quietly in

Although hunting had been prohibited in Tennessee since 1911, by the early 1930s the state's whitetail population had dwindled to less than 500.

Tennessee's autumn woods. The faint rustle of brittle, brown leaves grows, becoming punctuated with each footfall as the animal approaches. In a few moments, all grows quiet again, leaving one's memory etched with a mental picture to be framed, hung and viewed from time to time.

The white-tailed deer native to Tennessee almost became a memory, its numbers dwindling to less than 500 a by the time a few concerned sportsmen and wildlife enthusiasts began restoration attempts in the early 1930s. It is quite likely that some of these remaining remnant populations were gone before any restoration began, according to Tennessee Wildlife Resources Agency wildlife biologists.[4] It was reported by J.D. Newsom, that Tennessee's deer population was only

TENNESSEE

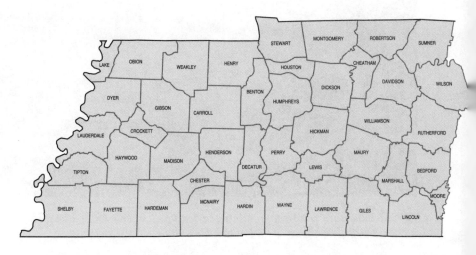

1,000 animals in 1946, several years after restoration attempts had begun and after several hundred deer had been stocked.[5]

Public agencies and private individuals made numerous efforts to revive Tennessee's deer population, but written records of the attempts are sketchy at best. Earliest records indicate that in 1931, five deer were purchased from a game farm and released on Andrew Johnson Wildlife Management Area (WMA) in Greene County. The following year 10 more whitetails were purchased from a game farm and released on the WMA, with an additional 25 deer purchased and stocked in 1933.[6]

Two years later, 14 whitetails were stocked on Shelby Forest and 12 in the Reelfoot Lake area amidst an inten-

sive reforestation and erosion control project led by the Work Progress Administration, according to A.J. Marsh, former chief of Game Management Division of the Tennessee Game and Fish Commission.[7]

According to TWRA Biologist Joe Farrar, unpublished data obtained from Game and Fish Commission files revealed a stocking from Pisgah National Forest in North Carolina in Lincoln County in 1936. However, information was not available as to the agency or individuals responsible for the stocking.[8]

The U.S. Forest Service released 178 Pisgah National Forest deer in 1936 and 1937 into the area now known as the Tellico WMA in Monroe County, and 10 Pisgah deer in 1937 into an area in Polk County now comprising the Ocoee Wildlife Management Area. A.R. Cahn reported that 14 Pisgah deer were released by the Tennessee Valley Authority (TVA) onto their lands on Norris Lake in 1936, and added three more in 1937. This is probably the release referred to elsewhere as occurring in Campbell and Claibourne counties, and including an area now known as the Chuck Swan WMA.[9]

Schultz also cited personal correspondence from A.J. Marsh that stated that stocking began on the Catoosa WMA in 1937 or 1938, and the Marsh released northern *borealis* subspecies white-tailed deer into this area in 1939.[10]

Many of the restoration attempts prior to the formation of the Tennessee Game and Fish Commission utilized deer from the Pisgah National Forest herd,

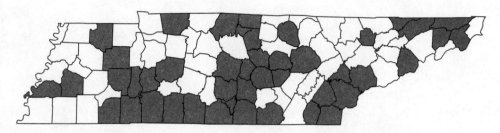

Areas of release for deer taken from the Fort Campbell Military Base: 1940-1985

which was comprised of a conglomeration of whitetail subspecies. These deer were descendants of three subspecies: *o.v.borealis* from New York; *o.v.virginianus* from coastal North Carolina; and o.v.osceola from coastal Florida.[11]

The early Tennessee deer restoration program relied upon sources that were readily available, primarily the Pisgah National Forest as well as donations from midwestern states also attempting restoration programs of their own. As stated, the Pisgah National Forest herd was a conglomeration of whitetail subspecies, which primarily exhibited the physical characteristics seen in deer from coastal North Carolina where the majority of Pisgah's deer originated. Typically, body weights and antler size was smaller than the northern borealis subspecies. Large, mature bucks from Pisgah weighed in the neighborhood of 200 pounds, whereas bucks originating from the Midwest often weighed over 300 pounds. Whitetails from northern climes are larger animals, which is a genetically-linked biological response to their environ-

A work crew from the Tennessee Game and Fish Commission watch eagerly as a whitetail is released into a state forest. Restocking efforts began in the late 1930s.

ment. Large bodies hold more heat, thus giving a deer a better chance of survival in harsh winter conditions. Conversely, whitetail subspecies from warmer southern regions have smaller bodies that retain less heat to fit into their biological niches. Decades later, the offspring of these different subspecies that have remained isolated still exhibit some of the same characteristics of body size and antler configuration of their ancestors. Antler coloration also differs between sub-species. The ancestors of bucks from Pisgah National Forest typically have yellow-ish white antlers, which is a contrast to the darker brown antlers found on northern bucks.

Today's Tennessee deer herd is an inter-mingling of different stocked whitetail sub-species in most areas of the state, which makes it difficult to directly link body size and antler con-figuration and col-oration to ancestral deer herds.

Chapter 7

Deer Restoration 1940 - 1959

*T*he Tennessee Wildlife Resources Agency's (TWRA) earliest attempts at stocking white-tailed deer met with both success and failure. Through trial and error, early game managers learned some hard lessons. Once initial hardships were overcome, stockings in East Tennessee quickly took hold and deer populations began to grow.

In 1940, Tennessee Game and Fish Commission (now the TWRA) personnel, led by Al Marsh, and Charles Pierle, purchased seven does and four bucks from Elmer J. Schowalter, owner of Schowalter Game Farm near Jackson, Wisconsin. In addition to these 11 Wisconsin deer, four does and four bucks were donated to Tennessee by the Wisconsin Department of Natural Resources. These 19 deer were released in an enclosure at Cheatham Wildlife Management Area in Cheatham County, south of the Cumberland River near Ashland City.

The following year, Tennessee received 154 deer

from two out-of-state sources. Fifty-two deer were donated by the Michigan Department of Natural Resources, but two succumbed to the stress of transport, leaving 38 does and 12 bucks for stocking at the Cheatham deer pens.

The Woodmont Rod and Gun Club in western Maryland also donated 82 deer during the state's second year of restoration. Woodmont, located near Hancock, Maryland, has a rich history as one of the few strongholds for whitetails and wild turkeys in the east. The club dates back to 1870, when it was formed

Deer shipped to Tennessee from Wisconsin, Maryland and Michigan were the large-bodied borealis subspecies.

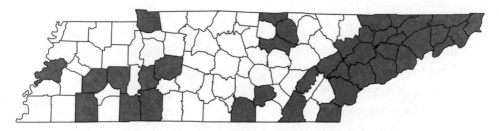

Areas of release for deer taken from the Chuck Swan WMA: 1940-1985

by Robert Lee Hill and Rear Admiral Robley D. Evans.
Woodmont's 8,000 acres, with 5,000 behind fence, was
created as a hunting preserve for the Washington, D.C.
elite, including presidents James A. Garfield, Chester A.
Arthur, William Henry Harrison, Grover Cleveland,
Herbert Hoover and Franklin D. Roosevelt, as well as
such as Babe Ruth. Under the guidance of Henry P.
Bridges, Sr., Woodmont gave 49 does and 33 bucks to
Tennessee to help reduce the surplus of game within
the 5,000-acre tract.[1]

Woodmont's deer were sought out by several states
for stocking purposes, owing to the large size of the
deer from the area. Bridges tells of selling deer to
Cuba, and Maryland, as well as Tennessee.[2] Bridges,
Woodmont's secretary for several years, claims the size
of the area's deer was due to an infusion of borealis
subspecies genes from stocking Michigan whitetails in
the early 1930s. The largest white-tailed buck killed on
Woodmont property prior to 1956 was a 320-pound,
18-point giant, bagged by Burt Knight of Fairmont,
West Virginia.

It is interesting to note that western Maryland is included in the southern-most range for *borealis* subspecies of whitetail. It is speculated that after a half century, the genetic variability of the deer within the Woodmont preserve had been reduced to a point where the average buck killed had become smaller than the norm for the subspecies. Bridges' stocking of deer from Michigan, still *borealis* subspecies, provided a boost through increased genetic variability, rather than

Tom Grelen (at right) and two companions observe a deer release. Grelen led the Game and Fish Commission's whitetail restoration program from 1953 to 1964.

a simple hybridization from a larger-bodied subspecies that Bridges credited as being the reason Woodmont's large-sized deer. High deer populations could also have contributed to the decline in body size prior to trapping excess deer.

Recent conversations with Bridges grandson, David Bridges, revealed that Woodmont's deer body and antler size has continued to decline over the past decades. Overpopulation and subsequent over browsing are the primary culprits for the physiological decline. Similar declines are evident in various localized Tennessee herds, such as the herd on Central Peninsula WMA. The average buck harvested there has also diminished over the past few years due to similar circumstances.

Instead of trying to restock Tennessee's hills and valleys with the state's native subspecies, *virginianus,* top game management officials were forced to get deer from wherever deer for stocking were available. It was fortunate that the subspecies available was *borealis,* which is a sort of "super" deer in body size when compared to the *virginianus* subspecies. When deer hunting began in the late 1940s and 1950s, some tremendous bucks were harvested. Several bucks killed were rumored to weigh over 300 pounds, with some approaching 400 pounds. Sonny Foster's state-record typical-antlered buck weighed 312 pounds field dressed, which would place this monstrous buck at or just over 400 pounds live weight. *Borealis* subspecies whitetails were stocked in the area where Foster killed his giant buck.

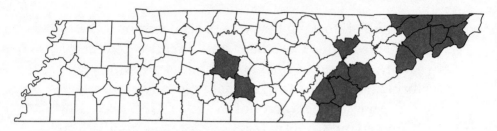

Areas of release for deer taken from the Arnold Engineering Development Center: 1940-1985

Reproduction in the Cheatham WMA pens went well, with 19 of these northern *borealis* subspecies deer stocked in Cumberland and Morgan counties on the Catoosa WMA in 1943. That same year 10 whitetails were stocked in the wilds on Cheatham WMA.

During 1944, Catoosa WMA received 33 more deer; Cheatham WMA nine; and Prentice Cooper WMA, located in Hamilton and Marion counties, received an initial stocking of 30 animals.

When all seemed to be going very well with the captive breeding program, tragedy struck in 1945. A disease outbreak decimated the deer population at the Cheatham pens, and the subsequent loss of the core breeding population prevented any stocking in 1945.

Having learned a hard lesson about the dangers of keeping a wild population in captivity and their subsequent susceptibility to diseases, the TWRA began stocking whitetails directly into the wild. Schowalter Farms sold 44 does and 38 bucks to Tennessee in 1946, with the entire lot being released into Catoosa WMA's 79,740 acres of near wilderness. Catoosa received an additional stocking that year of six deer from what remained at the Cheatham pens. Prentice Cooper WMA received 24 does and 22 bucks the same year bringing the total stocked that year to 134 animals.

An eyewitness account by Helen Krechniak, from Cumberland County, Tennessee, of the second release of 29 Wisconsin deer on Catoosa in November 1946,

Wildlife managers examine a plywood deer trap used by the Tennessee State Game and Fish Commission during restocking projects in the 1940s and 1950s.

revealed that, "Cars were left behind at Pine Orchards and the entire party got into jeeps and trucks for the final six miles of rough road to the release station. Some deer came swiftly out of the release box, some plunged in fright, a few looked casually about them, getting the lay of the land before trotting off down the woodland road along the top of Crab Orchard Mountain."

Trapped within 10 days before shipping, the deer were trucked down from northern Wisconsin in two days and a night of driving. This shipment, according to Jim Stingley, then Catoosa's area manager, was the second of three that year, 32 having been delivered in October. The October release included 18 fawns, 10 18-month-old yearlings and four mature deer. The deer (14 were bucks and 18 were does) ranged in weight from 60 to 200 pounds. Another shipment was scheduled for December to augment the previous releases. An entourage of Morgan and Roane county sportsmen joined the state and federal officials coordinating the November, 1946 Catoosa release: Dr. C.O. Johnson, president of the Roane County Sportsman's Club; C.A. Emerson, president of the Morgan County Sportsman's Club; Joe Freitag and several other members of each club. Tennessee Game and Fish Division District Supervisor of Conservation Officers, Ray Southard; State Game and Fish Division Deer, Turkey and Raccoon Project Leader, Fred Williams; State Game and Fish Educational Director, John Jared; and Federal Aid Section official, Al Hyder, led the release.

A whitetail "heads for the hills" following its release during a 1950s restocking operation.

Featured during the November stocking was a new release box devised by Deer Project Leader Williams it incorporated two top tagging doors and sliding panels at both ends to make releases easier and to reduce the possibility of injury—to both deer and people handling them. Each deer received a numbered identification tag at release.

Stingley stated that these Schowalter Farms deer were the cheapest good northern deer available, but they still cost $120 each; $30 from state funds and $90 from federal Pittman-Robertson matching funds.

Fall Creek Falls State Park, a 7,000-acre area in Bledsoe and Van Buren counties, got its first stocking of 25 does and 19 bucks in 1947 from Schowalter

Farms. Unicoi County in the Cherokee National Forest received a stocking of 54 does and 49 bucks from Schowalter Farms in 1947. That same year, Catoosa received an additional 83 deer, 56 does and 27 bucks, also from Schowalter Farms.

SCHOWALTER FARMS

Located 30 miles north of Milwaukee, off Highway 55 near Jackson, Wisconsin, was Schowalter Farms, primarily a dairy farm. Elmer J. Schowalter and his son Donald began raising deer in 1925 as a hobby. By 1931, they had a surplus of whitetails and shipped a small herd to northern Wisconsin's Eagle River area. In the following years Schowalter shipped deer to at least 17 states to assist in whitetail restoration programs. Schowalter Farms raised deer for 65 years, with the last deer being sold off by Donald's wife, Esther, in the early 1990s. During 1948, Schowalter Farms sold 54 more deer to Tennessee. Some were stocked on the Cherokee National Forest, 11 does and six bucks were released in the Laurel Fork area, and 16 does and 14 bucks went to the Andrew Johnson WMA. Wayne County got its first stocking—five does and two bucks—on Eagle Creek Refuge near Waynesboro. The final year of Tennessee's first decade of whitetail restoration saw the initial release on private land in the state. Morgan County received 24 does and 17 bucks from Schowalter Farms.

Also in 1949, Pickett County got 18 does and 14

Dairy farmer and deer breeder E. J Schowalter and his wife show off a rare set of whitetail triplets on the family's Wisconsin farm.

bucks from Schowalter Farms. The Cherokee National Forest received more deer that year: Laurel Fork area received 26 does and 10 bucks; and Kettlefoot WMA, 23 does and nine bucks; with another 19 deer going to Kettlefoot from Cheatham pens.

Overall, between 1940 and 1949, 830 deer from four major sources—Cheatham WMA breeding pens, Schowalter Farms in Wisconsin, the Woodmont Rod and Gun Club in western Maryland, and the state of Michigan were stocked in Tennessee.

The first decade of whitetail restoration cost approximately $100,000 of sportsman-funded money: 75 percent from federal Pittman-Robertson funds, excise taxes on firearms and ammunition; 25 percent came from Tennessee Game and Fish Commission coffers funded by sportsman license dollars.

DEER RESTORATION: 1950 — 1959

The second phase of the Volunteer State's deer restoration was characterized by a general expansion of stocking efforts. Several areas within 27 counties geographically distributed across the state received a total of 1,441 deer, under the guidance of Roy Anderson, Tennessee Game and Fish Commission chief.

During the 1950s, the Tennessee Game and Fish Commission Deer Project Leaders were Fred Williams in 1951, followed by Walter M. Weaver, and Tom Grelen

E.J. Schowalter, shown surrounded by deer in his farm's front feeding lot, began breeding whitetails in 1925. Schowalter sold his first shipment of deer in 1931.

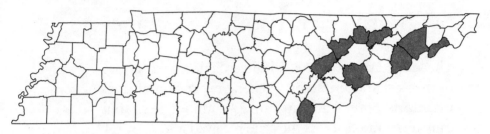

Areas of release for deer taken from the Department of Energy properties, Oak Ridge: 1940-1985

from 1953 until 1964. These men not only led the whitetail restoration program, they toiled long and hard trapping and transporting deer to new areas.

Counties in Tennessee's Western Valley, Coastal Plain and Mississippi River Valley got their first stockings during this decade. Aside from 1950, when 80 deer were purchased from Schowalter Farms in Wisconsin, all the deer released came from in-state sources. Of these areas, the most important was Chuck Swan WMA, which provided over 1,000 animals during this time period.

The source for Chuck Swan WMA, then known as Central Peninsula, was Pisgah National Forest in North Carolina. As mentioned before, the deer stocked from Pisgah National Forest were a mixture of *virginianus, borealis* and *osceola* subspecies.

Early Tennessee game managers' philosophies began to change concerning the upland hardwood climax forests, typically found in eastern Tennessee and the Cumberland Plateau, as being the best habitat for whitetails. This change in attitude is responsible for

E.J. Schowalter's farm was the source of more than a hundred deer purchased by Tennessee Game and Fish for its massive whitetail restocking project.

deer stocking in western counties with flatter, more open terrain characterized by small wooded areas broken up by land in a mixture of agricultural uses.

This shift in emphasis would bring a swift rise in Tennessee deer numbers. The agricultural practices in West Tennessee provided more food for deer to eat, and thus the area provided a higher carrying capacity.

Another characteristic of this decade was a shift in emphasis toward restoring deer populations on private lands. As deer populations became established on state-owned lands during the 1940s, these areas were used during from the mid-1950s as sources of deer to stock private lands in Tennessee. Today the success and wisdom of this strategy is unquestioned, as Tennessee now has a state-wide deer population over 800,000 animals, with over 90 percent of the state's deer harvest coming from private lands.

The method used to capture whitetails for relocation was to set several large, wooden box traps baited with salt. The dimensions of these traps were eight feet long, three feet high and three feet wide. One or two deer were normally taken from each trap, with as many as four being caught at one time. Once the deer were caught, they were moved into a holding box on a transport truck. They were immediately trucked to new areas and released.

Certain conditions had to be met before an area

Whitetail deer are transferred from a truck into shipping crates at the Schowalter Deer Farm in Wisconsin. The deer were transported to Tennessee for release.

received any deer. Protection was the first consideration when stocking on private lands. The local game warden was called upon to advise game managers which land owners would work cooperatively with the TWRA and protect the new herds. Oftentimes, a group of landowners would approach the TWRA and ask for deer to be stocked. A community meeting would be held by TWRA personnel to educate locals about the requirements of establishing new deer herds. During the 1940s, 1950s and early 1960s, an agreement was signed by local land owners, assuring wise stewardship of the new deer herds. Local magistrates were also key players in successful deer restoration. Their cooperation in assigning stiff fines for deer poachers was a deterrent for the few who might be tempted to break the law.

Bringing deer into new areas often created quite a stir with local media. Newspapers often gave the events top billing. Past TWRA game managers played the event for all it was worth, usually delaying release of a large-racked buck for last, then stopping to get everyone's attention. They would then explain that in about five years, hunting seasons would be opened in the area if the animals were given protection and allowed to thrive. Then they would release the big buck in front of their spellbound audience, giving them a brief glimpse of things to come.

In 1950, Catoosa WMA received a total of 92 deer: 45 does and 35 bucks purchased from Schowalter Farms; three does from Washington County; four does and two bucks trapped from a farm in Morgan County

Friendly 17 Point Buck on Farm

THIS buck on the Schowalter farm, near Jackson, Wis., had 17 points when 4 years old, proof that feed is the important factor in horn growth. The old rule that a deer will grow one added point on each beam per year still persists among hunters but was long ago abandoned by scientists as a means of determining age of deer.

owned by the Jones family; and three does trapped off the property of the Johnson City Veteran's Administration Hospital.

Deer trapping during 1951 slowed somewhat, with only 15 animals moved. The Jones farm in Morgan County provided seven does and four bucks for Catoosa WMA. Unicoi County in the Cherokee National Forest received three does and one buck.

Cove Creek WMA in Campbell County was the major contributor of whitetails in 1952. Cove Creek WMA provided 20 does and 11 bucks for Unicoi County; three does and two bucks for Natchez Trace WMA; and nine does and three bucks for Kettlefoot WMA. Morgan County sources also provided one doe for Unicoi, and Meeman-Shelby Forest State Park donated one doe for stocking on Natchez Trace WMA. In all, 50 deer were stocked in 1952.

Ninety-three deer were trapped from Chuck Swan WMA in 1953 for relocation in Natchez Trace and Kettlefoot WMAs. Natchez Trace received 22 does and 22 bucks, and Kettlefoot got 25 does and 24 bucks.

Between 1954 and 1959, Chuck Swan WMA provided 945 more deer for stocking in 19 new counties.
Grundy, Hardeman and Scott counties were release
sites for 164 deer in 1954, with Clay, Scott and Stewart
counties, and Anderson-Tully receiving 161 deer the
following year.

Perry, Putnam, Hickman and Blount counties
obtained 196 animals in 1956, with Franklin Hamilton,
Madison and Rhea counties receiving 154 deer in
1957. Franklin County got an additional 91 deer in
1958, as well as 52 for Overton County and 48 for
Hardin County, as well as one doe for Sewanee
University. In 1959, Carter and Hancock counties
received 60 and 51 whitetails, respectively.

As the decade of the 1950s drew to a close, Chuck
Swan WMA relinquished its spot as the leading produc-
er of deer for stocking purposes to Clarksville Naval
Base. The Naval Base has since been incorporated into
Fort Campbell, an
Army base located on
the Tennessee/
Kentucky border 60
miles north-west of
Nashville.

*Deer project leader Fred
Williams designed this
improved trap and release box
with sliding panels at both
ends to make releases easier
and reduce injuries.*

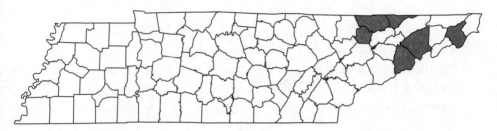

Areas of release for deer taken from Cades Cove, Great Smoky Mountains National Park: 1940-1985

The Clarksville Naval Base and Fort Campbell were originally stocked in 1948, with six whitetails of the *texanus* subspecies from Camp Bullis, an Army base in Bexar County, a few miles north of San Antonio, Texas. According to Mike Regan, a biologist with the Texas Parks and Wildlife Department, Camp Bullis was originally stocked with deer from the King Ranch and the Aransas National Wildlife Refuge near Corpus Christi in South Texas. South Texas is noted as being one of the top producers of large-antlered whitetails in North America, with over 100 bucks registered in the Boone & Crockett Club's record book. Fort Campbell later received an additional stocking of 24 deer from Fort Sill, near Lawton, Oklahoma, in 1955, with the source of Fort Sill's deer also being Texas' Camp Bullis.

Whitetails stocked on Fort Campbell played a part in national security during the Cold War. The reason the Army and Navy put whitetails on the base was for military security. The Navy had used goats and buffalo within the 2,500-acre, triple-fenced enclosure surrounding a nuclear weapons storage facility to control low vegetation, but they met with limited success. The deer within the enclosure quickly multiplied and ate a browse line about five feet high, allowing troops patrolling the area greater visibility.

The whitetails flourished within the "bird cage," as it is referred to by veteran TWRA biologists, like Region I's Joe Farrar, of Lexington, Tenn. It would later become the largest source of deer for Tennessee's restoration program.

As early as 1958, Fort Campbell's "bird cage" yielded four does and two bucks to augment deer releases in Hardin County. The following year Fort Campbell increased its role in the restoration with 57 animals going to Bradley County, 10 to Montgomery County, 95 to Weakley and 32 for White County, bringing the TWRA's second phase of whitetail restoration to a close.

Tennessee Deer Restoration Annual Summary

Area of Release	Source	Female	Male	Unknown	Total
Cheatham WMA	Schowalter Farms, WI	7	4		11
Cheatham WMA	Wisconsin Dept. of Cons.	4	4		8
Total for 1940		**11**	**8**		**19**
Cheatham WMA	Michigan Dept. of Cons.	38	12		50
Cheatham WMA	Maryland Dept. of Cons.	49	33		82
Total for 1941		**87**	**45**		**132**
Catoosa WMA	Cheatham WMA pens			19	19
Cheatham WMA	Cheatham WMA pens			10	10
Total for 1943				**29**	**29**
Catoosa WMA	Cheatham WMA pens			33	33
Cheatham WMA	Cheatham WMA pens			9	9
Prentice Cooper WMA	Cheatham WMA pens			30	30
Total for 1944				**72**	**72**

Area of Release	Source	Female	Male	Unknown	Total
Cheatham WMA	Schowalter Farms, WI	7	4		11
Cheatham WMA	Wisconsin Dept. of Cons.	4	4		8
Total for 1940		**11**	**8**		**19**
Catoosa WMA	Schowalter Farms, WI	44	38		82
Prentice Cooper WMA	Schowalter Farms, WI	24	22		46
Catoosa WMA	Cheatham WMA pens			6	6
Total for 194		**68**	**60**	**6**	**134**
Unicoi	Schowalter Farms, WI	54	49		103
Catoosa WMA	Schowalter Farms, WI	56	27		83
Fall Creek Falls	Schowalter Farms, WI	25	19		44
Total for 1947		**134**	**95**		**230**
Laurel Fork	Schowalter Farms, WI	11	6		17
Eagle Creek Refuge	Schowalter Farms, WI	5	2		7
Andrew Johnson WMA	Schowalter Farms, WI	16	14		30
Total for 1948		**32**	**22**		**54**
Morgan Co.	Schowalter Farms, WI	24	17		41
Pickett Co.	Schowalter Farms, WI	18	14		32
Laurel Fork	Schowalter Farms, WI	26	10		36
Kettlefoot WMA	Schowalter Farms, WI	23	9		32
Kettlefoot WMA	Cheatham WMA pens			19	19
Total for 1949		**91**	**50**	**19**	**160**

Area of Release	Source	Female	Male	Unknown	Total
Catoosa WMA	Jones Farm, Morgan Co.	4	2		6
Catoosa WMA	Washington Co.	3			3
Catoosa WMA	Schowalter Farms, WI	45	35		80
Catoosa WMA	Johnson City VA Hospital	3			3
Total for 1950		**55**	**37**		**92**
Unicoi	Cove Creek	3	1		4
Catoosa	Jones Farm, Morgan Co.	7	4		11
Total for 1951		**10**	**5**		**15**
Unicoi	Morgan County	1			1
Unicoi	Cove Creek	20	11		31
Natchez Trace WMA	Cove Creek	3	2		5
Natchez Trace WMA	Shelby Forest WMA	1			1
Kettlefoot WMA	Cove Creek	9	3		12
Total for 1952		**34**	**16**		**50**
Natchez Trace WMA	Chuck Swan	22	22		44
Kettlefoot WMA	Chuck Swan	25	24		49
Total for 1953		**47**	**46**		**93**
Grundy Co.	Chuck Swan	35	22	2	59
Hardeman Co.	Chuck Swan	39	14	2	55
Scott Co.	Chuck Swan	32	16	2	50
Total for 1954		**106**	**52**	**6**	**164**
Clay Co.	Chuck Swan	21	19		40
Scott Co.	Chuck Swan	3	1		4
Shelby Co.	McFadden Estates	9	4		13

Area of Release	Source	Female	Male	Unknown	Total
Stewart Co.	Chuck Swan	45	20	2	67
Anderson Tully	Chuck Swan	28	21	1	50
Total for 1955		**106**	**65**	**3**	**174**
Perry Co.	Chuck Swan	30	19		49
Putnam Co.	Chuck Swan	32	17	4	53
Hickman Co.	Chuck Swan	31	19		50
Blount Co.	Chuck Swan	29	15		44
Total for 1956		**122**	**70**	**4**	**196**
Franklin Co.	Chuck Swan	9	7		16
Hamilton Co.	Chuck Swan	22	16	12	50
Madison Co.	Chuck Swan	13	8	2	23
Rhea Co.	Chuck Swan	43	21	1	65
Total for 1957		**87**	**52**	**15**	**154**
Franklin Co.	Chuck Swan	56	32	3	91
Hardin Co.	Ft. Campbell	4	2		6
Hardin Co.	Chuck Swan	23	23	2	48
Overton Co.	Chuck Swan	31	20	1	52
Sewanee University	Chuck Swan	1			1
Total for 1958		**115**	**77**	**6**	**198**
Bradley Co.	Ft. Campbell	28	29		57
Carter Co.	Chuck Swan	41	18	1	60
Hancock Co.	Chuck Swan	31	19	1	51
Montgomery Co.	Ft. Campbell	5	5		10
Weakley Co.	Ft. Campbell	49	44	2	95
White Co.	Ft. Campbell	13	19		32
Total for 1959		**167**	**134**	**4**	**305**

Chapter 8

Deer Restoration 1960 - 1985

*C*ontinued expansion and accelerated trap and transfer efforts characterized the period from 1960 to 1972. During this 13-year stretch, more than 3,000 deer were transferred onto state and private lands. Heavy emphasis was placed on the establishment of deer populations in middle Tennessee, and the restoration program in middle and western counties was essentially completed.

The major source of deer for the releases in these areas came from Fort Campbell, with over 2,000 whitetails contributed during this phase. Deer releases continued in eastern Tennessee, with Chuck Swan WMA providing the majority of these deer.

This era of restoration was also a period of experimentation. In addition to the releases of white-tailed deer, approximately 75 black-tailed deer were brought in from the state of Oregon and released on Volunteer Army Ammunition Plant during 1966 and '67. These deer were used for a program of experimental breed-

A doe is released as part of the 1960s restocking program. In 1966 a number of black-tailed deer were introduced from Oregon as part of an experimental breeding program.

Ben Layton was the Deer Project leader from 1991 until 2002.

ing between white-tailed deer and black-tailed deer until 1973. The black-tailed deer breeding program was directed by TWRA biologists Bob Nichols and Cliff Whitehead.

In 1973, 46 black-tailed deer from Volunteer Army Ammunition Plant were released in Hamblen County, and all surviving hybrid deer from the breeding experiments were released at the Milan Arsenal. As far as is known, nearly all of the black-tailed and hybrid deer gene pool have been eliminated from Tennessee's deer populations because of their susceptibility to meningeal worm (*Parelaphostrongylus tenuis*) infestations.

Eagle Creek Refuge in Wayne County got two more deer from Chuck Swan WMA in 1960. These would be the last deer trapped at Chuck Swan until 1965. The remaining deer stocked during the first six years of TWRA's third phase of deer restoration would come exclusively from Fort Campbell. Cumberland, Haywood, Montgomery, Van Buren, and White counties, and Anderson Engineering Development Center WMA near Tullahoma received a total of 225 texanus subspecies deer from Fort Campbell in 1960. Caroll, Decatur, Franklin, Henderson, Rutherford and Marion counties got 214 animals in 1961, with Macon Smith, Sumner and Tipton

Deer project leaders Bob Pugh (foreground) and Jack Murrey prepare a whitetail for release.

receiving 200 the following year. TWRA's trap and transfer program stocked two counties, Giles and Lincoln, in 1963; Giles received 30 does and 31 bucks, and Lincoln got four does and seven bucks. Cannon, Dekalb, Lincoln, Smith and Sumner counties received a total of 169 animals in '64, with Bedford, Jefferson and Perry counties getting their initial stockings in 1965. The same year, Dekalb, Hawkins, Hickman and Smith received additional stockings, bringing the year's total to 263 animals translocated. Claiborne, Lawrence and Warren county sites were selected for new releases in 1966, and Perry and Wayne had their deer populations augmented with additional stockings that year.

Today's Tennessee Chief of Game Larry Marcum sorted through thousands of deer tags each year during his service as Deer Project Leader between 1977 and 1987 to determine the progress of the deer restoration project.

Jack Murrey (left) and Greg Wathen (below left) both served as deer project leaders during the 1970s and 1980s. Murrey focused on improving deer stocks in East Tennessee.

In 1967, four counties received deer: Campbell County got 57 animals from Chuck Swan WMA; Coffee County got 80 from Fort Campbell; Decatur County, 62 from Fort Campbell; and Warren County, 36, also from Fort Campbell.

The TWRA began introducing deer from Fort Campbell on Chuck Swan WMA, with 53 deer moved in 1968, and 94 more the following year. This was done for one basic reason; Roy Anderson, chief of game management for the TWRA during this period, felt that Chuck Swan needed an infusion of new blood from the *texanus* subspecies found at Fort Campbell.

To start the two-year experiment, a buck-only hunt was held prior to the normal breeding period, which would have been in late November 1968. This was done to reduce the number of existing bucks of breeding age at Chuck Swan, then deer from Fort Campbell were stocked after the hunting season. The bag limit for bucks was reduced for the 1969 hunting season on Chuck Swan, with additional *texanus* deer stocked after the hunting season.

During 1968, the counties of Anderson, Decatur, Jefferson, Knox, Moore, Morgan, and Scott and Kettlefoot WMA, received 237 deer from both Fort Campbell and Chuck Swan WMA. Aside from TWRA's stockpiling efforts on Chuck Swan, Morgan County received one female deer from Volunteer Army Ammunition Plant in 1969.

Grainger, Hardin, McNairy, and Trousdale counties received major stockings totaling 315 animals in 1970, as well as Andrew Johnson WMA, which received 48 deer from Chuck Swan. In 1971 and 1972, Coffee County received 97 deer from AEDC WMA; Grainger, 100 animals from Chuck Swan; Marshall and Trousdale counties, 206 from Fort Campbell. Polk County received a minor stocking of eight deer in 1970, but efforts led to a jump in 1972, with 55 coming from Fort Campbell and 136 more coming from Chuck Swan WMA. Coffee County also was the site for

TWRA Biologist Ed Penrod draws a bead on a whitetail with a dart gun. Sedative darts were used to capture selected deer for restocking projects.

*Workers disentangle a fawn from a
cannon propelled net. The mother
lies immobilized under the netting in
the foreground.*

release of 31 deer from AEDC WMA.

Protection of newly stocked deer was still a priori-
ty for a successful restoration program. Joe Farrar,
TWRA Deer Restoration Project leader from 1964 to
1970, related the sentiments of Judge Fred Durham
from Gallatin. "We stocked deer in Bug Hollow in
Sumner County, and Judge Durham was there," Farrar
said. "He told me, `If anyone comes before my court
and they've been harassing these deer, they better be
prepared to face the up to what they've done.'" Judge
Durham and other magistrates across the state understood their role in the whitetail restoration program,
and many were ready to hand down stiff penalties for
law violators.

The restoration program was highly successful
during the 1960s and early 1970s. The deer quickly
multiplied, but in some instances restocking proved
too successful. Farrar told of his experience in White
County, near McMinnville. "We were asked by several
people in White County to bring deer in for stocking.
We warned them that bringing deer to the area held
the potential for crop and plant damage to the local
nursery businesses. Eventually the deer did their thing
and began working on the nurseries. The local nurseries have since had to build deer-proof fencing
around their businesses to protect their property."

There is no doubt about the importance of Fort
Campbell's contribution to Tennessee's deer restoration,

so TWRA personnel returned the favor by stocking wild turkeys on the base. Biologist Farrar did the first stocking of turkeys, one hen and five poults, on the day President Johnson dedicated Percy Priest Dam. The initial stocking of wild turkeys was augmented with subsequent releases, and today Fort Campbell has a thriving population. In addition to the wild turkeys, TWRA stocked Kinzer Pool, near West Fork Creek, with rainbow trout, which allowed military personnel a chance at some fine fishing close at hand.

A doe feeds on a baited patch in front of a cannon net at left. The device, commonly used in the1970s, used small rockets to launch a net over the deer .

DEER RESTORATION: 1973 — 1985

The final phase of Tennessee's restoration program was led by four men who served as deer project leaders. Bob Pugh, Jack Murrey, Larry Marcum and Greg Wathen led the restoration during the 1970s and 1980s. Under Murrey's guidance, the Volunteer State returned its emphasis to stocking areas of East Tennessee that had not responded well to initial stockings. Whitetail populations were for the most part well established in middle and western counties by the mid 1970s, but much of eastern Tennessee still had only sparse populations. To rectify this situation, the thrust of the program was redirected to eastern counties, with large releases of deer into counties and areas with low whitetail populations.

Speculation surrounding East Tennessee's slow whitetail expansion points to harassment as a major limiting factor. A study was conducted from May 1973 to July 1977 by two TWRA biologists, Robert G. Nichols and Clifton J. Whitehead, at the Buffalo Springs Research Center in Grainger County, Tennessee. Thirteen deer were fitted with radio collars and released. Over 50 percent of the deer released in the simulated restoration at Buffalo Springs Research Center were killed either directly or indirectly because of dog harassment. The effects of a loss of this magnitude on an actual restoration would be significant. The minimal effect would be to slow the buildup of a herd in the area greatly. "When the loss of deer due to dogs is combined with

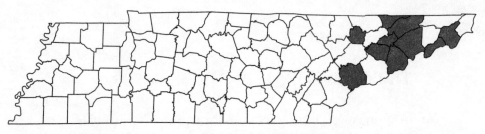

Areas of release for deer taken from the Holston Army Ammunition Plant: 1940-1985.

the loss due to illegal shooting, automobiles, and accidents, the restoration could easily fail."[1]

Another limiting factor to whitetail restoration in East Tennessee might have been "smaller than ideal numbers," Farrar said, of deer stocked in previous attempts. This was due to limited availability of whitetails for stocking during the early years of the program. In many instances, only 30 to 50 deer were stocked in a county, when five times that many would have been optimum for adequate herd expansion.[2]

The third limiting factor for eastern Tennessee's deer restoration could be attributed to the land itself. Early concepts of what constitutes good deer habitat have changed dramatically. Initially, it was believed that areas with large contiguous wooded areas (90 percent or more forest land), provided the best habitat for deer. However, restoration attempts have proven most successful in areas where forest and agriculture lands are mixed. It appears that the best habitat for deer occurs in areas of medium to high soil fertility with 40 to 70 percent forest coverage.[3] The diversity required in the deer food plant community throughout much of eastern Tennessee might be considered inferior in both nutritional quality and quantity to western and middle regions of the state.[4]

Though Chuck Swan WMA and AEDC WMA provided the most deer, other sources were located and used as additional reservoirs of deer. These new sources included Oak Ridge National Laboratory, which is a facility run by the U.S. Department of Energy; Cades Cove in the Great Smoky Mountains National Park; Holston Army Ammunition Plant; Henderson Island; and others. Supplementing these in-state sources, the state of Virginia donated 176 deer.

Chuck Swan WMA, AEDC WMA and Fort Campbell continued to be major sources of deer in 1973, with Cherokee Islands contributing its first whitetails to the restoration effort. Grainger, Hawkins, Monroe, Polk and Sullivan counties received a total of 295 deer. Fort Campbell donated 97 deer to the cause in 1973, but the military base declined in its support of the state's restoration program over the next several years.

The TWRA perfected several new capture techniques during this period of restoration. The use of cannon nets was widespread, where bait was placed in front of a net attached to several solid propellant rockets. When the desired deer came to feed, wildlife tech-

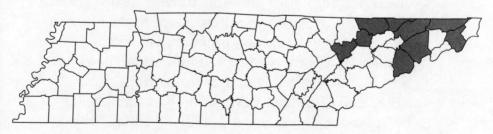

Areas of release for deer taken from the State of Virginia: 1940-1985.

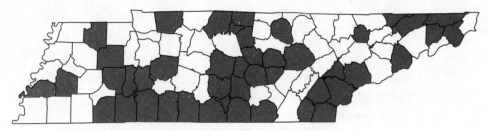

Areas of release for deer taken between 1960 - 1972.

nicians fired the net over them. When islands in East Tennessee lakes and rivers became deer sources, TWRA personnel simply drove the deer into the water and caught them with boats. Several deer from Cherokee Lake's islands were captured in this manner.

Carter County received 67 deer from Fort Campbell, AEDC WMA and Chuck Swan WMA in 1974. It had last been stocked with 60 whitetails from Chuck Swan in 1959. Other counties stocked in 1974 were: Cocke, 49 does and 20 bucks from Chuck Swan; Hawkins, 122 from Fort Campbell, AEDC and Holston Army Ammunition Plant; Sullivan, nine from AEDC and nine from Chuck Swan; and Unicoi County with 17 animals from Chuck Swan.

In 1975, four east Tennessee counties had additional stockings, with Johnson receiving its first. Then in 1976, Pickett and Sevier were added to the roster of counties in the restoration program. Three other counties, Claiborne, Coffee and Rutherford, had their herd numbers raised with deer from Chuck Swan, AEDC and Cheatham WMAs, and Fort Campbell. In 1977, Washington received its initial stocking, with Loudon, Monroe and Roane counties following in

1978. Blount County joined the effort in 1979, with 60 deer stocked in various areas. Four other counties also got additional deer that year. McMinn and Union counties were added to the list of those stocked in 1980, with Hamblen and Hancock coming on board in 1981. From 1982 through the end of the deer restoration project in 1985, only Greene County remained to

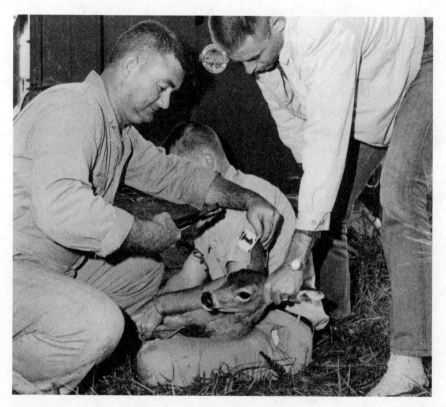

Joe Farrar, head of the TWRA Deer Restoration Project from 1964 to 1970, affixes an identification tag to a doe's ear prior to transportation and release.

receive whitetails. It was added to the counties stocked
in 1984. During the last four years of the program 11
eastern counties received supplemental numbers of
animals. In 1985, Tennessee's deer restoration program
was completed with the release of 360 deer into five
eastern counties. These releases were the crowning
touch for an effort that spanned 45 years and resulted
in the release of more than 9,000 animals.

The success of the program is measured in dramatic increases in the number of deer in the state,
which is estimated at nearly 800,000 animals today.
Another indicator of the successful program is annual
harvest rates currently topping 130,000 per year. By
1988, all 95 counties in the state had established deer
seasons, and in 1990 there were no areas in the state
with closed deer seasons.

Tennessee Deer Restoration Annual Summary 1960 - 1985

Area of Release	Source	Female	Male	Unknown	Total
Cumberland Co.	Ft. Campbell	5	6		11
Haywood Co.	Ft. Campbell	32	42		74
Montgomery Co.	Ft. Campbell	15	30	1	46
Van Buren Co.	Ft. Campbell	5	10		15
White Co.	Ft. Campbell	4	10		14
AEDC	Ft. Campbell	32	33		65
Eagle Creek Refuge	Chuck Swan	1	1		2
Total for 1960		**94**	**132**	**1**	**227**
Carroll Co.	Ft. Campbell	20	29		49
Decatur Co.	Ft. Campbell	14	26	1	41
Franklin Co.	Ft. Campbell	6	5		11
Henderson Co.	Ft. Campbell	17	38		55
Marion Co.	Ft. Campbell	25	29		54
Rutherford Co.	Ft. Campbell	1	3		4
Total for 1961		**83**	**130**	**1**	**214**

Macon Co.	Ft. Campbell	30	31		61
Smith Co.	Ft. Campbell	27	33		60
Sumner Co.	Ft. Campbell	35	30	4	69
Tipton Co.	Ft. Campbell	2	8		10
Total for 1962		**94**	**102**	**4**	**200**
Giles Co.	Ft. Campbell	30	31		61
Lincoln Co.	Ft. Campbell	4	7		11
Total for 1963		**34**	**38**		**72**
Cannon Co.	Ft. Campbell	24	18		42
Dekalb Co.	Ft. Campbell	29	29	1	59
Lincoln	Ft. Campbell	13	13	1	27
Smith Co.	Ft. Campbell	15	25		40
Sumner Co.	Ft. Campbell	1			1
Total for 1964		**82**	**85**	**2**	**169**
Bedford Co.	Ft. Campbell	24	29		53
Dekalb Co.	Ft. Campbell	1			1
Hawkins Co.	Ft. Campbell	37	6	4	47
Hickman Co.	Ft. Campbell	27	21	1	49
Jefferson Co.	Ft. Campbell	7	4		11
Perry Co.	Ft. Campbell	49	45	3	97
Smith Co.	Ft. Campbell	1	4		5
Total for 1965		**146**	**109**	**8**	**263**
Claiborne Co.	Chuck Swan	35	10	1	46
Lawrence Co.	Ft. Campbell	25	25		50
Perry Co.	Ft. Campbell	38	23		61
Warren Co.	Ft. Campbell	9	8		17

Wayne Co.	Ft. Campbell	23	26		49
Vol. Army Amm. Plt.	Oregon*	15	14	5	34
Total for 1966		**145**	**106**	**6**	**257**
Campbell Co.	Chuck Swan	45	10	2	57
Coffee Co.	Ft. Campbell	40	39	1	80
Decatur Co.	Ft. Campbell	35	27		62
Warren Co.	Ft. Campbell	16	20		36
Volunteer Army AP	Oregon*	23	18		41
Total for 1967		**159**	**114**	**3**	**276**
Anderson Co.	Chuck Swan			45	45
Decatur Co.	Ft. Campbell	6	1		7
Jefferson Co.	Chuck Swan			4	4
Knox Co.	Chuck Swan			5	5
Moore Co.	Ft. Campbell	32	39		71
Morgan Co.	Chuck Swan			45	45
Scott Co.	Chuck Swan			50	50
Chuck Swan	Ft. Campbell	19	34		53
Kettlefoot WMA	Chuck Swan	7	3		10
Total for 1968		**64**	**77**	**149**	**290**
Morgan Co.	Volunteer Army AP	1			1
Chuck Swan	Ft. Campbell	46	46	2	94
Total for 1969		**47**	**46**	**2**	**95**
Grainger Co.	Chuck Swan	80	25	1	106
Grainger Co.	Buffalo Springs		1		1
Hardin Co.	Ft. Campbell	51	34	2	87
McNairy Co.	Ft. Campbell	47	26	1	74

Polk Co.	Hamilton Co.		1		1
Polk Co.	Ft. Campbell	4	3		7
Trousdale Co.	Ft. Campbell	25	22		47
Andrew Johnson WMA	Chuck Swan	39	7	2	48
Total for 1970		**246**	**119**	**6**	**371**
Coffee Co.	AEDC	40	26		66
Grainger Co.	Chuck Swan	78	21	1	100
Marshall Co.	Ft. Campbell	66	51	2	119
Trousdale Co.	Ft. Campbell	22	17		39
Total	**for 1970**	**206**	**115**	**3**	**324**
Coffee Co.	AEDC	12	19		31
Marshall Co.	Ft. Campbell	21	18	1	40
Monroe Co.	Ft. Campbell	3	2		5
Monroe Co.	AEDC	8	1		9
Polk Co.	Ft. Campbell	29	26		55
Polk Co.	Chuck Swan	91	45		136
Trousdale Co.	Ft. Campbell	4	4		8
Total for 1972		**168**	**115**	**1**	**284**
Grainger Co.	Chuck Swan	5			5
Grainger Co.	Cherokee Islands	1			1
Hawkins Co.	AEDC	25	11		36
Monroe Co.	Ft. Campbell	4	9		13
Monroe Co.	AEDC	14	9		23
Monroe Co.	Chuck Swan	20	11		31
Polk Co.	Ft. Campbell	39	34		73
Polk Co.	AEDC	20	14		34
Polk Co.	Chuck Swan	43	25		68

Sullivan Co.	Ft. Campbell	8	3	11
Total for 1973		**179**	**116**	**295**
Carter Co.	Ft. Campbell	23	18	41
Carter Co.	AEDC	2		2
Carter Co.	Chuck Swan	14	10	24
Cocke Co.	Chuck Swan	49	20	69
Hawkins Co.	Ft. Campbell	9	2	11
Hawkins Co.	AEDC	80	27	107
Hawkins Co.	Holston Army AP	3	1	4
Sullivan Co.	AEDC	9		9
Sullivan Co.	Chuck Swan	6	3	9
Unicoi Co.	Chuck Swan	11	6	17
Total for 1974		**206**	**87**	**293**
Carter Co.	AEDC	5	2	7
Grainger Co.	Chuck Swan	5	1	6
Jefferson Co.	Chuck Swan	33	20	53
Johnson Co.	Chuck Swan	2	6	8
Sullivan Co.	AEDC	10	3	13
Sullivan Co.	Chuck Swan	15	10	25
Holston Army AP	Chuck Swan	6	2	8
Total for 1975		**76**	**44**	**120**
Claiborne Co.	Chuck Swan	34	21	55
Coffee Co.	AEDC	43	8	51
Coffee Co.	Cheatham WMA		2	2
Pickett Co.	Blythe Ferry	5	7	12
Rutherford Co.	Ft. Campbell	17	5	22
Rutherford Co.	AEDC	4	4	8

Sevier Co.	Chuck Swan	34	21	55
Total for 1976		**137**	**68**	**205**
Anderson Co.	Chuck Swan	32	23	55
Campbell Co.	Chuck Swan	22	5	27
Campbell Co.	Cherokee Islands	15	9	24
Cocke Co.	Ft. Campbell	14	8	22
Cocke Co.	AEDC	15	11	26
Cocke Co.	Chuck Swan	19	9	28
Pickett Co.	Blythe Ferry	15	1	16
Pickett Co.	Thiefneck Island	1	1	2
Washington Co.	Ft. Campbell	16	10	26
Washington Co.	AEDC	18	10	28
Total for 1977		**167**	**87**	**254**
Hawkins Co.	Holston Army AP	2	5	7
Hawkins Co.	Radford, VA.	11	6	17
Loudon Co.	Chuck Swan	13	11	24
Loudon Co.	Cherokee Islands	21	4	25
Monroe Co.	Chuck Swan	8	9	17
Monroe Co.	Cherokee Islands	6	4	10
Overton Co.	Ft. Campbell	28	10	38
Overton Co.	AEDC	38	22	60
Putnam Co.	Chuck Swan	1		1
Roane Co.	Blythe Ferry	12	5	17
Roane Co.	Chuck Swan	14	6	20
Roane Co.	Oak Ridge	7	6	13
Sullivan Co.	Radford, VA.	20	14	34
Sullivan Co.	Richmond, VA.	7	2	9
Totals for 1978		**188**	**104**	**292**

Blount Co.	Dickson Co.	1	1
Blount Co.	Ft. Campbell	17	7	24
Blount Co.	AEDC	13	8	21
Blount Co.	Chuck Swan	6	8	14
Hawkins Co.	Holston Army AP	17	16	33
Hawkins Co.	Debord	2	3	5
Johnson Co.	Chuck Swan	31	21	52
Loudon Co.	Dickson Co.		2	2
Loudon Co.	Ft. Campbell	6	2	8
Loudon Co.	AEDC	31	19	50
Roane Co.	Oak Ridge	9	13	22
Total for 1979		**132**	**100**	**232**
Bradley Co.	Ft. Campbell	11	1	12
Grainger Co.	Chuck Swan	31	18	49
Grainger Co.	Cherokee Islands	10	3	13
Hawkins Co.	Cheatham WMA	4	2	6
McMinn Co.	Ft. Campbell	13	4	17
McMinn Co.	AEDC	45	17	62
Union Co.	Holston Army AP	14	5	19
Union Co.	Chuck Swan	42	20	62
Union Co.	Oak Ridge	4	7	11
Total for 1980		**174**	**77**	**251**
Anderson Co.	Oak Ridge	16	12	28
Carter Co.	Cades Cove	50	1	51
Hamblen Co.	Henderson Island	2		2
Hamblen Co.	Holston Army AP	3	5	8
Hamblen Co.	Chuck Swan	30	14	44
Hancock Co.	Ft. Campbell	9	3	12

Hancock Co.	AEDC	20	14	34
Hancock Co.	Holston Army AP	4	3	7
Hancock Co.	Cades Cove	47	8	55
Hawkins Co.	AEDC	36	22	58
Hawkins Co.	Henderson Island	5	4	9
Hawkins Co.	Holston Army AP	16	12	28
Knox Co.	Chuck Swan	14	10	24
Sevier Co.	Henderson Island	13	4	17
Sevier Co.	Chuck Swan	36	19	55
Sevier Co.	Cherokee Islands	7	2	9
Total for 1981		**306**	**135**	**441**
Carter Co.	Holston Army AP	28	19	47
Carter Co.	Chuck Swan	31	18	49
Carter Co.	Cherokee Islands	16	7	23
Claiborne Co.	Cades Cove	63	15	78
Cocke Co.	Sevier Co.		1	1
Cocke Co.	Ft. Campbell	5	4	9
Cocke Co.	AEDC	37	26	63
Cocke Co.	Henderson Island	12	5	17
Cocke Co.	Chuck Swan	7	3	10
Cocke Co.	Cherokee Islands	2	1	3
Coffee. Co.	AEDC		1	1
Grainger Co.	Chuck Swan	39	16	55
Grainger Co.	Oak Ridge	18	18	36
Total for 1982		**258**	**134**	**392**
Anderson Co.	Henderson Island	8	7	15
Anderson Co.	Chuck Swan	22	8	30
Anderson Co.	Cherokee Island	15	8	23

Blount Co.	Henderson Island	27	10	37
Blount Co.	Holston Army AP	6	8	14
Blount Co.	Chuck Swan	40	8	48
Jefferson Co.	Henderson Island	6	2	8
Jefferson Co.	Holston Army AP	13	13	26
Jefferson Co.	Chuck Swan	35	6	41
Total for 1983		**200**	**92**	**292**
Bradley Co.	Kingston Refuge	9	6	15
Bradley Co.	Oak Ridge	22	14	36
Claiborne Co.	Henderson Island	8	5	13
Claiborne Co.	Chuck Swan	37	12	50
Cocke Co.	Oak Ridge	4	2	6
Cocke Co.	Cades Cove	26	5	31
Greene Co.	AEDC	12	8	20
Greene Co.	Holston Army AP	15	11	26
Greene Co.	Oak Ridge	2	2	4
Greene Co.	Cades Cove	11	3	14
Greene Co.	Phipps Bend	25	9	34
Monroe Co.	AEDC	22	8	30
Monroe Co.	Henderson Island	13	6	19
Monroe Co.	Chuck Swan	30	19	49
Monroe Co.	Phipps Bend	1	1	2
Union Co.	Cades Cove	52	14	66
Total for 1984		**289**	**126**	**415**
Anderson Co.	AEDC	7	3	10
Anderson Co.	AEDC	12	3	15
Anderson Co.	Dublin, VA	17	14	31
Anderson Co.	Radford, VA	10	7	17

Blount Co.	Chuck Swan	42	27		69
Blount Co.	Oak Ridge	2	4		6
Cocke Co.	Holston Army AP	9	5		14
Cocke Co.	Kingston Refuge	2			2
Cocke Co.	Oak Ridge	10	8		18
Cocke Co.	Cades Cove	27	6		33
Cocke Co.	Dublin, VA	14	4		18
Cocke Co.	Radford, VA	30	20		50
Greene Co.	Oak Ridge	3	2		5
Unicoi Co.	AEDC	11	2		13
Unicoi Co.	Holston Army AP	3	3		6
Unicoi Co.	Chuck Swan	22	10		32
Unicoi Co.	Oak Ridge	10	5		15
Unicoi Co.	Phipps Bend	3	3		6
Total for 1985		**234**	**126**		**360**

Total for Deer Restoration Program   5377   3414   334   9123

* Deer originated from Oregon were black-tailed deer brought into the state for breeding experiments

Source of this information is the Wildlife Research Report, *Deer Restoration in Tennessee 1940-1985*, Wildlife Resource Agency, Nashville, TN., 1991

Deer Restoration Areas of Deer Releases and Sources 1940-1985

Area of Release	Source	Female	Male	Unknown	Total
Anderson	AEDC	7	3		10
	Hend Is	8	7		15
	Chuck Swan	54	31	45	130
	Oak Ridge	28	15		43
	Dublin, VA	17	14		31
	Radford, VA	10	7		17
	Cherokee Islands	15	8		23
Bedford	Ft. Campbell	24	29		53
Blount	Dickson		1		1
	Ft. Campbell	17	7		24
	AEDC	13	8		21
	Hend Is	27	10		37
	Holston AAP	6	8		14
	Chuck Swan	117	58		175

Blount	Oakridge	2	4		6
Bradley	Ft. Campbell	39	30		69
	Kingston REF	14	14		28
	Oak Ridge	45	28		73
Campbell	Chuck Swan	67	15	2	84
	Cherokee Islands	15	9		24
Cannon	Ft. Campbell	24	18		42
Carroll	Ft. Campbell	20	29		49
Carter	Ft. Campbell	23	18		41
	AEDC	7	2		9
	Holston AAP	28	19		47
	Chuck Swan	86	46	1	133
	Cades Coves	50	1		51
	Cherokee Islands	16	7		23
Claiborne	Hend Island	8	5		13
	Chuck Swan	106	44	1	151
	Cades Coves	63	15		78
Clay	Chuck Swan	21	19		40
Cocke	Sevier		1		1
	Ft. Campbell	19	12		31
	AEDC	52	37		89
	Hend Island	12	5		17
	Holston AAP	9	5		14
	Chuck Swan	75	32		107
	Kingston REF	2			2
	Oakridge	14	10		24
	Cades Cove	53	11		64
	Dublin, VA	14	4		18
	Radford, VA	30	20		50
	Cherokee Islands	2	1		3
Coffee	Ft. Campbell	40	39	1	80
	AEDC	95	54		149
	Cheatham WMA		2		2

Cumberland	Ft. Campbell	5	6		11
Deacatur	Ft. Campbell	55	54	1	110
Frankin	Ft. Campbell	6	5		11
	Chuck Swan	65	39	3	107
Giles	Ft. Campbell	30	31		61
Grainger	Chuck Swan	238	81	2	321
	Oak Ridge	18	18		36
	Buffalo Springs		1		1
	Cherokee Islands	11	3		14
Greene	AEDC	12	8		20
	Holston AAP	15	11		26
	Oak Ridge	5	4		9
	Cades Cove	11	3		14
	Phipps Bend	25	9		34
Grundy	Chuck Swan	35	22	2	59
Hamblen	Hend Island		2		2
	Holston AAP	3	5		8
	Chuck Swan	30	14		41
Hamilton	Chuck Swan	22	16	12	50
Hancock	Ft. Campbell	9	3		12
	AEDC	20	14		34
	Holston AAP	4	3		7
	Chuck Swan	31	19	1	51
	Cades Cove	47	8		55
Hardeman	Chuck Swan	39	14	2	55
Hardin	Ft. Campbell	55	36	2	93
	Chuck Swan	23	23	2	48
Hawkins	Ft. Campbell	9	2		11
	AEDC	141	60		201
	Hend Island	5	4		9
	Holston AAP	38	34		72
	Chuck Swan	37	6	4	47
	Cheatham WMA	4	2		6

	Radford, VA	11	6		17
	Debord	2	3		5
Haywood	Ft. Campbell	32	42		74
Henderson	Ft. Campbell	17	38		55
Hickman	Ft. Campbell	27	21	1	49
	Chuck Swan	31	19		50
Jefferson	Hend Island	6	2		8
	Holston AAP	13	13		26
	Chuck Swan	75	30	4	109
Johnson	Chuck Swan	33	27		60
Knox	Chuck Swan	14	10	5	29
Lawrence	Ft. Campbell	25	25		50
Lincoln	Ft. Campbell	17	20	1	38
Loudon	Dickson		2		2
	Ft. Campbell	6	2		8
	AEDC	31	19		50
	Chuck Swan	13	11		24
	Cherokee Islands	21	4		25
McMinn	Ft. Campbell	13	4		17
	AEDC	45	17		62
McNairy	Ft. Campbell	47	26	1	74
Macon	Ft. Campbell	30	31		61
Madison	Chuck Swan	13	8	2	23
Marion	Ft. Campbell	25	29		54
Marshall	Ft. Campbell	87	69	3	159
Monroe	Ft. Campbell	7	11		18
	AEDC	44	18		62
	Hend Island	13	6		19
	Chuck Swan	58	39		97
	Cherokee Islands	6	4		10
	Phipps Bend	1	1		2
Montgomery	Ft. Campbell	20	35	1	56
Moore	Ft. Campbell	32	39		71

County	Source				Total
Morgan	Chuck Swan			45	45
	Volumteer AAP	1			1
	Schowalter, WI	22	17		39
Overton	Ft. Campbell	28	10		38
	AEDC	38	22		60
	Chuck Swan	31	20	1	52
Perry	Ft. Campbell	87	68	3	158
	Chuck Swan	30	19		49
Pickett	Blythe Ferry	20	8		28
	Schowalter, WI	19	14	2	35
	Thiefneck Island	1	1		2
Polk	Hamilton		1		1
	Ft. Campbell	72	63		135
	AEDC	20	14		34
	Chuck Swan	134	70		204
Putnam	Chuck Swan	33	17	4	54
Rhea	Chuck Swan	43	21	1	65
Roane	Blythe Ferry	12	5		17
	Chuck Swan	14	6		20
	Oak Ridge	16	19		20
Rutherford	Ft. Campbell	18	8		26
	AEDC	4	4		8
Scott	Chuck Swan	35	17	52	104
Sevier	Hend Island	13	4		17
	Chuck Swan	70	40		110
	Cherokee Islands	7	2		9
Shelby	McFadden Estates	9	4		13
Smith	Ft. Campbell	43	62		105
Stewart	Chuck Swan	45	20	2	67
Sullivan	Ft. Campbell	8	3		11
	AEDC	19	3		22
	Chuck Swan	21	13		34
	Radford, VA	20	14		34

	Richmond, VA	7	2		9
Sumner	Ft. Campbell	36	30	4	70
Tipton	Ft. Campbell	2	8		10
Trousdale	Ft. Campbell	51	43		94
Unicoi	Morgan	1			1
	AEDC	11	2		13
	Cove Creek	23	12		35
	Holston AAP	3	3		6
	Chuck Swan	33	16		49
	Oak Ridge	10	5		15
	Schowalter, WI	54	49	3	106
	Phipps Bend	3	3		6
Union	Holston AAP	14	5		19
	Chuck Swan	42	20		62
	Oak Ridge	4	7		11
	Cades Cove	52	14		66
Van Buren	Ft. Campbell	5	10		15
Warren	Ft. Campbell	25	28		53
Washington	Ft. Campbell	16	10		26
	AEDC	18	10		28
Wayne	Ft. Campbell	23	26		49
Weakley	Ft. Campbell	49	44	2	95
White	Ft. Campbell	17	29		46
AEDC	Ft. Campbell	32	33		65
And-Tully	Chuck Swan	28	21	1	50
Holston AAP	Chuck Swan	6	2		8
Catoosa	Morgan	12	7		19
	Washington	3			3
	Cheatham WMA			52	52
	Schowalter, WI	144	100	1	245
Eagle Creek	Chuck Swan	1	1		2
Chuck Swan	Ft. Campbell	65	80	2	147
Cheatham WMA	Cheatham WMA			19	19

	Schowalter, WI	9	7		16
	State of Michigan	25	25		50
	Woodmont	59	17		76
Falls Creek FLS	Schowalter, WI	25	19		44
Natches TR	Cove Creek	3	2		5
	Chuck Swan	22	22		44
	Shelby For	1			1
PR Cooper	Cheatham WMA			30	30
	Schowalter, WI	2322		1	46
Volunteer AAP	Oregon	38	32	5	75
Laurel Fork	Schowalter, WI	42	18		60
Eagle Creek Refuge	Chuck Swan	5	2		7
Andrew Johnson WMA	Chuck Swan	39	7	2	48
	Schowalter, WI	16	14		3
Kettlefoot WMA	Cove Creek	9	3		12
	Chuck Swan	32	27		59
	Schowalter, WI	18	6		24
Sewanee UNIV	Chuck Swan	1			1
TOTAL		5377	3414	332	9123

Section III

Habits &
Habitat

Chapter 9

Life Cycle of Tennessee Deer

*I*ndian summer's shorter days and cooler nights were having a profound effect on a buck we'll call Eight Ball, a 28-month-old 8-pointer whose rack has grown to the width of a basketball hoop. Now mid-September, only a few bloody shreds of velvet clung to his antlers. Seemingly annoyed, he rises from his bed deep in the heart of a young pine plantation and saunters up to a two-inch thick tree. Weaving his rack among its lower branches, he twists his head side to the side, sparring with its springy limbs and snapping a few off in the process.

Leaning his 175-pound muscular body into it, Eight Ball catches the young pine's trunk with his right antler solidly raking it up and down. Neck muscles bulging, eyes rolled back, Eight Ball continues his relentless attack on the tree. After three minutes he backs away panting, mouth agape. A twisted pine bough clings to his antlers, so he shakes his head like a soggy dog, tossing the offending branch to the ground.

EAR TAG AGED HER

Tennessee Wildlife RA officer Dick Hurd was surprised to discover the age of a doe shot during the 1993 muzzleloader season by Cookeville, Tennessee hunter Gwynn Medlin. Medlin, on a hunting trip in Pickett County near the Kentucky border, noticed an ear tag on his kill and called Hurd with the information. Records revealed that the doe had been trapped in the Arnold Engineering Development Center and released in Overton County, bordering on Pickett, in 1978 as a six-to-nine-month-old fawn. Hurd was able to confirm that the doe, who had been released as part of the state's deer restoration program, was at least 15 years old.

As the sun dips toward the western horizon Eight Ball walks from his pine-thicket sanctuary shadow boxing with an even dozen saplings before arriving in his favored feeding area, a honeysuckle-carpeted hardwood bottom a quarter mile away.

Attracted by the succulent food source, several other deer mill about. Three mature does and their twin offspring are joined by a yearling doe and her lone fawn. The acorn crop was abundant the previous winter, and reproduction followed suit. Three 16-month-old bucks soon arrive, a basket-racked 8-pointer, a spindly 6-pointer and a spike. All four bucks are feeling the effects of the changing seasons and corresponding higher levels of testosterone coursing through their veins. Each feeds, alternately testing the wind for the aroma of a "hot" doe, but the coming breeding season is still two months away, so the herd feeds together peacefully.

After feeding for an hour, the small 8-point buck turns and walks toward Eight Ball. Lifting his head from a clump of honeysuckle, Eight Ball pivots to meet the other buck half way. Lowering their heads, the two bucks spar lightly with each other while the herd watches and idly chews their browse.

As the breeding season grows nearer these half-hearted sparring sessions will transform into more aggressive bouts, with the mature, larger-bodied bucks asserting their dominance and the younger bucks sorting out the pecking order. Each buck will quickly learn his place, the strongest earning the right to pass on his genes to future generations.

RUT

A topic of conversation often heard around Volunteer State deer camps is whether on not the bucks are in "rut." Many a campfire discussion has centered around this phenomena of the whitetail world and how it affects hunting. According to Clarence Coffey, Region III information officer for the Tennessee Wildlife Resources Agency, "The rut can be defined as an annually recurrent state of sexual excitement in male deer. The rut lasts from three to four months during which time a buck is capable of servicing a doe. Peak rutting activity lasts several days."

Certain whitetail markers are made signifying the rut has commenced. Trees and bushes are stripped of their bark with by antlers, and oval depressions are pawed out of the leaf litter on the ground. Marked trees are referred to as "rubs," and the pawed places are called "scrapes."

RUBS

The scene portrayed at beginning of this chapter is typical for Tennessee whitetails during the pre-estrus stage. As day length decreases, the amount of light entering a deer's eyes triggers the pineal gland, with testosterone and androgen flooding the circulatory system. Bucks' antlers stop growing, their velvet covering dries, cracks and peels off. To hasten the removal of velvet bucks begin rubbing trees and brush. Rubbing increases daily as testosterone levels skyrocket, pump-

A hunter points to a well-used rub on a small cedar tree. Whitetail bucks often prefer shrubs and saplings with aromatic bark or wood .

ing up the buck's body size, much the same as an athlete on steroids.

Rubs serve both as visual and olfactory signposts to other area whitetails. Once the bark is rubbed from a tree, bucks rub their foreheads on the denuded trunk, depositing a glandular secretion. The stark, light-colored rub serves as a long-distance visual marker, while the scent left behind serves as close-range marker that probably identifies the individual buck making the rub and his readiness to breed. Occasionally, several bucks will rub the same tree, which may serve as a "bulletin board" of sorts. Does have also been observed to sniff, lick and rub their reproductive organs on rubs.

On several occasions the author has watched bucks rubbing saplings of various size and species. Rubs are commonly made on trees ranging from one to four inches in diameter, and occasionally up to 12 inches in diameter. Rubs on larger trees signify the presence of a large, dominant buck in the area. Although rubs can be found on practically any type tree in Tennessee, a buck's preference for odiferous species like red cedar and pine are apparent.

SCRAPES

As the end of September approaches bucks begin making "scrapes," pawed out oval patches of bare earth. Bucks urinate in their scrapes to leave a calling card for area does ready to breed. When a doe comes into estrus she will also urinate in scrapes announcing her readiness to be bred. Bucks continue rubbing and increase scrape making activity in areas where does frequent throughout the month of October in Tennessee. Scrapes are often found along field edges or trails within a buck's territory. They can vary greatly in size. Some Tennessee bucks' home range can be as small as two to three square miles, or as large as nine or 10 square miles.

The size of scrapes ranges from about one to two feet in diameter, but in rare instances can be as large as a car. The largest scrapes are often communal hubs of activity for several whitetails.

I have found two of these "super scrapes," and both were on a club where I frequently hunt in South Carolina. The first scrape of this magnitude was found beneath a low, bushy dogwood tree adjacent to a thick stand of young pines. It started out as four or five separate scrapes in a 15-foot wide circle around the squat dogwood. Over a four-week period at least two different bucks worked the scrape, as well as a doe, and by the middle of the hunting season it was one continuous ring around the dogwood. The "dogwood scrape" was first discovered in 1990. It was reopened and used again in 1991.

Another "super scrape" was found about a half mile from the first scrape in 1991. It measured nine feet wide and 30 feet long. Standing in the middle of the scrape I counted more than 20 fresh rubs in the immediate area. This scrape probably started out as average in size but was greatly enlarged by a tremendous buck fight. The entire area was practically swept clean, the ground looking like a disc harrow had been used to turn the soil. Several bucks and does were seen using the scrape during the course of the hunting season, and a few were tagged by lucky hunters.

If you look closely at a scrape, it is nearly always accompanied by an overhanging branch three to six feet above the ground that is usually twisted or broken. When a buck makes a scrape he begins by grasping a branch in his mouth and lightly chewing on it. He will also lick it and rub his forehead on the branch depositing saliva and scent. Next he will take a forefoot and paw at a place on the ground beneath the branch until all leaves and debris are removed. Then he will step forward and urinate down the inside of his rear legs, the stream running across his tarsal glands on the inside of his hocks onto the bare ground. The whole process usually takes about a minute.

PRE-ESTRUS DEER ACTIVITY

During the rubbing and scraping period, or pre-estrus, bucks have abandoned their summer bachelor groups and become loners. Yearling bucks, those approaching 18 months old, are driven from doe groups, which reduces the chance for inbreeding.

The "fall shuffle," a phrase coined by Montana whitetail expert David Morris, aptly describes the helter skelter scattering of yearling bucks from their former home ranges. At this time of the year yearling bucks bounce between territories dominated by differ-

A buck checks out a scrape beneath the branches of a pine tree. In September bucks paw oval patches of bare earth to use as scent marking stations.

A whitetail buck leaps a farmer's barbed wire fence at the edge of a pasture. Most man-made barriers pose little obstacle to wide-ranging O. Virginianus.

ent doe groups and mature bucks like a pinball. The associated increase in movement for yearling bucks is one of the reasons why Tennessee hunters are able to harvest these age class bucks so readily. The other reason more yearling bucks are harvested is that they comprise the majority of all legal bucks in most areas.

Feeding still dominates daily activity for both bucks and does, consequently hunters should locate deer food sources when pursuing whitetails during October and early November. As peak estrus approaches with the first does coming into heat during late October, bucks can be located by stand hunting on trails between area doe groups. Bucks will make a circuitous route daily from their core bedding areas to doe bedding and feeding areas to check for does coming into estrus. This is the best time to hunt near scrapes in areas frequented by does, as bucks will stay on fairly predictable schedules while checking scrapes.

ESTRUS AND THE RUT

When the first does begin visiting scrapes, leaving their calling cards for amorous bucks, the onset of estrus, or the breeding period, has arrived. Estrus activity builds slowly over a three-to-four-week period, peaking in a flurry of breeding activity lasting about a week. After the peak of estrus a lull of deer activity follows, with

An amorous buck pursues a doe in estrus. A dominant buck will attempt to isolate females in estrus from other bucks and will breed with the doe several times

Pre-rut activity includes light sparring matches between bucks as they test their strength and assert dominance prior to the breeding phase.

worn-out bucks seeking sanctuary in thick cover. After a few days rest, usually a week to 10 days, and bucks resume normal feeding patterns.

Female whitetails show very little stress from rutting activities, and their daytime activity centers around feeding. The exception for females is the three to four-day period prior to their actual estrus, which lasts about 24 hours. As estrus approaches the doe will be chased by one or more bucks, with the dominant buck fending off the does' other amorous suitors. The dominant buck will attempt to isolate his mate from other bucks, and frequently will breed the doe several times during the 24-hour period she will stand for copulation. As soon as the doe goes out of estrus her suitor will immediately go on the prowl seeking other willing mates.

Does that don't become pregnant during their first estrus will come into estrus again 28 days later. This accounts for a secondary peak in breeding activity for many areas in Tennessee. (See chart beginning on page 172 for peak breeding dates for selected counties and WMAs.) Does will come into estrus a third and sometimes a fourth time if they don't become pregnant.

In some areas doe fawns also come into estrus, but this usually doesn't contribute significantly to the first peak in breeding activity. If doe fawns are bred during their first winter, it usually takes place in late December, January or February. This concentration of breeding effort over a short time span is a survival mechanism. It allows a large percentage of the population's offspring to be born during a corresponding period 200 to 205 days later. This mass delivery of offspring helps overcome losses to predators.

The dates of peak estrus vary throughout Tennessee and can be attributed to several factors. Generally, does in East Tennessee and the northern tier of counties will have the greatest breeding activity from the second to the fourth week in November. Does in West Tennessee and the southern tier of counties tend to come into estrus near Thanksgiving and throughout the month of December.

The timing of peak estrus can vary about a week

In one of nature's ancient rites, two mature bucks challenge each other during the fall rut. At this time yearling bucks scatter and seek opportunities to breed.

in a particular area, depending on temperatures and the physical condition of the area's herd. Cooler than average temperatures will speed up the breeding process, while warmer than average temperatures tend to slow things down.

Areas where whitetails are heavily dependent on acorns for their fall and winter food supply show a significant difference in peak breeding dates, depending on the scarcity of food. "Poor nutrition will delay the rut for that year," Larry Marcum, assistant chief of wildlife for the TWRA says, "but the following year, the peak of estrus for the majority of the area's herd will be earlier, due to does that did not have fawns. Lactating does will not come into estrus until fawns are weaned, thus the does that didn't have any fawns will breed earlier."

Hunters wanting to predict the peak of estrus to plan their hunting strategy should consider acorn availability in areas were deer depend heavily on hard mast. The fall following a poor mast crop females will come into estrus earlier than normal. If the previous fall's mast crop was heavy and the current acorn crop is poor, does will come into estrus later than normal. If acorn crops were average the year before and are good during the current year, breeding will predictably take place during the normal time frames for that area. Localities where deer feed heavily on agricultural crops seldom show a breeding cycle influenced by food scarcity.

Another influence on timing of peak estrus is the source of the subspecies stocked into a particular area. Counties and wildlife management areas where a majority of the deer stocked were from Wisconsin and Michigan will have a peak in breeding activity earlier than areas stocked with deer from Fort Campbell. Fort Campbell's whitetail population came from South Texas, where peak breeding activity takes place in mid- to late December. For example, Cheatham WMA's deer are descendants of the *borealis* subspecies from Wisconsin, and peak estrus occurs during the second and third weeks in November. McNairy County only received whitetails from Fort Campbell, which is the *texanus* subspecies, and typically have a peak in breeding activity in mid to late December. Peak estrus for deer herds in counties that have a wide cross section of whitetail subspecies in their gene pool is influenced very little, if at all, by their genetic ancestry.

HUNTING THE RUT

Hunters have long associated the peak of estrus, and its corresponding high level of daytime whitetail activity, with the best time to be afield. During this period bucks will forego eating in their drive to breed every doe they can. Bucks will abandon their normal travel patterns to chase does. Fairly predictable a few weeks before, bucks are liable to show up anywhere. Distracted by their lust, bucks lose their cautious nature and become highly aggressive. Find the females and you'll find the bucks. Locating food sources frequented by does is one of the best approaches to bagging a buck during this time.

POST RUT

"Post rut" is characterized as the rest and feeding period for bucks during lulls in breeding activity and when the area's does quit coming into estrus. Bucks will hide in thick cover and rest for several days, then resume normal feeding patterns. During the months of January and February, depending on where they are located, bucks work overtime consuming foods that will help them recover from the rigors of the rut to prepare for the lean times of winter.

WINTER ACTIVITIES

During the winter months, whitetails resume their normal schedules of feeding and resting. After breeding ceases a buck's hormonal level comes back to normal and his antlers are cast, or shed, as the process is commonly described. Shed antlers are often found along trails and in agriculture fields, much to the chagrin of farmers during spring planting. A whitetail antler can do quite a bit of damage to a tractor or implement tire.

Simply put, whitetails concentrate their winter feeding activities around the best food sources available, primarily waste grain, acorns, and woody browse. An in-depth description of food sources is given in a later chapter. High-quality winter food sources plays an important role in body and antler growth in bucks, and in birth weight of fawns the following spring.

James M. Wentworth determined in a 1992 study of Tennessee whitetails in the Appalachian Mountains that "the influence of the acorn crop on reproduction was reflected most strongly in the yearling age class. Ovulation rates, and presumably fetal rates were lower during poor acorn years. The proportion of yearlings (1½-year-olds) breeding also seemed to be reduced when acorns were scarce. Younger animals are generally more responsive to nutritional deficiencies than prime-aged animals, and under nourishment of yearling does results in both lowered fertility and fawning rates. Dietary restriction in adults generally causes

A buck searches a fallow field for forage. Bucks tend to have more points, longer beams and heavier racks if they have access to good winter food sources.

more moderate reductions in fawning rates, and unless severe, doesn't reduce fertility." Wentworth also found that recruitment of yearling animals suffered, which was evidenced by a lower percentage of 1½-year-old deer in the harvest two years after a poor mast crop.

In a concurrent study, Wentworth found that "antler development was reduced significantly following years of poor acorn availability" in the southern Appalachians. He found that bucks tended to have more points, longer beams and heavier racks if acorn crops were good. He also learned that the field-dressed weight bucks fluctuated about 10 pounds between poor and good mast crop years.[1]

SPRING AND SUMMER PATTERNS

Spring is a great time for whitetails. Over the course of a few days spring green-up of foliage brings a much needed improvement in diet. Pregnant does consume a lot of the new, green browse to feed their unborn fawns. The nutritious, succulent browse contributes to rapid body growth for both bucks and does, young and old.

About 202 days after conception, does give birth. Mature females commonly give birth to twins, some-

A doe nuzzles her newborn fawn in the Cheatham WMA. Gestation in whitetail deer generally takes 202 days following conception.

times triplets, and on rare occasions quadruplets. If triplets are commonly sighted in an area, it's a sure bet fall and winter food sources, normally acorns, were in great abundance. Frequent late winter and early spring rains, which promoted rapid plant growth, also contribute to triplet fawning. Conversely, if most of the does in an area only have one fawn, or are barren, times were pretty harsh.

When a doe is ready to give birth, she frequently seeks a secluded spot and will often drive other deer from the area. During labor, does will pace about, and when the time has come, will deliver their first fawn in less than 30 minutes.

After delivery is complete the doe will eat the afterbirth to reduce the chance that predators will catch the scent of a vulnerable situation. Nursing begins as soon as fawns learn to stand, normally about 30 minutes after birth. While nursing, a doe will persistently lick her fawn's anal region to stimulate defecation, and will eat her offspring's feces. This habit also works to hide a fawn's scent from predators.

The fact that whitetails in a normal environment concentrate their breeding activity around a brief period, and later their fawning dates, is a simple survival mechanism for the species. It puts a large number of offspring on the ground over a short period, and this helps to negate the effects of predation. The whitetail has always been a crucial link in the food chain. They are a prey species, pure and simple. Little has changed in this regard for the whitetail across thousands of

Within a half-hour of its birth the fawn becomes alert to its surroundings. This doe's single fawn implies that food sources were in short supply the previous winter.

Shortly after birth the fawn stands unsteadily on all four feet. As a prey species, locomotion at an early age in young whitetails is a definite survival trait.

Nursing begins about 30 minutes after birth, as soon the fawn is able to stand.

A whitetail fawn's white spots serve as effective camouflage in the dappled light of Tennessee's woodlands. The spots will fade as the deer matures.

years, only the prey specie have shifted in their relationship — man rising from an equal among other large predators once the large carnivores were eradicated.

Spring and summer months are a special time for bucks. Beginning in late April, bucks start growing in size and sprout new antlers. Antlers are among the fastest growing of living materials, with some mature bucks being capable of growing enormous racks over a 16-week period. Lots of nutritious browse, high soil fertility and the acquisition of essential minerals such as calcium are necessary for good antler growth.

Bucks grow their first sets of antlers during the spring following their first winter, and they repeat the process each spring until they die. Antlers are made of true bone and sprout from pedicels located on top of the skull above the eyes and in front of the ears. A buck's first set of antlers can range from spikes to a total of 10 points, with four being average.

It is a common misconception that if a buck grows a set of spikes his first year, each year following he will again only produce spikes. Research has shown that a high percentage of yearling spike bucks will later produce branched antlers. In many instances, "spikeism" is a result of does having been bred during a late breeding cycle and their male offspring having a shorter summer growth period. These more immature bucks were basically short-changed in their growth cycle, and to assure survival, their bodies dedicated more nutrients to body growth than antler production. If a buck's second set of antlers are spikes, it is a good indication that he is a genetically inferior animal.

Growing antlers are composed of bone filled with blood vessels and nerve tissue surrounded by a fuzzy skin called velvet. Antlers in velvet are susceptible to injury and may sprout odd formations if damaged.

During the spring and summer months bucks and does shift their social behavior. Large doe groups seen in winter break apart to raise their fawns, and bucks tend to congregate in "bachelor groups." As September approaches, bucks' antlers harden as their testosterone levels rise, and bachelor groups break up.

TENNESSEE'S WHITETAIL PREDATORS

Besides man, several other predators found in Tennessee seize the opportunity on occasion to include venison in their diets. Bears, bobcats, free-ranging dogs, and a newcomer, coyotes, are all whitetail predators. It is a rare occasion when any of these predators overcomes a mature deer. Most losses are young fawns, crippled, sick or aged deer.

WHITETAIL DISEASE

Tennessee's whitetail population also experiences natural losses to disease. Typically, when an area's population reaches a critical level, disease outbreaks can occur. Although whitetails are susceptible to several diseases, two viruses, epizootic hemorrhagic disease (EHD), and bluetongue are the top whitetail killers. In mid-1991, a severe outbreak of EHD in Hardeman County killed a large portion of the area's population. Other areas in Tennessee have had EHD-related die-offs in the past. Unless hunter harvest continues to reduce the population in other areas of the state, EHD may cause further whitetail die-offs.

LIFE SPAN

Generally, whitetails in an unhunted population will live to be about nine years old, with a few living as long as 20 years. Tennessee's thriving whitetail population has a rather young age structure. Losses due to natural mortality, i.e. predation and disease, highway and farming mortality and hunting pressure combine to keep the age structure low.

Harvest data taken from Oak Ridge WMA's 1992-1993 season is a good barometer for herd age structures in Tennessee. Thirty-five percent of the bucks taken were less than one year old; 42 percent were 1½-year-olds; 17 percent were 2½; 4 percent were 3½; with the remaining 2 percent 4½ or older.

Does on Oak Ridge live longer. Thirty percent were less than one year old when harvested; 23 percent were 1½; 30 percent were 2½; 9 percent were 3½; 2 percent were 4½; and 6 percent were 5½ or older.

The oldest deer on record in Tennessee was a 19½-year-old doe killed in Overton County in 1992. The doe was 2½ when captured on Catoosa WMA in 1972 for stocking in Clay County. Another senior citizen whitetail lived to be 15 years old. A Cookville hunter, participating in the Unit B muzzleloader season, killed a deer in Pickett County which turned out to be a veteran of many hunting seasons. The hunter, Gwynn Medlin, noticed an ear tag on the animal and called TWRA Biologist Dick Hurd with the information. Hurd did some research and found that the doe had been trapped from AEDC and released as a six- to nine-month-old fawn in northern Overton County in 1978.

Peak Estrus
Dates

Region	Counties or WMAs	Peak Estrus
Mississippi River	Anderson-Tully WMA	After 12/3/89
	Chickasaw NWR	After 12/3/89
	Shelby Forest WMA	11/25/90-12/1/90
Gulf Coastal Plain	Fayette Co.	12/11/83-12/17/83
	Hardeman Co.	12/11/83-12/17/83
	Hardeman Co.	*Most bred after 12/18/83
	Hardeman Co.	12/2/84-12/8/84
	Hardeman Co.	*Most bred after 12/16/84
	Haywood Co.	11/25/84-12/1/84
	Haywood Co.	Significant peak after 12/18/84
	Weakley Co.	11/27/83-12/3/83
	Weakley Co.	Sig. peak after 12/18/83
	Weakley Co.	11/11/84-11/17/84
	Weakley Co.	Sig. peak after 12/16/84
	Natchez Trace WMA	12/10/84-12/16/84
	Natchez Trace WMA	11/19/88-11/25/88
	Natchez Trace WMA	Sig. peak after 12/3/88
	Natchez Trace WMA	After 12/1/91
	Natchez Trace WMA	11/23/92-11/29/92
Western Valley	McNairy Co.	After 12/18/83
	McNairy Co.	After 12/16/84
W. Highland Rim	Cheatham WMA	11/11/91-11/24/91
	Hickman Co.	11/27/83-12/17/83
	Hickman Co.	12/2/85-12/8/85
	Hickman Co.	Sig. peak after 12/18/85
	Humphreys Co.	11/27/83-12/3/83

	Humphreys Co.	11/25/84-12/1/84
	Humphreys Co.	Sig. peak after 12/18/84
	Perry Co.	11/25/84-12/8/84
	Perry Co.	Peak after 12/16/84
Central Basin	Giles Co.	12/11/83-12/17/83
	Giles Co.	Peak after 12/18/84
	Giles Co.	11/25/84-12/1/84
	Henry Co.	11/17/85-11/23/85
	Jackson Co.	12/4/83-12/10/83
	Jackson Co.	Peak after 12/18/83
	Jackson Co.	After 12/16/84
	Lincoln Co.	After 12/18/83
	Lincoln Co.	After 12/16/84
E. Highland Rim	AEDC WMA	12/4/83-12/10/83
	AEDC WMA	11/25/84-12/1/84
	Coffee Co.	11/27/83-12/3/83
	Coffee Co.	Sig. peak after 12/18/83
	Franklin Co.	After 12/18/83
	Franklin Co.	After 12/16/84
	Franklin Co.	After 12/4/87
		(83% had not ovulated)
Cumberland Plateau	Catoosa WMA	11/4/92-11/17/92
Ridge & Valley	Chuck Swan WMA	After 12/16/84
	Chuck Swan WMA	11/21/87-11/27/87
	Chuck Swan WMA	11/18/88-11/24/88
	Chuck Swan WMA	Peak after 12/3/88
	Chuck Swan WMA	11/26/89-12/3/89
	Chuck Swan WMA	11/25/90-12/1/90
	Chuck Swan WMA	11/23/91-12/6/91
	Hawkins Co.	11/28/87-12/4/87
	Hawkins Co.	Sig. peak after 12/4/87
	Prentice Cooper WMA	11/18/91-11/24/91
Unaka Mtns.	Johnson Co.	11/21/87-11/27/87

173

Breeding and Fawning Dates based on Fetal Development January 4 - 6, 1985

FRANKLIN COUNTY			
Week of Conception	# of Does	% of Sample	Week of Fawning
Oct. 28-Nov 3	0	0	May 17-May 23
Nov 4-Nov. 10	1	1.1	May 24-May 30
Nov. 11-Nov. 17	1	1.1	May 31-June 5
Nov. 18-Nov. 24	0	0	June 6-June 13
Nov. 25-Dec. 1	1	1.1	June 14-June 20
Dec. 2-Dec. 8	0	0	June 21- July 27
Dec. 10-Dec. 16	1	1.1	June 28-July 4
After Dec. 16*	50	56.2	After July 5
Did not ovulate	35	39.3	
	89		

For all charts listed:

* Does had ovulated too recently to determine when or if pregnancy had resulted.

(Data from reproductive tracts from fawns not included- no tracts from fawns showed fetal development.)

GILES COUNTY

Week of Conception	# of Does	% of Sample	Week of Fawning
Oct. 28-Nov 3	0	0	May 17-May 23
Nov 4-Nov. 10	0	0	May 24-May 30
Nov. 11-Nov. 17	0	0	May 31-June 5
Nov. 18-Nov. 24	0	0	June 6-June 13
Nov. 25-Dec. 1	3	37.5	June 14-June 20
Dec. 2-Dec. 8	2	25	June 21- July 27
Dec. 10-Dec. 16	1	12.5	June 28-July 4
After Dec. 16*	2	25.0	After July 5
Did not ovulate	0	0	
	8		

HARDEMAN COUNTY

Week of Conception	# of Does	% of Sample	Week of Fawning
Oct. 28-Nov 3	0	0	May 17-May 23
Nov 4-Nov. 10	0	0	May 24-May 30
Nov. 11-Nov. 17	0	0	May 31-June 5
Nov. 18-Nov. 24	0	0	June 6-June 13
Nov. 25-Dec. 1	4	11.8	June 14-June 20
Dec. 2-Dec. 8	9	26.5	June 21- July 27
Dec. 10-Dec. 16	8	23.5	June 28-July 4
After Dec. 16*	13	38.2	After July 5
Did not ovulate	0	0	
	34		

HAYWOOD COUNTY			
Week of Conception	# of Does	% of Sample	Week of Fawning
Oct. 28-Nov 3	0	0	May 17-May 23
Nov 4-Nov. 10	0	0	May 24-May 30
Nov. 11-Nov. 17	1	5.9	May 31-June 5
Nov. 18-Nov. 24	3	17.6	June 6-June 13
Nov. 25-Dec. 1	4	23.5	June 14-June 20
Dec. 2-Dec. 8	3	17.6	June 21- July 27
Dec. 10-Dec. 16	2	11.8	June 28-July 4
After Dec. 16*	4	23.5	After July 5
Did not ovulate	0	0	
	17		

HICKMAN COUNTY			
Week of Conception	# of Does	% of Sample	Week of Fawning
Oct. 28-Nov 3	0	0	May 17-May 23
Nov 4-Nov. 10	0	0	May 24-May 30
Nov. 11-Nov. 17	0	0	May 31-June 5
Nov. 18-Nov. 24	0	0	June 6-June 13
Nov. 25-Dec. 1	2	11.1	June 14-June 20
Dec. 2-Dec. 8	6	33.3	June 21- July 27
Dec. 10-Dec. 16	4	22.2	June 28-July 4
After Dec. 16*	6	33.3	After July 5
Did not ovulate	0	0	
	18		

HUMPHREYS COUNTY			
Week of Conception	# of Does	% of Sample	Week of Fawning
Oct. 28-Nov 3	0	0	May 17-May 23
Nov 4-Nov. 10	0	0	May 24-May 30
Nov. 11-Nov. 17	0	0	May 31-June 5
Nov. 18-Nov. 24	4	13.3	June 6-June 13
Nov. 25-Dec. 1	7	23.3	June 14-June 20
Dec. 2-Dec. 8	4	13.3	June 21- July 27
Dec. 10-Dec. 16	5	16.7	June 28-July 4
After Dec. 16*	10	33.3	After July 5
Did not ovulate	0	0	
	30		

JACKSON COUNTY			
Week of Conception	# of Does	% of Sample	Week of Fawning
Oct. 28-Nov 3	0	0	May 17-May 23
Nov 4-Nov. 10	0	0	May 24-May 30
Nov. 11-Nov. 17	0	0	May 31-June 5
Nov. 18-Nov. 24	1	3.7	June 6-June 13
Nov. 25-Dec. 1	4	14.8	June 14-June 20
Dec. 2-Dec. 8	3	11.1	June 21- July 27
Dec. 10-Dec. 16	2	7.4	June 28-July 4
After Dec. 16*	17	63.0	After July 5
Did not ovulate	0	0	
	27		

LINCOLN COUNTY			
Week of Conception	# of Does	% of Sample	Week of Fawning
Oct. 28-Nov 3	0	0	May 17-May 23
Nov 4-Nov. 10	0	0	May 24-May 30
Nov. 11-Nov. 17	4	6.3	May 31-June 5
Nov. 18-Nov. 24	0	0	June 6-June 13
Nov. 25-Dec. 1	9	14.1	June 14-June 20
Dec. 2-Dec. 8	6	9.4	June 21- July 27
Dec. 10-Dec. 16	9	14.1	June 28-July 4
After Dec. 16*	33	51.6	After July 5
Did not ovulate	3	4.7	
	64		

McNAIRY COUNTY			
Week of Conception	# of Does	% of Sample	Week of Fawning
Oct. 28-Nov 3	0	0	May 17-May 23
Nov 4-Nov. 10	0	0	May 24-May 30
Nov. 11-Nov. 17	0	0	May 31-June 5
Nov. 18-Nov. 24	1	6.3	June 6-June 13
Nov. 25-Dec. 1	1	6.3	June 14-June 20
Dec. 2-Dec. 8	1	6.3	June 21- July 27
Dec. 10-Dec. 16	2	12.5	June 28-July 4
After Dec. 16*	11	68.8	After July 5
Did not ovulate	0	0	
	16		

NATCHEZ TRACE WMA			
Week of Conception	# of Does	% of Sample	Week of Fawning
Oct. 28-Nov 3	0	0	May 17-May 23
Nov 4-Nov. 10	0	0	May 24-May 30
Nov. 11-Nov. 17	0	0	May 31-June 5
Nov. 18-Nov. 24	0	0	June 6-June 13
Nov. 25-Dec. 1	1	11.1	June 14-June 20
Dec. 2-Dec. 8	1	11.1	June 21- July 27
Dec. 10-Dec. 16	4	44.4	June 28-July 4
After Dec. 16*	2	22.2	After July 5
Did not ovulate	1	11.1	
	9		

PERRY COUNTY			
Week of Conception	# of Does	% of Sample	Week of Fawning
Oct. 28-Nov 3	0	0	May 17-May 23
Nov 4-Nov. 10	0	0	May 24-May 30
Nov. 11-Nov. 17	0	0	May 31-June 5
Nov. 18-Nov. 24	0	0	June 6-June 13
Nov. 25-Dec. 1	1	20.0	June 14-June 20
Dec. 2-Dec. 8	1	20.0	June 21- July 27
Dec. 10-Dec. 16	0	0	June 28-July 4
After Dec. 16*	3	60.0	After July 5
Did not ovulate	0	0	
	5		

WEAKLEY COUNTY			
Week of Conception	# of Does	% of Sample	Week of Fawning
Oct. 28-Nov 3	2	8.3	May 17-May 23
Nov 4-Nov. 10	0	0	May 24-May 30
Nov. 11-Nov. 17	5	20.8	May 31-June 5
Nov. 18-Nov. 24	3	12.5	June 6-June 13
Nov. 25-Dec. 1	3	12.5	June 14-June 20
Dec. 2-Dec. 8	2	8.3	June 21- July 27
Dec. 10-Dec. 16	2	8.3	June 28-July 4
After Dec. 16*	7	29.2	After July 5
Did not ovulate	0	0	
	24		

A E D C WMA			
Week of Conception	# of Does	% of Sample	Week of Fawning
Oct. 28-Nov 3	3	0	May 17-May 23
Nov 4-Nov. 10	3	0	May 24-May 30
Nov. 11-Nov. 17	5	0	May 31-June 5
Nov. 18-Nov. 24	13	2.4	June 6-June 13
Nov. 25-Dec. 1	21	4.9	June 14-June 20
Dec. 2-Dec. 8	18	12.2	June 21- July 27
Dec. 10-Dec. 16	14	22.0	June 28-July 4
Dec. 16-Dec. 22	6	41.5	July 5-July 11
After Dec. 23*	15	14.7	After July 5
Did not ovulate	4	3.9	
	102		

CHUCK SWAN WMA			
Week of Conception	# of Does	% of Sample	Week of Fawning
Oct. 28-Nov 3	0	0	May 17-May 23
Nov 4-Nov. 10	0	0	May 24-May 30
Nov. 11-Nov. 17	0	0	May 31-June 5
Nov. 18-Nov. 24	1	2.4	June 6-June 13
Nov. 25-Dec. 1	2	4.9	June 14-June 20
Dec. 2-Dec. 8	5	12.2	June 21- July 27
Dec. 10-Dec. 16	9	22.0	June 28-July 4
After Dec. 16*	17	41.5	After July 5
Did not ovulate	7	17.1	
	41		

Chapter 10

Preferred
Foods

Solving the riddle of what deer eat is paramount for understanding the habits of whitetails, as is the case with any other wildlife species. Much research has been devoted to what foods are important to deer and when and why they eat them. When it is all boiled down, Tennessee's whitetail enthusiasts have a wealth of knowledge about deer feeding habits to help manage this renewable resource.

The relationship between white-tailed deer and their food sources is important to several groups. Farmers, concerned about their crops, want to know how to avoid or reduce the negative impact deer can have on their income. Forestry resource managers in Tennessee have broadened their focus on land management over the past two decades to include wildlife species, most notably whitetails. Timber companies have realized that managing their timber lands for wildlife casts them in a favorable public relations light and can earn added income from the lease of hunting rights.

Naturally, the availability and nutritional quality of whitetail food sources are the most important factors in herd health and reproduction. Wildlife biologists are curious about deer eating habits and how they affect their habitats. Biologists evaluate food sources to determine "carrying capacity" and set hunting season lengths and bag limits to keep the burgeoning whitetail population in check. Annual mast and browse surveys tell them a lot about herd abundance and health as

Whitetails switch from one preferred food source to another rather quickly as the nutritional quality drops in one and rises in another.

Although it is toxic to humans, white-tailed deer find poison ivy palatable and a valuable source of nutrition during the spring and summer months.

well as playing a big role in determining whether a herd is in balance with its habitat. As we proceed, we will dig deeper into the influence an abundant or limited food supply has on the animal itself.

People who enjoy the whitetail resource, whether they be casual observers, wildlife photographers or hunters, can learn a lot about this fantastic animal by increasing their knowledge of what deer prefer to dine on and when they utilize various food sources. Contrary to popular opinion, deer are picky eaters. At first glance, everything that is green during the spring and summer might seem a likely candidate for whitetail food. In reality, deer have "ice cream," "meat and potatoes" and "broccoli" in their diets, and like young children, have a preference for eating them in that order. The "ice cream" foods are highly nutritious and highly palatable. The "meat and potatoes" serve common nutritive needs, but are less palatable, and the "broccoli" foods are characterized as fillers, eaten only when the other food sources have been depleted and starvation is near.

Leaves, stems and buds of woody plants, collectively referred to as browse, are the mainstay of a white-tail's diet. Deer are ruminants (cud chewers) like cows, with the difference being that deer are browsers instead of grazers, which depend on grasses for their diet. Other common deer foods include fruits of trees and shrubs and the foliage of herbaceous plants, or weeds, commonly referred to as "forbs." Whitetails also relish farm crops, seeds, fungi, mosses, lichens, succulent grasses, and sometimes small amounts of meat such as snails, fish and mice. Although the author has never seen deer eat animals, he learned from a reliable source

Clovers, both native and introduced, are valuable food sources for deer. Clovers are high in protein and contain large amounts of calcium and other minerals.

that deer in a captive herd in southwest Mississippi would chase down mice, catch and eat them. Researchers in the Great Lakes region have discovered that whitetails will eat minnows, sometimes finding several hundred in a single deer's digestive tract.

Sam Munro, the lands manager for the large tract in southwest Mississippi and the caretaker for the captive herd with the peculiar taste for mice, has also observed other interesting whitetail food choices. "These deer love fried chicken, and will knock you down for a pair of fried frog legs," Munro said. "They like squash too, but won't eat it unless it's boiled. They'll eat venison roast, but they don't act like they really like it." In addition, Munro has observed the deer picking ticks off each other and eating them. Why whitetails eat meat is unclear, but a protein deficiency may be the reason.

Over 450 different kinds of plants are known to be eaten by white-tailed deer, but of these only a few

Several species of green brier, also called smilax or cat-briar, thrives in wooded or thicket areas of Tennessee. Green briar is an important component of whitetail browse.

are used extensively.[1] A deer's diet is limited by what it can reach, typically from the ground to 55 inches, but their reach can be extended to well over six feet if they take a notion to stand on their hind feet to stretch for a lofty morsel.

The author witnessed this peculiar habit several years ago while hunting in Henderson County near Lexington. It was late December, and what little honeysuckle remained along the edge of a fallow field was draped among lower tree branches. Honeysuckle being one of the "ice cream" foods, the doe being observed was determined to make a meal of this prime food source. She reared up and stood in place for about a half minute while she plucked several mouthfuls. She would drop back to all fours, move a few steps and resume her elevated dining. After her appetite was satisfied, she quietly moved off.

Not all plants are deer food. Wildlife researchers in the Southeast have learned that when certain "broccoli" foods are eaten, such as pine, deer populations are too high for the habitat to support. Biologists conduct browse surveys during February and March each year when food availability is at its lowest to determine herd densities. If too many of the plant species in the "broccoli" category have been eaten, they know deer have outstripped the area's carrying capacity.

Differing habitat types dominate Tennessee's landscape. These habitats are easily defined by categorizing them into 10 different major physiographic regions. Accordingly, whitetail diets differ by locality.

The Unaka Mountain Region along the North
Carolina border in East Tennessee is characterized by
steep, expansive hardwoods interspersed with a few
coniferous trees, and the understory is composed of
evergreens like rosebay rhododendron and mountain
laurel. Virtually no agriculture exists in the Unaka
Mountains. Moving west, we find the Ridge and Valley
Region that extends to the edge of the Cumberland
Plateau Region. The Ridge and Valley Region is comprised mainly of hardwoods interspersed with pastures

Acorns, particularly those of the white oak (above) with its lower level of tannic
acid, are preferred deer food. Acorns are are high in fats and carbohydrates.

and limited agriculture. The Cumberland Plateau is primarily hardwoods, with the Eastern Highland Rim, Central Basin and Western Highland Rim regions also being dominated by hardwoods. The composition of these four regions is changing on an annual basis with the emphasis on timber management leaning toward removal of hardwoods and replacement with faster growing pine species.

The dominance of agriculture grows as we travel into West Tennessee. The Western Valley Region, which lies along the Tennessee River corridor, and the Mississippi River Valley Region share a mix of hardwoods and agriculture. The Coastal Plain regions, both Upland and Plain, lie in between the river valleys and are comprised mostly of agriculture interspersed with broken hardwoods, and lately, pine.

Like people, deer require variety in their diets to stay healthy. Forbs and grasses have high levels of protein, phosphorous, and potassium. Fruits, acorns and crops such as corn are high in energy-producing fats and protein. Leaves from woody plants provide calcium and roughage to aid in digestion. Browse and certain forbs, grasses and fungi provide some mineral requirements.

The pursuit of food is the most important factor controlling year-round deer movement, and is the key to locating this shy, reclusive animal. We'll start by dividing whitetail foods into two categories — fall/winter and spring/summer. Then we will cover how the scarcity or abundance of food sources in different regions of Tennessee affect individual deer growth and reproduction. Hunters should take special note of how food sources influence herd numbers, body weights and antler growth, and during the fall and winter hunting seasons, how deer move and react to their food sources.

FALL AND WINTER

Memphis State researchers collected stomach samples from 254 deer between 1981 and 1990 in west Tennessee to ascertain fall and winter diets. What they found can help hunters concentrate their efforts in the right direction. Major deer foods for fall and winter include acorns, soybeans, corn, cross vine and honeysuckle. Persimmons, pokeberries, and grapes were the most commonly found fruits, or "soft mast" in deer diets. In areas where samples were taken for more than one year, they found that the percentages of the most desirable food sources changed according to availability. In general, if the preferred food source was in short supply, deer switched to the next best thing they could find.

At present population levels, finding enough food to survive is not a problem for most of Tennessee's deer herd. When they have enough to eat, deer are more selective, hence their nutritional needs have a greater influence on their diets than the availability of food. Predominantly agricultural areas provide enough of what deer need, but in other areas native plants must fulfill energy requirements when acorns are not available.

A whitetail buck forages in a grove of hardwoods. In the fall many deer switch their diet to fallen mast crops—the nuts of oak and beech.

Woody browse then becomes the main food source.

Carrying capacity for whitetails is greater in the western part of the state, which is substantiated by the larger deer harvests there each year. This condition could change, as the carrying capacity could be reduced in areas dominated by agriculture. For instance, a sharp decline in deer the harvest was recorded on highly agricultural areas such as Ames Plantation when area farmers switched from soybeans to cotton as their major crop. Other significant shifts in land use practices could also reduce carrying capacity on a large scale. In general, highly nutritious agricultural crops are eaten by deer when they are available. They are even preferred to acorns in instances such as on Ames Plantation, where acorns are present but rarely used. Areas where soybeans are harvested may yield a fantastic opportunity for hunters if special weather conditions exist. If soil moisture is high in harvested soybean fields and a few days of warm temperatures occur, soybean plants may sprout giving a succulent food source that will attract whitetails like a magnet.

MAST SURVEYS

During late summer each year, TWRA personnel take to the woods to assess the type and quantity of hard mast from oaks and other nut bearing trees. The data they collect tell biologists about the availability of acorns, primarily, for the coming fall and winter, which has a bearing on hunter success that fall, and reproduction and growth trends the following year. Astute wildlife observers have learned that whitetails tend to range farther and move more frequently during years of low mast production. Current local mast production can be learned by personal observation or by contacting TWRA biologists.

SPRING AND SUMMER

During the spring and summer the foods available to whitetails in Tennessee include both naturally available forages and planted crops. These can be categorized into seven types; acorns, agricultural crops, browse, forbs, fruit, fungi and grass. In 1991, an extensive study

While not grazing animals, deer, such as the buck shown above, will seek out agricultural crops such as soybeans, beans, corn, squash plants and grains.

was completed by Memphis State wildlife researchers, Dr. Phyllis K. Kennedy, Dr. Michael Kennedy and Diana A. Garland, on the year-round diet of whitetails in Tennessee. The Memphis State researchers collected stomach samples from 355 deer during spring and summer from 23 locations across the state over an 11-year period. The major foods consumed included honeysuckle, soybeans, poison ivy, green briar, lespedeza, and a host of minor plants. During the summer, deer in the western half of the state depended on agricultural crops more than deer in the eastern half. Where crops were in short supply, browse took over as the major component of their warm-season diet.

When they analyzed their data, they also found

that Tennessee's whitetails prefer different foods depending on where they live. Across the state, browse, agriculture crops and forbs were eaten in the highest quantities, and acorns did not occur in most samples; the exceptions were Shelby Forest and Johnson County. Fungi and fruits were rarely found, except in Johnson

Alert for danger, a spike buck feeds on honeysuckle at the edge of a clearing. Honeysuckle is a major deer food year-round.

County, where 26 percent of a whitetail's diet consisted of fruit, and Catoosa WMA, where deer foods sampled were 23 percent fungi in their summer diets. Grass was a minor food source for all areas except the Tennessee National Wildlife Refuge. Coming as no surprise, no agricultural crops were found in samples from Oak Ridge or Chuck Swan WMAs, but McNairy County deer diets were comprised of 77 percent crops.

WILDLIFE OPENINGS

The whitetail's dietary preference for crops gives credence to the practice of creating wildlife openings, or food plots, for deer and maintaining them on a year-round basis to attract and hold whitetails in a particular area. A wide array of other wildlife species also benefit from planted wildlife openings, especially if they are maintained throughout the year. The first step in preparing a wildlife opening is to take soil samples to check for pH levels and fertility. To do this, take a cupful of topsoil from several spots in the opening and mix them in a container. Obtain soil sample shipping containers from your local Soil Conservation office and ship them to the lab specified. In a few weeks the results will come back telling you the amount of lime and fertilizer needed to bring soil fertility to good levels. Soil sampling is an important step, since whitetails show a preference for planted foods from areas with good soil fertility. A general rule for forested land converted to openings is to apply 400 pounds of 10-10-10

A spike pauses at the edge of a cleared area. Whitetails prefer the margins of fields and clearings due to the greater variety of food plants found there and the sense of security afforded by access to cover.

fertilizer and two tons of lime per acre.

The size and shape of wildlife openings is important, too. Two acres is the minimum, with three or more being the optimum size. Southern wildlife biologists have noticed that deer seem to avoid food plots under two acres in size. Wildlife openings should be irregular in shape. A long, winding opening about 40 feet wide is better than one which is rectangular in shape. Whitetails love "edges" of all descriptions, owing to their greater plant diversity, and a field with irregular borders gives them a greater sense of security. If danger approaches, a couple of quick bounds put them in thick cover.

Five major plant types can be planted for year-round wildlife food sources: Warm season species; plants put out in the spring or summer which provide forage during the warm months and, when mature, produce seeds by early fall that are used by wildlife; cool season species, planted in late summer or early fall to provide fall, limited winter and spring foods; annuals, a species that has to be replanted each year; perennials, plants that when established will continue to grow for several years without having to be replanted; and legumes, those plants that have the ability to fix nitrogen from the air and incorporate it in the soil and are therefore excellent soil builders. Openings planted with these various species will attract and hold wildlife throughout the year.

Popular cool season plantings for deer include annuals such as iron clay cow peas, soybeans, rye grass, cobe lespedeza and crimson clover. Cool season perennials such as alfalfa, Redland II clover and the Ladino clovers; Osceola, Tillman and Regal, which perform better on wet soils, are prime wildlife food sources. Bicolor lespedeza (strain 101) is a perennial, shrubby legume that grows to a height of nine feet and is heavily browsed by deer.

Various trees species that produce hard or soft mast are also candidates for a portion of wildlife openings. Sawtooth oak, an introduced tree that is native to Asia, grow to a height of 55 feet and produces acorns annually and often in its sixth or seventh growing season. Persimmon is an excellent soft mast producer.

A wide variety of seeds and seedlings, as well as planting information, are available through the National Wild Turkey Federation's Project HELP

(Habitat Enhancement Land Program); 1-803-637-3106. Office hours are Monday through Friday, 8:30 a.m. to 5:00 p.m. EST.

Another method to attract whitetails is to mow existing areas with natural whitetail foods to stimulate growth, then fertilize these areas. Deer will be quick to recognize the added nutrients, dining on the plants with relish.

In recent years, the timber industry's practice of clearcutting has received a lot of attention from sportsmen and other groups. A study conducted in 1989 by University of Georgia researcher James M. Wentworth sheds light on the whitetail's use of clearcuts in the southern Appalachians. Wentworth included the Tellico unit of the Cherokee WMA as part of the study.

Wentworth found that deer used clearcuts most intensively during the summer, when woody and herbaceous forages were abundant. Use of clearcuts was very low in winter, as deer relied heavily on acorns in the surrounding forested areas.

Throughout the rest of Tennessee, clearcuts between one and five years old provide both cover and an excellent food source, owing to the abundance of herbaceous growth, primarily honeysuckle and cat green briar. As canopy closure develops, the amount of low browse decreases annually.

In the mountainous regions of Tennessee, timber harvest to increase the availability of winter browse appears to be of little benefit. Woody twigs, which account for most of the forage produced, are a minor component of the fall and winter diet of deer in the southern Appalachians.[2]

EFFECTS ON REPRODUCTION, BODY WEIGHTS AND ANTLER SIZE

The effects of an abundant or scarce food supply can be dramatic. Reproduction, body weight and antler size can all be affected. Research has shown that body weights of male and female fawns were tied to acorn crops from the previous year. During good acorn crop years East Tennessee deer herds' conception dates were typically nine days earlier than in poor acorn crop years. As a rule, if acorn crops are abundant, peak estrus, or peak rut, will come earlier than in low mast production years. Yearling does also had fewer fawns following poor mast crop years, and if the mast crop failed in areas where few other food sources were available, fetuses were sometimes absorbed, with no fawns being born. Buck weights and antler development were significantly lower following years of poor acorn production.

Hunter success is tied to acorn production, too. During good acorn years, due to lower deer activity levels, hunters harvest fewer deer. During poor years, whitetails have to range farther to find food, exposing themselves to hunters more often.

Top Food Sources*

Area	Spring/Summer	Fall/Winter
Lake County	soybeans	honeysuckle
Reelfoot NWR	crops	corn
Shelby Forest	honeysuckle	acorns
Anderson-Tully WMA	cross vine	acorns
Chickasaw NWR	cross vine	acorns
Hatchie NWR	poison ivy	acorns
Ames Plantation	soybeans	honeysuckle
Chickasaw WMA	soybeans	honeysuckle
McNairy County	soybeans	acorns
Natchez Trace WMA	honeysuckle	acorns
Decatur Co.	honeysuckle	corn
Tenn. NWR	lespedeza	acorns
LBL	corn	acorns
Hickman County	clover	acorns
Laurel Hill WMA	soybean	acorns
Cheatham WMA	flowering dogwood	acorns
Giles County	honeysuckle	acorns
Lincoln County	honeysuckle	acorns
Smith County	honeysuckle	acorns
Jackson County	honeysuckle	acorns
A.E.D.C.	green briar	acorns
Franklin County	browse	acorns
Dekalb County	honeysuckle	acorns
Catoosa WMA	cat green briar	acorns
Oak Ridge WMA	honeysuckle	acorns
Chuck Swan WMA	honeysuckle	acorns
Johnson County	green briar and apples	acorns

* It is assumed that samples taken from wildlife management areas are typical for deer in the surrounding county areas, owing to the whitetail's mobile nature. Data derived from TWRA Technical Report No. 91-6, *Spatial Variation in the diet of White-Tailed Deer in Tennessee;* Phyllis K. Kennedy, Diana A. Garland and Michael L. Kennedy, 1991.

(The food sources in parenthesis are from personal observation and reliable sources in those areas.)

Chapter 11

Herd Management

$\mathcal{F}$ive decades ago the mere sight of a whitetail in Tennessee was a rare treat. Over the years the deer herd grew and a few hunters benefited from the resource. As the popularity of the sport grew, so did hunter numbers. Successful deer hunters were scarce commodities for several years. Just knowing a successful hunter was a treat.

Reflecting back on the 1981 season, I remember cutting morning classes at Freed-Hardeman University in Henderson to try my luck on Chickasaw WMA. My roommate, James Pilgrim and I, tried in earnest to put our tag on any legal deer. We saw a few, or their rear ends as they bounded over the next ridge. Almost every day we would stop by Robertson's Pawn Shop or Webster's Sporting Goods, local big-game checking stations, to see if anyone had been lucky enough to bag a deer. Then one day word on campus got around that a student, Paul Cook, had tagged a deer with his bow. It wasn't long before we tracked down this whitetail wizard to convince him to share some of his methods for success.

Time passed and Tennessee's deer herd grew, raising our odds for success. We were finally able to bag deer, as were other hunters throughout the state as their numbers increased, too.

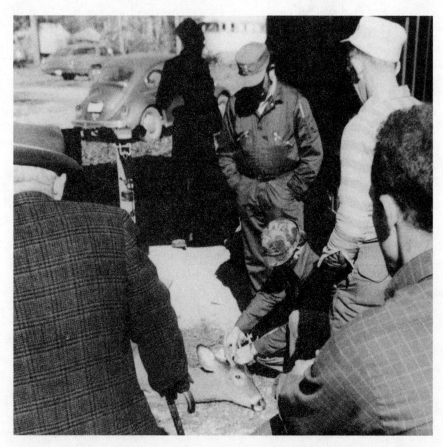

A hunter detaches his state deer tag at a Tennessee game checking station. His buck will be weighed and aged and the antlers will be measured.

Today, the white-tailed deer is the most sought after game animal in Tennessee. The number of deer hunters in the state grew from about 16,000 in 1955 to 197,661 during the 1988 - 1989 hunting season. By 1992, the number of deer hunters had dropped to 191,099. As deer populations have increased and expanded their range in the state, the harvest has also grown, from less than 200 deer in 1949 to nearly 127,000 in 1993. Huntable deer populations now exist in all 95 counties of the Volunteer State.

In addition to increasing harvests, hunter opportunities and success have increased as a result of the expanding deer herds. Deer hunters in Tennessee are provided the opportunity to harvest deer during archery, muzzleloader, and regular firearms seasons. A survey conducted in 1987 found that most of the deer hunters surveyed hunted during at least two different seasons, and a significant portion used all three weapon types in their hunting. There is also a statewide Young Sportsman's hunt, designed to promote hunting and proper sportsmanship to the state's younger hunters.

Hunter success rates have increased dramatically in the last 15 years. In 1974, deer hunter success was estimated to be about 9 percent. Only 8 percent of all successful hunters killed more than one deer. In 1988, the overall success rate was 32 percent with more than 30 percent of successful hunters harvesting two or more deer. By 1992, hunter success had grown to 41 percent with 28 percent of successful hunters bagging two or more deer. While the dramatic increase of deer populations in Tennessee has greatly benefited sportsmen and has contributed to the economy of Tennessee, it has also created some challenging issues for the Tennessee Wildlife Resources Agency that were unforeseen during the earlier stages of deer herd establishment. As deer herds have expanded, crop depredation complaints and vehicle/deer collisions have increased, especially in areas with dense deer populations. Also, some herds are apparently approaching carrying capacity, insofar as the tolerance of landowners is concerned, and the TWRA is attempting to stabilize these herds. Establishing control of some of these herds may prove to be the most difficult challenge the Agency will face in the upcoming years. To complicate matters further, the leasing of private lands for hunting rights is becoming more prevalent in Tennessee, which may prove to reduce the Agency's ability to control the state's deer populations effectively .

RANGE AND DISTRIBUTION

In the 1940s, Tennessee's deer population was estimated to be about 1,000 animals, existing in several small isolated populations in East Tennessee, and with a few deer present on Catoosa and Cheatham WMAs, and perhaps along to Tennessee River in the western portion of the state. Organized deer restoration efforts were initiated in 1940, with most of the early stockings occurring in the eastern and plateau regions of the state. By the late 1950s and 1960s, the emphasis of deer restoration activities had shifted to the counties in the middle and western counties of Tennessee. In the late 1970s and early 1980s, restoration was resumed in the

Successful hunters indicate the achievements of Tennessee's deer restoration. The harvest has increased from 200 deer in 1949 to more than 158,000 in 2003.

eastern counties, with this work finished in 1985.

As a result of the restoration activities and effective game management, Tennessee's whitetail herd is now estimated to number about 750,000 animals, with huntable populations existing in all of the state's 95 counties. The bulk of the population is located in the middle and western counties of the state, evidenced by the fact that Regions I and II account for approximately 75 percent of the statewide harvest.

Tennessee's potential carrying capacity in terms of deer populations is unknown at this time, primarily due to a lack of knowledge on the available quantity and quality of sustainable deer habitat in the state. Since the first restoration attempts in the state, opinions on what constitutes "good" deer habitat have changed dramatically. Early on it was believed that areas with large expanses of wooded areas (90 percent or more forest land) provided superior habitat for deer. However, restoration attempts have been most successful in areas where forest land and agriculture are interspersed. It appears that the best habitat for deer occurs in areas of medium to high soil fertility with 40 percent to 70 percent forest coverage. However, there remains much to learn and work on to improve understanding in this area.

SUPPLY AND DEMAND

The number of deer hunters in Tennessee has grown steadily since 1955, currently numbering about

191,000. Between 1975 and 1989, the number of deer hunters increased dramatically, from 123,277 to 197,661. The number of hunters took a dip in 1990, falling to 190,000, and fell again to 188,064 in 1991. The number of hunters rose to 191,099 in 1992.

Between 1975 and 1989, the number of deer hunters has increased at an average annual rate of 3.9 percent. However, during the 1975 - 1981, hunter numbers increased an average of 5.7 percent each year, then slowed to average 2.4 percent increase during 1982-1988. Deer hunter numbers fell 3.9 percent in 1990. The slight decline continued in 1991, falling 1 percent, but hunter numbers rose 1.6 percent in 1992.

According to the TWRA's 1989 *Strategic Plan for Wildlife Resources Management* for the 1990s, fourth revision, from which the vast majority of this text is derived, the Agency expected to have a slight growth of deer hunters through 1993.

SLOWING THE GROWTH

As the state's deer herds have continued to expand, the Agency has attempted to slow herd growth in some areas through the use of either-sex and antlerless-only quota hunts. Region I Big Game Biologist Joe Farrar was the farsighted manager that pushed for either-sex deer hunting in the early 1970s. Farrar conferred with Tom Greeland, chief of game management, and decided that the female deer population needed to be thinned to slow herd growth in portions of West Tennessee.

Working closely with Elmore Price, lands management biologist at Big Sandy WMA in Benton County, and Wilbur Baughn, regional manager for Region I stationed in Weakley County, Farrar led the first either-sex hunts in those counties.

The early hunts were controversial. It was a new concept for hunters who had been taught that protecting the female segment of the deer population was the key to successful whitetail restoration and management. Hunters in the two counties were slow to come around to the new management concepts, many clinging to the "sacred doe" philosophy.

Farrar wanted to get as broad a base of data together in as short a time period as possible, fearing that political pressure would halt the hunts. Opting to "play Weakley County by the book," as Farrar put it, he set initial either-sex quotas low to offset any public backlash, characterizing the effort as a "soft sell" from the public relations standpoint.

Farrar went to the extreme in Benton County. "We turned the screws" on the either-sex permits in Benton County, the biologist said. "We wanted to find out if we could actually impact the deer herd. The Agency went from passively managing the Benton County deer herd, to allowing the deer hunters there to manage the whitetail herd through seasonal harvest."

It took three years to convince top TWRA management that either-sex herd management could be a vital tool for whitetail population control. The concept finally took hold, and two decades of harvest data has

A hunter downs a buck from his tree stand. Tennessee game authorities estimate that approximately 190,000 hunters harvest more than 150,000 deer each season.

proven its merit. Since 1982, the number of permits available for these hunts has increased from 10,000 to a high of 98,150 in 1990. The number of either-sex quota tags dropped to 80,650 in 1991, when post-season landowner/tenant hunts began. The need for more antlerless harvest was apparent, and the quota was raised to 86,550 in 1992.

As a result of the either-sex quota hunts and other either-sex opportunities, the antlerless portion of Tennessee's total harvest increased from 25.8 percent in 1982, to 36 percent during 1988. The trend for increased antlerless harvests is expected to continue as either-sex hunting is initiated in additional counties.

BIOLOGICAL DATA COLLECTION

Each hunting season, many TWRA staffers and graduate students studying wildlife biology man big game checking stations to collect biological data from deer that are harvested. Thousands of deer are weighed and aged. Bucks' antlers are measured and does are checked to collect breeding success data. This information serves as a barometer of state-wide herd health as well as local population performance. This data is critical to managing whitetails in Tennessee successfully.

THE HARVEST GROWS

Tennessee's deer harvest increased an average of 15.5 percent each year between 1975 and 1987, when another record harvest of 98,817 was realized. Harvests have increased dramatically, rising from 108,762 in 1989, to 126,999 in 1992. Current annual harvest exceeds 150,000 each season.

As the statewide harvest has increased, the harvest on wildlife management areas has remained relatively constant, comprising a smaller percentage of the over-

Sporting a tracking collar, a young doe looks alertly toward the camera. By tracking and studying deer population trends, TWRA biologists can manage herd size and ensure healthy populations.

all kill each year. In 1988, the deer harvest on WMAs made up less than 10 percent of the state's total. By 1992, the percentage of deer taken on WMAs had dropped to 4.6 percent of the state's total harvest, excluding deer taken from Land Between the Lakes and Fort Campbell.

WMAs continue to be popular areas for deer hunters to pursue their sport. However, some have experienced declining participation on their hunts during the last few years. As WMAs continue to represent a less significant portion of Tennessee's deer harvest, the TWRA has begun to improve the quality of hunting and encourage better hunter participation. The decrease of WMA use is due in part to the increase in leased hunting lands in the state. When hunters invest their money in hunting rights, they tend to concentrate their efforts on the land they lease.

GOALS AND OBJECTIVES

The goals and objectives of the TWRA's whitetail management program are simple; they wish to maintain healthy, viable deer populations at optimum levels and improve the quality of deer hunting. Their overall objective, as set forth in their five-year wildlife resources management plan written in 1989, was to achieve a harvest of 137,450 deer by 222,675 hunters at an individual success rate of 35 percent by 1993. Although TWRA's expectations of hunter participation were rather optimistic, the collective wisdom of their wildlife management techniques has yielded hunter success rates in excess of their predictions. Individual hunter success rose to 38 percent in 1990, 40 percent in 1991, and 41 percent in 1992. Generally, the TWRA has managed its whitetail population as a renewable resource, focused on providing the highest possible hunter satisfaction. This boils down to providing the highest possible hunter opportunity, balanced against land use practices that are negatively impacted by the whitetail's presence. Most Tennessee residents want deer, but their numbers must be controlled to maintain acceptable levels that are compatible with human interests and herd carrying capacities that differ throughout the state.

PUBLIC HUNTING

The Volunteer State is blessed with a vast cumulative land base in their wildlife management area system. Over a million acres of public land is maintained for both game and non-game species. Hunter dollars pay for the management and maintenance of this land, but the benefit to the general public for enjoying vast array of flora and fauna comes at virtually no cost.

In addition to WMAs, Tennessee's hunters are fortunate to have access to al-most 235,000 acres of pub-

Careful management of deer populations and the health of deer herds can guarantee more trophies such as this extraordinary Volunteer State drop-tined buck.

lic hunting lands through cooperative effort with several large timber companies. An agreement has been made with the TWRA to enforce rules and regulations on these lands, while individual timber companies realize a profit through the sale of hunting permits.

Spread across the state, these lands are as varied as Tennessee and are within a short distance for every Tennessee hunter. Although all wildlife species are not found on each tract, excellent hunting is available. Depending on the location, hunters can expect to find deer, boar, black bear, wild turkey, waterfowl, grouse, squirrel, quail and rabbit.

Champion International Corporation, Hiwassee Land Company (Bowater), Packaging Corporation of America (PCA), Westvaco Corporation and Willamette Industries, Inc. had land in the public hunting area program.

Today, these timber companies have either been sold to other corporations, or have put their land into private hunting lease programs. Over the last decade, this program has dwindled from 600,000 acres to its present size. The trend toward downsizing is sure to continue.

A free brochure describing local permit purchase points is available from the TWRA, Ellington Agriculture Center, P.O. Box 40747, Nashville, TN 37204.

FEDERAL HUNTING LANDS

Public hunting opportunities are still available on federal lands like military reservations and National Wildlife refuges. Contact area managers for specific hunting information.

Fort Campbell (270) 798-2175

Federal Refuges
Federal refuge seasons and regulations may be different from the ones listed in the general hunting regulations. Contact the individual refuge for their specific seasons and regulations.
Chickasaw National Wildlife Refuge (731) 635-7621
Cross Creeks National Wildlife Refuge (931) 232-7477
Lower Hatchie National Wildlife Refuge (731) 635-7621
Hatchie National Wildlife Refuge (731) 772-0501
Reelfoot and Lake Isom National Wildlife Refuges
      (731) 538-2481
Tennessee National Wildlife Refuge (731) 642-2091

Chapter 12

Quality Deer Management

$\mathcal{A}$s the Volunteer State's whitetail population has expanded, hunter success has followed. Past management practices have focused on increasing hunter opportunity, which is interpreted as putting as many legal bucks in front of the hunter as possible. The result was a management program that opted for a rather young buck age structure, mostly 1½ years old at harvest.

This has been a highly successful plan, as evidenced by annually increasing harvest figures. From the ranks of successful deer hunters has come a call for more opportunities to bag larger-bodied, bigger-antlered bucks—a need for quality deer management.

The natural progression for many deer hunters is a maturation process. Many deer hunters go through stages; the first few seasons they strive to harvest the first legal buck that walks by their stand. As seasons pass and they have taken several smaller sized bucks, they expand their hunting experiences by taking up the use of weapons, like bows and blackpowder rifles. When they have mastered these other methods of hunting they frequently turn look to the greater challenges presented by hunting mature, heavy-bodied, large-antlered bucks. It is at this point that merely killing a legal buck takes a back seat to the total outdoors experience, and the added challenge and time required to bag a mature, quality buck serves to extend

In recent years many hunters have turned their attention to trophy or quality whitetail bucks -- mature, heavy-bodied, large-antlered animals.

the enjoyment of time afield.

Following close on the heels of Tennessee's expanding whitetail herd is a new breed of deer hunters who want to pit their skills against high-quality, trophy bucks with heavier bodies and bigger antlers. For bucks to reach this lofty status three chief criteria must be met; age, genetics and nutrition. Of these three ingredients, age is the most important. If a buck doesn't reach maturity, at least 3½ years old, good genetics and nutrition never have a chance to factor into the equation. By 3½ years of age, white-tailed bucks are nearly as heavy as they'll ever grow. Once body growth slows, more nutrients are dedicated to putting on additional antler mass.

Bucks generally have their largest racks at 5½ to 7½ years of age. Bucks living longer than 7½ years often begin to decline in body and antler size, due to the natural aging process. By the time a buck reaches 3½ years of age he has three hunting seasons behind him, and that makes him one of the most challenging big game animal on the earth. Hunting mature white-tailed bucks is rivaled in difficulty by other big game species only because of their remote habitats, harsh climates, or relative scarcity within large, trackless regions. Whitetails, the "all American" big game animal, are available to practically anyone wishing to hunt for them, and they provide world-class challenges for discriminating sportsmen who want the ultimate challenge hunting the mature buck brings.

On the other side of the coin, today's deer hunter

also wants a quality hunting experience, usually described as a place to hunt where deer can be observed in a relatively undisturbed setting and with a minimum of interference from other hunters. Sometimes labeled "trophy" hunter, this new breed of deer hunter is more aptly termed a "quality" deer hunter. "Trophy" hunting has become a target of controversy for an urbanized liberal media that is out of touch with rural lifestyles. The liberal media has taken a self-appointed role to determine what is politically correct for the rest of us. They have proposed such nonsense as calling guns the main culprit in today's skyrocketing crime rates. On another front, they have proclaimed that all hunting — with special emphasis on trophy hunting — is responsible for any decline in wildlife populations. Their "ivory tower" perceptions of hunting ignore the fact that America's game populations have made amazing comebacks since the turn of this century. Largely ignored is the fact that hunters and energies have been the leading saviors of declining wildlife habitats, and their collective resources are responsible for the management, preservation and restoration of many non-game species.

Nearly all Volunteer State hunters enjoy a good venison roast and still rank harvesting a deer for consumption extremely high. Most deer hunters who desire to shoot a quality buck understand modern deer herd management and recognize the importance of harvesting does to keep herds in balance with their habitat.

Another intangible "trophy" gained by those who hunt mature, quality whitetails is the added pleasure of

In Tennessee a quality buck can be considered a branch-antlered buck that has reached 3½ years of age.

passing up young bucks to observe and learn the whitetail's elusive habits. Learning the small intricate workings of nature helps us to understand what makes nature "tick" and ultimately gives us a deeper understanding of our role in the overall scheme of nature.

DEFINITION OF A QUALITY DEER

My personal definition of a quality buck in Tennessee is any branch-antlered buck that has reached 3½ years of age. Even though good genetics and proper nutrition are required for large antlers and bodies, the difficulty of pursuing and tagging a buck 3½ years old or older presents the ultimate challenge to a hunter's skills. As a whole, Tennessee's whitetail herd has present a strong genetic makeup from whitetails imported from South Texas and northern deer from Wisconsin and Michigan. Broad habitat diversity along with a high agricultural presence in many regions provides ample, high-quality food supplies to build large bodies and big racks. There's no doubt that Tennessee has what it takes to produce a high number of quality bucks, as seen by the growing number of deer added to the Tennessee Deer Registry (TDR) each year. The TDR, described in great detail in the Appendix, is a record-keeping system of the largest-antlered white-tailed bucks from the Volunteer State.

FIELD JUDGING TROPHY BUCKS

The best way to determine if a live buck fits the criterion of a "quality" deer is to judge the animal's antler size. Although body weights are a good measure of maturity, good genetics and nutrition, weight is difficult to assess before you pull the trigger.

The typical 3½-year-old Tennessee buck carries a rack with eight points, four per side, with beams measuring about 20 inches around the curve. His antler bases measure from 3¼ to 4 inches in circumference. A good rule of thumb for field judging a buck is to discern if the antler tips extend to the end of his nose when you get a side view. The width of a quality buck's rack measures at least 18 inches, or a couple of inches beyond his ears if viewed from the front or rear.

BODY SIZE FOR QUALITY BUCKS

Field-dressed weights for 3½ year-old bucks in good habitat usually range between 175 and 185 pounds, which interprets to live weights between 215 and 230 pounds. That's an exceptional buck in anyone's book. If we consider these bucks as "average" 3½ year-olds, it really gives credence to the philosophy of letting bucks mature. Exceptions to this criteria for quality bucks are found in areas where acorn crops are sparse, and the spring and summer ranges are nutritionally lacking. Another limiting factor noticed is when reviewing wildlife management area harvest data where deer herd genetic ancestry originated in North Carolina during the 1930s and 1940s. These deer are a mixed breed from the coastal region of North Carolina, Florida and New York. Two examples are Chuck Swan WMA and Natchez Trace WMA. High population densities and stiff competition for food also factor into the equation, pointing to the need for more harvest of females from these areas. Mature bucks from Chuck Swan average almost 50 pounds lighter than bucks from most other areas of Tennessee. Natchez Trace bucks in the older age classes typically weigh 20 to 30 pounds less than bucks from elsewhere. A trend I have noticed is that bucks from areas with acorns as the primary fall and winter food source tend to reach their largest body weights at 3½ years of age. Bucks in the 4½ age class and older may weigh less than bucks just one year younger. Although these older age class bucks

A Tennessee hunter displays a quality 8-pointer taken in the fall of 1972. Such mature bucks generally average around 200 to 230 pounds, live weight.

tend to be lighter in weight, they usually exhibit larger antlers than 3½ year-olds. It is my opinion that these older bucks are the dominant breeders in their areas, and subsequently spend less time feeding and more time in pursuit of does.

TWRA'S QUALITY DEER MANAGEMENT SURVEY

Personnel from the TWRA identified Natchez Trace as the most likely WMA to initiate a quality management program. Natchez Trace is one of the largest WMAs, with about 48,000 acres located in Henderson and Carroll counties. TWRA wildlife managers felt they

A statewide survey of 1,800 deer hunters in 1987 indicated that the most common hunting strategy was to shoot the first legal deer that came within range.

should first evaluate how widespread the interest in such a program really was and whether different types of deer hunters would continue to support such a program under a variety of conditions that might be necessary for the program's success. The purpose of the study, conducted by Bruce C. Hastings and Michael R. Pelton of the University of Tennessee, was to help TWRA personnel understand what Tennessee deer hunters want and need in general and how they view trophy or quality deer management in particular.[1]

A total of 1,800 deer hunters were sent six slightly varying questionnaires in April 1987. The questionnaires were mailed to statewide sportsman license holders, statewide gun hunters, statewide muzzleloader hunters, statewide bow hunters, Natchez Trace gun hunters, and Natchez Trace muzzleloader hunters. Response rate for the survey was rather high, totaling 74.6 percent.

Typical hunters from most survey groups were males in their 30s, were blue collar workers and were raised in rural areas or in small cities and towns. About 75 percent of Natchez Trace hunters, and 43 to 60 percent of hunters statewide, lived within 100 miles of Natchez Trace.

Respondents from most survey groups averaged deer hunting 20-21 days during the 1986 season, while statewide hunters spent about 15 days doing so. Respondents generally hunted with friends, and often walked ¼ to ⅓ mile from their vehicle to their favorite hunting spot. Their most common hunting strategy was to shoot the first legal deer that came within range. Success rates were rather high, ranging from 15.5percent for statewide bow hunters to over 50-percent for sportsman license holders.

More than 25 percent of each statewide survey group hunted WMAs. Sportsman license holders not only hunted WMAs more frequently than other statewide groups, they also hunted a greater number of WMAs than any other group, including Natchez Trace hunters.

When statewide hunters who had used WMAs during 1986 were asked what TWRA should change to improve deer hunting on these areas, the most common responses related to improvement of food availability, improvement of law enforcement, reduction or better distribution of hunters, acquisition of deer from

A combination of diet, maturity and heredity has produced the massive rack of typical antlers on this big Tennessee whitetail buck.

elsewhere for stocking, or no change at all because of confidence in TWRA's existing program. Nearly all these responses are manageable, with the exception of stocking large-racked, heavyweight deer. The effects of stocking big "northern" deer would have little if any impact on the Natchez Trace herd, owing to the high deer densities already present on the area. The most commonly hunted WMAs for statewide hunters were Cherokee, Catoosa, AEDC, LBL, and Chuck Swan. The areas they rated highest in quality were LBL, Oak Ridge, and Fort Campbell.

Natchez Trace hunters surveyed felt very strongly that there were not enough trophy bucks.

Some attitudes toward deer management were

assessed by asking deer hunters how much they agreed with each of nine alternatives for managing an over-populated deer herd. The least popular alternative by all six groups was for TWRA to do nothing.

Most hunters believed that harvesting a trophy buck was at least moderately important, but not significantly more than bagging a buck of any size or taking deer just for consumption.

About 60-75 percent of each survey group wanted at least one WMA in Tennessee managed for quality deer. Statewide groups usually were somewhat in favor of trophy management in at least one WMA, even if bucks were not hunted for a few years, if hunters saw fewer deer, or if more spikes of any size had to be shot. They were mildly opposed to initiation of quality deer management if more does were shot, although very few were opposed to doe hunting in general. Natchez Trace hunters were affected by the "not in my back yard" syndrome, and were mildly opposed to quality deer management there under the four previously mentioned conditions. Acceptance for these management strategies was much higher when the question was left open to an unnamed WMA in the state.

Statewide hunters listed Natchez Trace as the primary candidate for quality management, along with LBL, Catoosa, Cherokee, Oak Ridge, AEDC, Cheatham and Chuck Swan. Statewide groups were more likely to hunt Natchez Trace if a quality management program was started, but they were unlikely to hunt the area without the program.

THE PROGRAM BEGINS

After much deliberation, TWRA wildlife managers decided to begin a quality deer management program on the portion of Natchez Trace WMA that lies south of I-40 in 1989. At the same time they liberalized hunting on the northern portion of the WMA to allow open hunts concurrent with West Tennessee's seasons. This allowed Natchez Trace area hunters access to hunt the northern area at will, while restricting hunting dates and imposing buck harvest restrictions on the southern portion. This helped alleviate fears of local hunters who might have responded unfavorably to the new management program if they thought they would lose access to a hunting area close to home.

Harvest restrictions for South Natchez Trace limited hunters to taking only bucks with six points or more. The doe harvest quota was also raised to lower herd densities, making available more food to potentially fewer deer. These management strategies were aimed at carrying more bucks into the older age classes, thereby raising the likelihood of more bucks reaching maturity.

During the 1992 season, Natchez Trace South produced at least 13 bucks 3½ years old or older. Twenty-two of 51 bucks harvested were not aged. Eight 2½ year-old bucks were harvested that had at least six points. The average field-dressed weights were 136.9 and 145.8 pounds for 2½ and 3½+ year-old bucks, respectively.

Controlling vehicular access is an important aspect

Harvest restrictions in some areas allow hunters to take only bucks with six or more points, a strategy aimed at permitting more bucks to reach maturity.

in managing for quality bucks. South Natchez Trace may have too many roads open to travel to provide the protection needed from wildlife thieves who ride the roads and kill deer indiscriminately. If control and protection by law enforcement can't be maintained, the quality management program on the area may be jeopardy.

Implementing a quality deer management program is a slow process. Some may feel that too few quality bucks have been harvested but don't take into account how difficult it is to kill a mature buck. South Natchez Trace has what it takes to produce mega bucks. Billy Mays of Darden, Tennessee, is convinced. He bagged a buck on Natchez Trace in 1987 that scores 160⅞ on the Boone & Crockett scale, a tremendous buck by any standard of measurement.

From a personal viewpoint, I know for a fact that really big bucks are present in the South Natchez Trace area. During the second segment of the hunting season in December 1991, I watched a 150 B&C-class buck feed in a private corn field less than a mile from South Natchez Trace. The massive 10-pointer's rack was conservatively 22 inches wide and his longest tines were over a foot long. Unfortunately, the buck came no closer than 550 yards from my tree stand, so I had to settle for watching him through binoculars for nearly

Management of herd size and protection of deer populations from poaching is vital to the success of any quality deer management program.

20 minutes. It was a great temptation to try a shot, but I held fire not wanting to risk wounding such a magnificent animal. Later that day I moved my stand within 150 yards of where the buck fed, but three consecutive days spent hunting from daylight to dark in 10- to 15-degree weather yielded nothing more than sightings of small bucks and does.

EARLY ATTEMPTS AT QUALITY MANAGEMENT

The current management program on South Natchez Trace isn't the TWRA's first attempt at managing a wildlife management area for quality whitetails. In 1968, Roy Anderson, chief of Game Management for the Tennessee Game and Fish Commission, spearheaded an effort to increase the antler and body size of deer on Chuck Swan WMA. An early hunt was held that year to reduce the number of bucks in the breeding population on the WMA. Then, 34 bucks and 19 does from Fort Campbell were released on Chuck Swan. The following year, 94 more Fort Campbell deer were released on the WMA. The theory of infusing genetically superior deer into a current population is a "quick fix" that doesn't work, game managers have learned. Today, body and antler size for Chuck Swan deer are typically smaller than average for whitetails statewide.

CREATING YOUR OWN QUALITY DEER MANAGEMENT AREA

Tennessee hunters wishing to implement quality deer management on the land where they hunt should consider what is required for a successful program. As stated before, age, nutrition and genetics play major roles in producing quality whitetails.

Having a large contiguous land area with controlled access is another key ingredient for managing a quality herd. About 5,000 acres in one block is the minimum size parcel of land to provide protection from neighboring hunters who prefer to shoot any legal buck that comes their way. Sometimes, several smaller hunting clubs can pool their acreage and collectively manage for quality animals. This is a more difficult proposition, but worth the effort after a few years of management.

Passing up the opportunity to bag a buck during the first and second year he carries antlers is the most important management tool the quality manager has to work with. Providing alternative food sources by planting wildlife openings is the second most important step. Mature bucks with enough high-quality food to eat will most often do their part of growing big bodies and racks. Keeping deer herd numbers in balance with their habitat is achieved by harvesting surplus females in the herd. Under the TWRA's present either-sex quota system this management tool is rather difficult to use, but harvesting enough does on areas is possible if a concerted effort is made. Other

Southeastern states, such as Alabama, Mississippi and South Carolina, have implemented a special program for landowners and hunting clubs wishing to manage for quality deer. They send a biologist to survey the land in question and then issue a set number of tags allow the harvest of surplus does. The acceptance and success of this tagging system has proven its merit for many clubs in these states.

MANAGEMENT PRACTICES AT WORK

Packaging Corporation of America, Inc. (PCA) biologists have implemented a quality deer management program on some of their land holdings in southwest Tennessee, near Pickwick Lake in Hardin County. The program was led by PCA Wildlife and Lands Manager Dean Stewart, and PCA Wildlife Technicians David McArthur and Mark Day.

The Rochelle family signed a long-term lease and cutting agreement in 1975, giving PCA full rights to timber and wildlife resources, and access control. This 6,049-acre tract is in one block, and borders close to 8,000 acres of PCA-owned land. Prior to lease of the land, the tract was mostly pasture with scattered natural stands of pine, hardwood and hardwood bottoms. In 1975, after the lease, natural stands and pastures were converted to pine plantation—roughly 4,700 acres—composed of two consecutive year age classes. Many of the hardwood drains were left intact, providing mast for area wildlife.

From 1975 to 1990, the tract was in public hunting, but the growing deer population was not properly managed and a few area residents abused the area by destroying roads and dumping trash along roadsides. The abused area was fenced and gated off for a period of one year with no hunting allowed, and then leased in 1991 to four groups with long-term plans of integrating a quality deer management program with an intensively managed pine pulpwood plantation.

One of the problems managers faced on the tract is canopy closure with limited openings, causing severe competition for browse among an already dense deer herd. PCA utilized all available roadside and natural open space and has begun creating more wildlife openings as timbering progresses.

The Rochelle quality deer management program is now aimed at harvesting a buck with a minimum of six points with a 12-inch inside spread, or a common 2½ year-old buck, and an intensive harvest of does to help lower an already highly skewed buck to doe ratio of approximately 1 to 8 or higher. This harvest regime will bring herd ratios back toward a natural balance. Future regulation of bucks harvested may increase to four points per side, with a wider inside spread.

To monitor the progress of the program, harvest data are being collected. Dressed weights, jawbones for aging, lactation in does, beam circumferences and lengths, inside spreads and number of points are being collected. Other data collected by PCA wildlife staff includes census data, incidental deer observations,

Quality deer management programs on both public and private lands can increase the likelihood to finding trophy size bucks such as this one.

235

browse surveys, kidney fat and bone marrow checks, and abomasal parasite counts.

Deer population on the Rochelle tract is estimated to be approximately 550 animals — 7 percent bucks, 53 percent does and 40 percent fawns — which translates to one deer per 12 acres. During the 1991 and 1992 seasons, 20 antlered bucks and 111 antlerless deer were harvested toward management goals on the Rochelle tract. Four hunting clubs participated in the program. Browse surveys in 1991 showed a heavy utilization of third-choice foods — cedar and mountain laurel — which means that the habitat was over browsed. In 1992, the browse line wasn't quite as harsh as the year before, which was due to a reduced deer population and higher moisture content in area vegetation. Correspondingly, body weights increased in 1992 over those for deer harvested in 1991.

To achieve management goals, PCA wildlife managers have determined that only 18 bucks could be harvested (50 percent of buck population); no fawns should be harvested; and one doe per 56 acres should be harvested (109 does) each year.

Special habitat treatments are also required. Prescribed burns of ⅓ of the pine plantations, roughly 1,530 acres, will help release lush browse. They are also creating openings that will total about 10 percent of the total land area. To increase browse quality further, roadsides and larger clumps of natural vegetation are being fertilized. Mineral licks have been distributed to supplement dietary requirements. The last step is the clearing and planting of all natural or secondary pine/hardwood openings.

SMALL QUALITY DEER MANAGEMENT AREAS

A new management strategy for small land holdings that is still in its experimental stages is called "core area management," which recommends the harvest of "alpha" does to keep bucks in an area. New research has found that alpha, or matriarch does, will force young bucks to abandon the area where they were raised, but allow their female offspring to stay in the area. It has been found that buck fawns will remain in the area where they were raised if the maternal doe is absent. Harvesting mature does and creating highly nutritious wildlife openings may be the best quality management tool available for small areas.

Top 10 Counties for Trophy Bucks

1. Montgomery 75
2. Stewart 66
3. Williamson 58
4. Humphreys 55
5. Fayette 46
6. Fentress 46
7. Cumberland 40
8. Cheatham 38
9. Dickson 36
10. Hardeman 33

* Counties ranked according to the number of deer entered in the Tennessee Deer Registry as of 2003.

Top 10 WMAs for Trophy Bucks

1. Land Between the Lakes   47
2. Ft. Campbell   47
3. Oak Ridge   42
4. Catoosa   17
5. Holston   14
6. Eagle Creek   4
7. Falls Creek Falls   3
8. AEDC   3
9. Cheatham   3
10. Tellico   3

* Wildlife management areas ranked according to the number of deer entered in the Tennessee Deer Registry as of 2003.

Chapter 13

Economic and Social Impact of Whitetails in Tennessee

*W*hite-tailed deer were the farthest things from her thoughts as Susan Wilson and her two young daughters, Hallie and Becca, drove through a drizzly, cold, late November night in Tennessee's northwest corner. Susan, a nurse, was driving north along Highway 79 near Paris, on her way home from family Thanksgiving festivities. Her mind drifted between the day's activities and unfinished Christmas shopping. Suddenly, a large white-tailed buck bounded into her path. Her first reaction was to swerve to miss the big animal, but the wet conditions caused her to lose control of her Toyota Cressida. The little, black car slid from the pavement. It rolled over and over, accompanied by the sound of twisting metal and shattering glass as it tumbled down a steep embankment. The car came to rest upside down at the bottom of the ravine, leaving Susan hanging in mid-air, suspended by her seat belt.

Susan's first thoughts were for her two children

The rise in deer numbers throughout the Volunteer State over the past
five decades has created an increasing hazard for motorists.

241

who had been asleep in the back seat. Susan could hear
Hallie crying, but couldn't hear Becca as she frantically
fought to free herself. Finally she found the latch and
fell to the ceiling of the overturned car. Susan scram-
bled for the children and quickly found Hallie, scared,
but with no serious injuries. Desperately, Susan dug
through piles of pillows and blankets trying to find
Becca. Finally she uncovered her sleepy, frightened
child whose cries were the sweetest sound she had ever
heard. Susan quickly assessed her injuries and those of
her children and determined they would be safer outside the destroyed car, its gas tank now leaking. Several
minutes later she was able to crawl up the hill and
summon help.

Practically every driver in Tennessee has either had
a near miss, struck a whitetail, or knows someone else
who has. The Wilsons were lucky, escaping their scary
highway encounter with only minor cuts and bruises.
Other motorists have not been so fortunate. The number of people killed by animals worldwide each year is
very small, with the majority of such deaths attributed
to species not commonly though of as dangerous,
according to a report by Tim A Snyder.[1]

On average, grizzly bears and alligators kill one
person every seven years. The venomous coral snake
accounts for one death every five years, and the man-
eating shark claims but one victim in a typical year.

Bee stings claim 11 times as many people as the
more notorious poisonous spiders, 43 to 4. Rattlesnake
bites result in 10 deaths, but man's best friend, the dog,

A whitetail lies by the side of a state highway in Tennessee. The doe is one of thousands of deer killed each year by collisions with automobiles.

gets 14 of us in the same time. Which is the most dangerous animal, the one that accounts for 131 deaths each year? The common white-tailed deer. The majority of deer-related deaths result from automobile collisions. The number of deer/auto collisions have become so numerous in recent years that the Tennessee Highway Patrol is no longer able to keep record of the accidents. To get an idea of how significant auto/deer collisions are to Tennessee motorists, let's look at some statistics compiled by William Creed, Frank Haberland, Bruce Kohn and Keith McCaffery, biologists with the Wisconsin Department of Natural Resources. While there's a world of difference between Wisconsin and Tennessee, mainly more people, more

Bucks browse near a farmer's storage shed. As Tennessee deer populations approach one million, crop damage through feeding, trampling and bedding rises.

deer and a larger state, enough similarities exist in their research for the comparison.

These researchers found that Wisconsin motorists killed 62,182 deer from 1978 through 1980, averaging 20,727 deer/auto collisions per year where the deer were killed.[2] These figures don't take into account the collisions where the deer staggered off, but the vehicle was damaged.

During this period, Wisconsin's deer population numbered about 750,000 animals, also the current whitetail population for Tennessee. If you compare Wisconsin's land mass of 54,426 square miles with Tennessee's 41,155 square miles, then factor in 3/4 million deer, you see Wisconsin had 13.7 deer per square mile, whereas Tennessee now has about 18.2 deer per square mile. Wisconsin has quite a few more vehicles on the road, but Tennessee has more deer crammed into a smaller state.

For the statistical purists among us, I'll take the conservative highroad and estimate that at least 10,000 whitetails meet their demise each year on Tennessee highways. That's a pile of auto insurance claims, any way you look at it. Rest assured, the people who set your auto insurance premiums know that whitetails pose a threat. In some areas of the northeast, whitetails have become so numerous that they have overpopulated their habitat and have started eating ornamental plants and shrubs in urban areas. Quite a few anti-hunting zealots have learned first hand, at the expense of their prize rose bushes, why professional wildlife managers actively manage whitetails by hunting to keep their numbers within the land's carrying capacity. Some of the folks who have experienced deer damage have changed their perspective of whitetails from that of the soft, cuddly, brown-eyed Bambi type, to what one enraged landowner termed "rats with hooves."

WHITETAILS AND THE FARMER

In 1977, when Tennessee's deer population numbered about 125,000 animals, there were only 20 to 30 crop damage complaints filed. With the state's whitetail population about six times higher today, complaints have risen with them.

A 1984 University of Tennessee (Knoxville) study conducted by graduate student Gary Tanner, under the direction of Professor Ralph Dimmick, found that farmers' opinions varied greatly toward deer on their land. Responses from farmers surveyed in Stewart, Montgomery and Henry counties ranged from no damage to severe damage on primarily soybean and corn crops. Farmers who derived the majority of their income from their crops tended to have larger farms and experienced the most damage. The incidence of crop damage was also higher in fields bordered by woods.

Approximately 41 percent of all respondents reported no damage to their crops, 50 percent reported light to moderate damage, and 9 percent reported severe damage. The majority of farmers (62 percent) reported that they enjoyed having deer on their land, but 15.4 percent felt that deer were a nuisance. In highly agricultural areas, Tennessee's whitetails can and do pose an economic threat to farming incomes.

Another research project conducted by Tanner and Dimmick during the early 1980s centered around the effectiveness of applying deer repellents to soybeans. This project was conducted on Land Between the Lakes, a TVA recreation area on Tennessee's northwest border with Kentucky. Hinder, a chemical odor repellent, was sprayed along the outer six border rows and a strip a meter wide in the foliage along field edges. Open jugs of Hinder were also placed about 30 meters (33 feet) apart in a ring around treated fields. What the researchers found was that deer didn't eat the treated fields as fast, but they soon completely destroyed the treated plants anyway.

DEER, DISEASE AND MAN

Whitetails can sometimes be carriers of diseases that affect man and livestock, but the impacts are minuscule for Tennesseeans. Occasionally, farmers are mistakenly quick to point a finger at deer as carriers of livestock diseases between infected and healthy herds. One example was brucellosis scare a few years ago. Also known as Bang's, this serious cattle disease causes abortions, infertility and reduced milk yields in cattle. After 50 years of research and testing nearly 20,000 deer, doctors at the Southeastern Cooperative Wildlife Disease Study at the University of Georgia, said whitetails are not involved in the problem.

As recently as 1990, veterinarians in Franklin County suspected deer as carriers for anaplasmosis between local cattle herds. Several blood samples were taken from deer in the area of infected cattle. When the results came back, it was determined that none of the deer were infected with the disease.

LYME DISEASE

Lyme disease in humans, caused by bacteria primarily transmitted by ticks, has slowly come to the attention of people who frequently expose themselves to tick bites during summer months. Lyme disease is usually associated with deer because the adult forms of the ticks that transmit the disease prefer deer as hosts. The disease is characterized by skin rash, flu-like illness and possible arthritic syndrome, that if left untreated, may develop into a syphilis-like illness. Lyme disease is treatable by antibiotics. The Centers for Disease Control has been studying Lyme for the last five or six years, but has recently abandoned its Lyme's research when the present political climate swayed their attention toward the AIDS epidemic. This move has left America's outdoors enthusiasts in somewhat of a bind, as many physicians still know little about the disease and its treatment. If you receive a tick bite and a rash develops, the safest bet is to contact a doctor who understands something about Lyme disease.

On rare occasions, deer do become infected with diseases that can be transmitted to man. When field-dressing deer it a safe practice to wear rubber gloves, which reduces the chances of blood-borne pathogens being transmitted to open cuts in the hands.

POSITIVE IMPACTS FROM DEER AND DEER HUNTING

The positive economic impacts on local and state economies from deer and deer hunting is rather large in Tennessee. Millions of dollars are collected each year in the form of excise taxes on hunting equipment and ammunition. The Pittman-Robertson Act, established

The product of a successful hunt, this magnificent buck is both a source of pride for the hunter and a source of delicious meat for his table.

in 1933 to help state agencies bring many game species back from the verge of extinction, is funded by these previously mentioned sporting goods taxes. Pittman-Robertson funding is paid on a 75:25 matching basis to each state, according to its size and number of hunters. With every dollar spent on wildlife management in Tennessee, Pittman-Robertson adds three. Without this money, Tennesseeans wouldn't have their present whitetail resource.

The money derived from the sale of hunting licenses also helps purchase critical wildlife habitat in Tennessee. The state now manages over 1.2 million acres of public wildlife habitat, enjoyed by hunters and non-hunters alike. Hunting for whitetails has a strong impact on practically every community in Tennessee. Hunters purchase equipment, vehicles, and as a whole, spend large sums on travel, food and lodging in their pursuit of deer. All this activity creates jobs. Everyone who enjoys whitetails, whether they be photographers, or just casual observers, have hunters to thank for the tremendous wildlife resources we enjoy today.

HUNTING'S REALLY BIG BUCKS

Besides the personal attributes of hunting, the sport is a vital part of our nation's economy. Most hunters, and certainly most anti-hunters, would be surprised to learn that the sport of hunting pumps more into our national economy each year than corporate giants like Coca-Cola, RJR Nabisco, Anheuser-Busch and

Goodyear Tire and Rubber. Every 81 seconds, hunters contribute about $36,000 to the nation's economy. That's on par with the United State's median annual household income of $35,975. That translates into some $1.6 million an hour, nearly $40 million a day and $14 billion a year.

Whether it's a young hunter using his lawn-mowing earnings to buy his first shotgun, a middle-aged businessperson writing out a $4,000 check for the elk hunt of a lifetime, or your local deer hunter paying $4.50 for an early morning breakfast of grits, eggs, bacon and biscuits at an all-night diner, our hunting heritage feeds the economy at a pace that is rivaled by few sports and few industries.

In this era of layoffs and downsizing, government officials may be interested to know that:

- More than 380,000 jobs are directly or indirectly supported by hunting.
- Each day, hunting produces enough economic activity to support 1,000 jobs.
- Hunting employs as many people as all Sears Roebuck stores — and then some.
- Hunting employs as many people as Northwest Airlines with enough workers left over to staff Delta and USAir.
- The people employed by hunting could fully staff the Turner Broadcasting Company—and 1,000 more just like it.
- For each 50 hunters, enough economic activity is generated to create one job. Think about that.

Each time you and I can do something that
encourages one additional person in each state to
go hunting, we create one job—and each time an
anti-hunting advocate prompts one person in
each state to stop hunting they put one person
out of work.
• Put in one place, the people employed by hunting would create a city the size of Minneapolis,
or Colorado Springs or Sacramento.

Of course, dollars and cents alone do not represent
hunting's true worth. Wealthier than all the Fortune
500 CEO's is the man who has a greater awareness and
respect of the natural environment and the game he
pursues. Wealthier still is the hunter who can share this
treasure with a youngster.

"The NSSF does not maintain that hunting is an
acceptable activity in our modern society merely
because it makes a significant contribution to our
national and local economies," Bob Delfay, president of
the National Shooting Sports Foundation, said.
"Hunting is an acceptable and desirable ingredient of
our nation's heritage because wildlife management pro-
fessionals and our conservation experience over the past
century tells us so. The economic value of hunting is
only a bonus to its spiritual, social and environmental
worth. If a penny did not change hands, hunting would
be no less acceptable or vital to our nation's fabric. But
pennies and dollars do change hands. Lots of them."

The average hunter contributes some $850 to the
economy each year. That is significant money and

A hunter takes aim at a whitetail. In 2001 some 230,000 Tennessee hunters used a firearm to successfully hunt white-tailed deer.

Fortune magazine recently explained how hunters can afford it. According to Fortune, "A demographic profile of the roughly 20 million Americans who hunt may surprise you! Urbanites may think of hunters as yahoos, but the truth, demographically, is that they get less yahoo-like all the time. Compared with the hunter of five years ago, today's hunter is better educated, more likely to be a professional or manager, and earns more. The average hunter has an income of $43,120 per year, compared to the national average of around $29,000, and 80 percent of all hunters own their homes."

Hunting contributes to the economy in many ways. Among the more obvious are:

- Hunters spend $7 billion annually on guns, ammunition, scopes, binoculars, clothing, reloading equipment and countless accessories.
- Hunters will spend approximately $3 billion annually on food and lodging in association with their hunting trips—be they half-day outings near home or a 10-day hunt of a lifetime.
- Hunters acquire or lease more than $1 billion in real estate for their outdoor pursuits each year.
- Hunters spend $520 million annually on permits, licenses, duck stamps and other government fees directly associated with their sport.

These national statistics, while impressive, don't adequately express the economic significance of hunting because, so often, hunting's economic benefit is concentrated in rural, economically sensitive areas where even modest incremental expenditure by hunters can have a pivotal effect on the success, or failure, of a local merchant. As stated in Fortune, "The dollars spent by hunters pack special oomph, because they hit small towns, far off the interstate. There, merchants look to hunting season the way Macy's looks to Christmas. It can make or break the year."

Those who are eager to bring an end to hunting in America might consider what substitute they could offer for the $14 billion loss in overall economic value that would result.

As hunters, we should not argue that hunting is

Deer hunters enjoy a moment in camp during Tennessee's fall deer hunt. Hunting is a time-honored Tennessee and American tradition.

good or hunting is acceptable in our modern society simply because it provides jobs for 380,000 Americans and funnels $14 billion into the economy. But it is certainly an element that should be factored into the equation when a politician in Washington, an animal rights advocate in Boston, or an anti-hunting activist in San Francisco decides that "NO HUNTING" signs should be posted all across America just because he or she doesn't like hunting.

An observation I have made is that hunters are the "doers" of our society. Not content with merely observing nature from the sidelines, hunters become part of it. America's first inhabitants became a part of nature, or perished. Today, many have fooled themselves into thinking the human race can keep our natural world "under glass," a curiosity to be viewed occasionally, but usually set aside, neglected and abused. Without a strong bond with nature — our own habitat — life as we know it will perish in time.

Section IV

Tennessee Deer Registry

Chapter 14

Tennessee's Record-Book Bucks

$\mathcal{A}$ tapestry woven from unbroken threads links today's Tennessee deer hunter with both aboriginal and pioneer hunters of yesteryear. Pursuit of this fine game animal for food is still the principal theme, with the thrill of the hunt providing an stimulating story line through the ages. Closer study will reveal, to the uninitiated, man's fascination with the crowning adornment found atop every mature white-tailed buck's head—those marvelous antlers. As distinctive and unique as a fingerprint, a white-tailed buck's antlers, surrendered in fair chase, serve as fond reminders of exciting days spent afield long after the venison has been eaten. Whether a tiny pair of spikes or a heavy-beamed, long-tined rack, hunters proudly display their trophies in a wide array of places and manners. Take for instance the farmer who tacks his trophy over his barn door, or the urban businessman who exhibits his prize for all his customers to view, or as most commonly seen, on a hunter's den wall at home. Antlers from a healthy, mature buck on display evoke a keen sense of wonder, with a simple inquiry often producing a lengthy hunting tale from the proud hunter.

Man's innate curiosity tempered with his competitive nature leads many hunters as to ask how a particular buck compares with others of his species.

In 1984, Tennessee Wildlife Resources Agency biologist Larry Marcum, then the state's leading whitetail manager, initiated the Tennessee Deer Registry (TDR) in cooperation with the Tennessee Conservation

Memphis hunter, the late Paul Blankenship, stands in a barn door flanked by several trophies placed in the Tennessee Deer Registry.

One of the author's favorite hunting companion, Kenneth Talbert, from Collierville, kneels next to a fine Shelby County buck taken in the Wolf River bottoms.

League, to rank the best bucks from the Volunteer State. Marcum adopted a scoring mechanism based on the Boone & Crockett Club's system for ranking North American big game animals. In 1887, President Theodore Roosevelt and other conservation leaders of the day formed the Boone & Crockett Club, one of the nation's first conservation organizations. Early members — men such as naturalist George Bird Grinnell, artist Albert Bierstadt, author Owen Wister, forester and governor Gifford Pinchot and ecologist Aldo Leopold — shaped the course of conservation in America. The Boone & Crockett Club's earliest achievements — protection of Yellowstone National Park, establishment of Forest Reserves, which later became National Forests, support of the wildlife refuge system, and framing of wildlife protection laws — are monuments to all conservationists and hunters today. In 1932, the Boone & Crockett Club began to recognize outstanding trophies of North American big game animals formally. In 1950, the current scoring system was devised to rank and give recognition to the finest specimens of North America's big game species.

Using the Boone & Crockett Club's scoring system as a basis, Marcum sought to accomplish three goals. First, he and other wildlife researchers wanted to provide the TWRA with a meaningful and understandable record of the number of quality white-tailed deer taken annually in Tennessee. Simply put, antler growth rates serve as a barometer of the state's deer herd health. Harvest data have been recorded in annual reports since 1952, but they lacked a focused interpretation that could be understood by the layman. Secondly, the TDR provides important data concerning Tennessee's expanding deer herd. After only 10 years, trends have developed that quickly point to several areas in the state as top producers of quality bucks. Further research programs should shed some light on why some of these areas consistently produce larger deer. The third goal of the TDR is to recognize successful deer hunters who bag quality deer. The 2001 update of the TDR lists 1,674 bucks that have met the qualifications for entry. TWRA personnel measure and keep appropriate records of each entry. The Tennessee Conservation League also recognizes all successful Tennessee Deer Registry participants with a certification plate. This plate, designed to be placed on the mount, includes the hunter's name and total points scored on the Boone & Crockett scale.

DEER REGISTRY RULES

The first rule governing a buck's entry in the TDR is that it was taken within Tennessee by legal sport hunting. Once that criteria is met, it must further qualify under the "fair chase" rules and guidelines set forth by the Boone & Crockett Club.

Fair Chase
Fair Chase is the ethical, sportsmanlike and lawful pursuit and taking of any free-ranging wild game animal in a manner that does not give the hunter an improper or unfair advantage over such game animals. Use of any of the following methods in the taking of game are deemed unfair chase and unsportsmanlike:

1. Spotting or herding game from the air, followed by landing in its vicinity for the purpose of shooting.
2. Herding, pursuing, or shooting game from any motor boat or vehicle.
3. Use of electronic devices for attracting, locating, or observing game, or for guiding the hunter to such game.
4. Hunting game confined by artificial barriers, including escape-proof fenced enclosures, or hunting game transplanted solely for the purpose of commercial shooting.
5. Taking of game in a manner not in full compliance with the game laws or regulations of the federal government or any state, province, territory,

or tribal council on reservations or tribal lands.
6. Or as may otherwise be deemed unfair or unsportsmanlike by the Executive Committee of the Boone & Crockett Club.

The TDR is divided into four classifications: Typical configuration taken by archery tackle; non-typicals taken by archery tackle; typicals taken by gun and non-typicals taken by gun. The minimum scores for each category are:

Archery Typical — 115
Archery Non-Typical — 140
Gun Typical — 140
Gun Non-Typical — 165

All antlers must have dried for a minimum of 60 days to allow for uniform shrinkage prior to being scored. All scoring must be done by qualified TWRA personnel. Deer from previous seasons can be entered provided you have proof of legal harvest in Tennessee.

HOW DEER ARE SCORED *

To derive a score for a white-tailed deer, four categories of measurements are taken: Total main beam lengths from the antler bases to beam tips; widest inside spread between the main beams; total length of all "normal" points; and total of circumferences of taken from specific places on the main beam. Penalties are assessed for non-symmetry. Simply put, if a rack has an uneven number of points that protrude from the

Deer that qualify for the Tennessee Deer Registry must be taken during a "fair chase." Confined deer and those stocked on hunting preserves do not qualify.

top of the main beam, only those with a corresponding point on the other beam are used in the final net score. If there is a difference in lengths between matching points, only the length of the shortest point is used for both tines in the final score. Correspondingly, if matching circumferences differ, the smaller of the two measurements are used for both in the final net score.

For example, if the first two tines on each main beam measure five inches for the left and six inches for the right, five inches or "points" are assigned to each tine in tabulating a final net score.

In the "typical" category, the length of any abnormal points are subtracted from the "gross" score obtained by adding the previously mentioned categories together. "Non-typical" racks have the total length of all abnormal points, those not originating from the top of the main beam, added to their "typical" score to achieve a final score.

HOW AND WHERE TO GET DEER MEASURED

Throughout the year, measuring rallies are held across the state where official scorers are available to measure deer. Local newspapers regularly publish date, time and location of these scoring rallies. If you can not attend a rally in your area, you may take your deer to an official scorer to have it measured. For more information about the TDR or the location of a scorer near you, write Deer Registry, T.W.R.A., P.O. Box 40747, Nashville, TN 37204, or Deer Registry, Tennessee Conservation League, 11 Music Circle S., Suite 5, Nashville, TN 37203. The telephone numbers for TWRA Regional offices and the TCL are:

Region I - 1-800-372-3928
Region II - 1-800-624-7406
Region III - 1-800-262-6704
Region IV - 1-800-332-0900
TCL - 1-615-353-1133

Although not the oldest trophy listed in the TDR, J.C. Myers of Jackson, TN, killed a fine buck on Fall Creek Falls State Park in 1954. Myers' trophy deserves special recognition as being the first TDR qualifier following whitetail reintroduction and subsequent open hunting seasons in 1949. The Myers buck scored 148⅜ points on the Boone & Crockett scale.

Fourteen TDR qualifiers were harvested during the 1950s. The largest typical, killed by Rockwood, TN resident W.A. "Sonny" Foster in 1959, scored 186⅛ points. Foster's Hawkins County monster buck still reigns as the typical state record and currently ranks as the No. 185 typical in North America, according to the 1999 edition of the Boone & Crockett Club's Records of North American Whitetail Deer. The year 1956 was a special one for world-class trophies in East Tennessee. Kingston's John Crosby bagged a 204⅝ point non-typical that reigned for 18 years as the state's record. The Crosby buck was taken from Catoosa WMA, as was Charles A. Ford's 197-point non-typical, killed that same year.

A total of 36 bucks are listed from the 1960s. The largest was John J. Herigs' buck shot in 1962. The Herigs buck came from Shelby County and scored 173⅛ points.

As deer populations quickly grew, the entries from the 1970s followed suit. There are 123 bucks listed from the 1970s, with Benny Johnson from Collierville bagging the biggest typical in 1979. Johnson's Fayette County buck scores 184⅛, ranking a close second to the Foster buck. The largest non-typical of the decade was Clarence McElhaney's 198⅜ point bruiser. McElhaney, a Crossville, TN resident, bagged his best buck on Ft. Campbell. Another notable buck is Jimmy

This buck is a candidate for the Tennessee Deer Registry. The Registry rates the state's best bucks following the scoring system of the Boone & Crockett Club.

Ray Woods' bow-killed buck from 1978. Woods arrowed the 170⅜ point buck in Montgomery County. The significance of this buck is that it ranks as the current No. 3 bow kill in the TDR, it also qualifies for Boone & Crockett's all-time record book, which lists 170 as the minimum for entry. That it was killed with a bow puts it among an even more elite class of bucks.

The decade of the 1980s saw a tremendous jump in TDR bucks. According to the 1991 update of the TDR, there were 510 bucks entered during the 1980s. The largest of the decade was Luther Fuller's state-record non-typical. Killed in 1984, in Hawkins County, the Fuller buck scored 223 points and also ranks high in the Boone & Crockett records. James Cobb of

Jackson, TN, killed a tremendous buck in 1988 on the Reelfoot National Wildlife Refuge that scores 203⅜. Currently ranked as the No. 9 non-typical, the Cobb buck involves a small bit of mystery. It seems that since it was killed so close to the Tennessee/Kentucky state line that both states have claimed the Cobb buck in both of their respective state's deer registries. Tennessee's No. 2 ranking archery-bagged typical was harvested in 1984 in Sullivan County by Kingsport's Alan C. Altizer, and scored 173 Boone & Crockett points. Two other top ranking deer were killed in 1984; Roger Kelly of Franklin, TN, bagged a 175⅝ point buck in Williamson County, and Joe K. Sanders of Goodletsville, TN, traveled to Land Between the Lakes Wildlife Management Area to bag his 172⅝ point buck of a lifetime.

As the decade of the 1990s moves toward the 21st century, entries in the TDR continue to steadily climb. Eighty new TDR deer were entered into its ranks by 1992, almost 10 percent of the total award-winning bucks. By the close of the 2002 season 1,673 deer were scored and qualified for the TDR.

History has a way of repeating itself. That last sentence might sound somewhat cliché, but when a serious deer hunter wants to hunt for an outstanding buck—hunt areas that have produced big bucks—it is the most common-sense approach to success. Reviewing 1992 statistics reveal 14 wildlife management areas and counties with at least 15 deer in the TDR. Deer hunters focusing their efforts on the top quality deer-producing areas will up their chances of bagging a buck that contends for the TDR. Tables on pages 238-239 list the top ranking counties and WMAs for TDR bucks taken through the 2002 deer season. Following the steady increase in state-wide deer harvests, the historical data provided by the TDR gives hunters a glance back in time. Any Tennessee deer hunter can scan the records listed in the beginning and review highlights of the best whitetails Tennessee has to offer.

* Staying with the TDR theme of simplicity, a point of clarification is owed the reader. When the author refers to a particular buck that scores "145⅜ points," etc., this means the buck's rack had 145⅜ inches of measurable antler. This is not to be confused with the term "point," when speaking in reference to an antler tine.

ENTRIES BY COUNTY OR WMA

Area	Antler Type	Weapon	Score	Name	City	Year
AEDC	T	Gun	161 2/8	Gene Currin	Tullahoma	1966
WMA	T	Gun	151 5/8	R E Stoudt	Chatt.	1966
	T	Gun	150 5/8	Dick Besancenez	Winchester	1971
Anderson	NT	Gun	177 3/8	Bruce Fox	Knoxville	1996
	T	Gun	156 2/8	Freddy E Griffith	Petros	1990
	T	Gun	152 0/8	Jack Southard	Clinton	1993
	T	Gun	151 3/8	Frank Phillips	Knoxville	1993
	T	Gun	149 0/8	Bill Young	Lake City	2000
	T	Gun	147 1/8	Harley D Swafford	Dayton	1996
	T	Gun	146 4/8	Daniel D Jones II	Oliver Springs	1990
	NT	Bow	145 3/8	Mark Sircy	Madisonville	1989
	T	Bow	144 3/8	Johnny W. Jobe	Lake City	1985
	T	Gun	144 2/8	Randy Foster	Petros	1994
	T	Gun	140 2/8	Virgil Lee Andrews, Jr.	Clinton	1985
	T	Gun	139 7/8	Donnie Watson	Ten Mile	1997
	T	Bow	134 7/8	Robert Hendren	Clinton	1987
And-Tully WMA	T	Gun	155 4/8	Robert Childs	Mphs.	1964
Bedford	T	Gun	157 6/8	Rick Parsons	Shelbyville	1976
	T	Gun	155 0/8	Ken E Parker	Bell Buckle	1990
	T	Gun	143 1/8	Wayne Simons	Shelbyville	1987
	T	Gun	142 4/8	Kevin Butts	Bell Buckle	1986
	T	Gun	141 3/8	Sammie Heard	Daisy	1984
	T	Bow	125 1/8	John Mckeon	Chapel Hill	1999
	T	Bow	122 6/8	Bobby Cunningham	Shlbville	1991
	T	Bow	118 1/8	Larry Moore	Shelbyville	1998
Benton	NT	Gun	189 6/8	Eddie Medlin	Camden	1989
	NT	Gun	182 5/8	Robert Mcpeake	Parsons	1996
	T	Gun	165 5/8	Keith Matlock	Camden	1987
	T	Gun	161 3/8	Don Bell	Jackson	1971
	T	Gun	152 0/8	Rick Acosta	Mphs.	1978
	T	Gun	152 1/8	Cantrell Phifer	Eva	1978
	T	Gun	151 0/8	Marshall Hicks	Camden	1976
	T	Gun	151 3/8	Harold D Douglas	Holladay	1976
	T	Gun	148 0/8	David Patty	Camden	1988
	T	Gun	148 1/8	Larry Hollingswort	Bruceton	1983
	T	Gun	146 4/8	Jerry Ward	Camden	1990
	T	Gun	145 1/8	Danny Hudson	Big Sandy	1989
	T	Bow	144 4/8	Willard Young III	Nashville	1995
	T	Gun	144 7/8	Larry E Frazier	New John'ville	1981
	T	Gun	142 2/8	Rick Acosta	Mphs.	1982
	T	Gun	141 1/8	Joe Ted Lynch	Camden	1998
	T	Gun	140 7/8	Wallace Cole	Camden	1998
	T	Gun	140 2/8	J. R. Mcknight	Union City	1975
	T	Gun	140 6/8	Curtis Marshall	Camden	1982
	T	Gun	140 0/8	Bobby Hollingswrth	Bruceton	1988
	T	Bow	135 4/8	Michael Pruett	Nashville	1999
	T	Bow	133 4/8	Daniel Cooper	Camden	1997
	T	Bow	130 7/8	Donald Umstead	Camden	1978
	T	Bow	115 7/8	Charles Cobb	Jackson	1987
Bledsoe	NT	Bow	170 6/8	Michael Castle II	Whitwell	1995
	T	Gun	168 1/8	Richard Edmons	Pikeville	1996
	T	Gun	152 2/8	Tim Cunningham	Soddy-Daisy	1985
	T	Gun	151 0/8	L.C. Dykes	Pikeville	1991
	T	Gun	149 6/8	James R. Brewer	Pikeville	1984

Area	Antler Type	Weapon	Score	Name	City	Year
	T	Bow	148 0/8	William Manery	Pikeville	1986
	T	Gun	146 7/8	James Songer	Dunlap	1976
	T	Gun	146 2/8	Philip T Walker	Crossville	1989
	T	Gun	145 6/8	Larry Frady	Pikeville	1995
	T	Gun	142 6/8	Brad Pendegrass	Pikeville	1994
	T	Gun	141 0/8	Dwayne Walker	Pikeville	1986
	T	Gun	141 7/8	Larry Frady	Pikeville	1994
	T	Gun	140 6/8	Garry E. Songer	Dunlap	1967
	T	Bow	134 1/8	Robert Fann	Evensville	1994
	T	Bow	116 2/8	Scott Earls	Russellville	2001
Blount	NT	Bow	191 2/8	Skip Coppinger	Rockford	1994
	T	Gun	151 0/8	Gabe Brown	Louisville	1997
	T	Bow	142 4/8	Dewayne Holloway	Louisville	1992
	T	Bow	134 2/8	Troy Cable	Alcoa	1999
	T	Bow	130 1/8	Roy Haun	Knox	1996
	T	Bow	117 2/8	Dana Keeble	Maryville	1991
	T	Bow	115 1/8	Charles Tipton	Townsend	1997
	T	Bow	115 6/8	Terry Skeen	Seymour	1995
Bradley	T	Gun	143 1/8	Clarence Smith	Charleston	1985
	T	Bow	139 1/8	Danny Peels	Cleveland	2000
	T	Bow	133 2/8	Royce Fugate	Calhoun	1990
Campbell	NT	Gun	190 4/8	James Metcalf	Eagan	1992
	NT	Gun	176 5/8	Sam Ward	Jacksboro	1989
	T	Gun	159 0/8	Charles M Green	Caryville	1998
	T	Gun	150 2/8	Bill Mccreary	Jacksboro	1992
	T	Gun	145 0/8	Anthony Spradlin	Knoxville	1991
	T	Gun	145 3/8	Donny Shelby	Duff	1998
	T	Gun	143 1/8	Randall Pierce	Lafollette	1984
	T	Gun	142 6/8	Maynard Wallace	Lafollette	1997
	T	Gun	141 2/8	Dennis Cotton	Helenwood	2001
	T	Bow	125 1/8	Truman Wilson	Caryville	1987
	T	Bow	121 1/8	Chris Sharp	Powell	1986
Cannon	NT	Gun	175 7/8	Tim Underwood	Woodbury	1991
	T	Gun	140 2/8	Darrell Young	Mcminnville	1983
	T	Bow	122 6/8	David Hughes	Bradyville	1998
Carroll	NT	Gun	168 3/8	Wayne Moore	Humboldt	1994
	T	Gun	164 4/8	Rex Allen Berry	Huntington	1990
	T	Gun	160 3/8	Marvin R Lord	Lexington	2001
	T	Gun	154 5/8	J. V. Mcalexander	Milan	1975
	T	Gun	149 5/8	Kenny Summers	Hollow Rock	1988
	T	Gun	149 5/8	Chris Williams	Lexington	1999
	T	Gun	148 4/8	Johnny W Tucker	Huntington	1978
	T	Gun	147 6/8	Randall M Clarke	Cedar Grove	1982
	T	Gun	145 2/8	Thomas Allen	Trezevant	1989
	T	Gun	145 5/8	Eddie Harris	Atwood	1990
	T	Gun	145 4/8	Tim Boyd	Huntingdon	1998
	T	Gun	144 6/8	Ed Tubbs	Parsons	1984
	T	Gun	140 6/8	Joe M Smith	Bruceton	1974
	T	Gun	140 1/8	Dennis Beecham	Lexington	1985
	T	Gun	140 0/8	Randy Lessenberry	Mckenzie	1985
	T	Bow	115 1/8	Tim Carlton	Huntingdon	1995
Carter	T	Gun	148 5/8	Vic Harrison	Elizabethton	1986

Area	Antler Type	Weapon	Score	Name	City	Year
Catoosa WMA	NT	Gun	204 5/8	Terry Crosby	Kingston	1956
	NT	Gun	197 0/8	Charles A. Ford	Seymour	1956
	NT	Gun	181 3/8	O. B. Jr. Sorrell	Sparta	1959
	T	Gun	166 7/8	Sam Bible	Kodak	1995
	T	Gun	162 4/8	Col. Edgar Snodgrass	Oak Ridge	1955
	T	Gun	160 6/8	W. A. Campbell	Athens	1958
	T	Gun	159 5/8	Jerry Windle	Livingston	1965
	T	Gun	159 5/8	Walter A. Turner	Smyrna	1958
	T	Gun	154 3/8	Ken Butcher	Knoxville	1992
	T	Gun	153 6/8	Harry Wilkerson	Athens	1971
	T	Gun	151 6/8	Joe Setser	Knoxville	1962
	T	Gun	149 3/8	Dwayne Porterfield	White Pine	1982
	T	Gun	149 5/8	Darryl R Hall	Heiskell	1982
	T	Gun	148 1/8	Randy Vanzant	Knoxville	1999
	T	Gun	144 3/8	Fred Foster	Knoxville	1956
	T	Gun	141 3/8	Cecil N. Smith	Rockwood	1982
	T	Gun	140 5/8	J.P. Johnson, Jr	Maryville	1987
Cheatham	NT	Gun	175 0/8	Daniel Conatser	Ashland City	1991
	NT	Gun	167 3/8	Hilda Bracey	Ashland City	2000
	T	Gun	166 5/8	Roy Pulley	Chapmansboro	1993
	T	Gun	161 7/8	Andrew Gleaves	Ashland City	1963
	T	Gun	156 7/8	Kenneth Pinson	Clarksville	2000
	T	Gun	154 4/8	Eugene King	Ashland City	1989
	T	Gun	152 7/8	Joe Townsend	Kingston Sprg	2000
	T	Gun	152 5/8	Paul Watson	Ashland City	1979
	T	Gun	149 5/8	Chris Collingsworth	Ashl Cty	2000
	T	Gun	147 5/8	Brian A. Chester	Nashville	1994
	T	Gun	147 2/8	Poole Hillous	Ashland City	1978
	T	Gun	146 1/8	Calvin Bell	Ashland City	2000
	T	Gun	146 5/8	Eldridge Murphy	Pegram	1968
	T	Gun	146 7/8	David Brown	Clarksville	1984
	T	Gun	146 4/8	Darren Holt	Ashland City	1971
	T	Gun	145 5/8	Robert Akin	Madison	1980
	T	Gun	143 5/8	Joe Townsend	Kingston Sprg	2000
	T	Gun	142 6/8	T W Meadows	Ashland City	1989
	T	Gun	142 6/8	Ronald Carney	Joelton	1996
	T	Bow	139 0/8	Mark Wagner	Ashland City	1999
	T	Bow	138 7/8	Joe Townsend	Kingston Sprg	1999
	T	Bow	136 4/8	Ricky Orange	Ashland City	1999
	T	Bow	136 2/8	Chris Hunt	Chapmansboro	1993
	T	Bow	134 5/8	Scott Stamps	Pleasant View	1996
	T	Bow	133 5/8	Ray Morris	Ashland City	1990
	T	Bow	132 1/8	Chuck Elean	Nashville	1987
	T	Bow	131 7/8	Carl Wood	Ashland City	1992
	T	Bow	129 2/8	Chris Ferguson	Ashland City	2000
	T	Bow	129 0/8	Bill Herbert	Kingston Sprg	1994
	T	Bow	125 0/8	Phil Ware	Old Hickory	1999
	T	Bow	123 7/8	Kevin Carney	Clarksville	1997
	T	Bow	122 7/8	James Bibee	Pegram	1990
	T	Bow	122 1/8	Robert Coker	Murrayville	1997
	T	Gun	122 1/8	Joshua Bell	Kingston Sprg	1998
	T	Bow	120 7/8	Chris Collingsworth	Ashlnd City	1997
	T	Bow	119 3/8	Bobby Shepard	Bon Aqua	1999
	T	Bow	115 0/8	Brian Collingsworth	Pleasant V	1991
	T	Bow	115 7/8	John Fudge	Madison	1994
Cheatham WMA	T	Gun	167 3/8	James B Mercer	Clarksville	1959
	T	Gun	142 5/8	Randy Butts	Gallatin	1973
	T	Bow	136 3/8	Monty Bartel	Crossville	1999
Chester	NT	Gun	178 1/8	Bobby Mc Earl	Henderson	1999
	T	Gun	147 7/8	Larry Busby	Henderson	1990
	T	Gun	147 4/8	David Mcbride	Jackson	1996
	T	Gun	144 0/8	David Stoltzfus	Bethel Sprgs	1994
	T	Gun	143 1/8	Ralph Alexander	Reagan	1992
	T	Gun	142 6/8	Danny Jobe	Cornith	1999
	T	Gun	141 7/8	David Mcbride	Jackson	1997
Chuck Swan WMA	T	Bow	123 7/8	Randall Epperson	Washburn	1987
	T	Bow	123 3/8	Dwayne Archer	Knoxville	1988
Claiborne	T	Gun	158 6/8	James Maiden	Harrogate	1994
	T	Gun	154 5/8	Harold Bolden	Tazewell	1984
	T	Gun	145 2/8	Jeff Brown	Maynardville	1995
	T	Gun	141 0/8	Jackie Southerland	Morristown	2001
Clay	T	Gun	155 7/8	James Likens	Red Bling Spg	1983
	T	Gun	152 1/8	Michael Sweezy	Moss	1995
	T	Gun	150 0/8	Johnny Allen	Hilham	2001
	T	Gun	148 4/8	Tim Mcdonald	Livingston	2000
	T	Gun	142 4/8	Ray Nelson Boles	Celina	1993
	T	Gun	142 0/8	Steve Monroe	Celina	1987
	T	Bow	136 2/8	Junior Smith	Thompkinsville	1991
	T	Bow	134 5/8	David A Allred	Celina	1993
Cocke	T	Gun	147 6/8	Allen Fowler	White Pine	1987
	T	Gun	141 3/8	Billy Hill	Newport	1984
	T	Bow	117 2/8	Michael Brooks	Parrottsville	1995
	T	Bow	115 6/8	Doug Cameron	Newport	1985
Coffee	T	Gun	146 5/8	Pat W. Spangler	Manchester	1987
	T	Gun	144 2/8	Eddie Stinnet	Ft Oglethorpe	1995
	T	Gun	143 1/8	Mark Kirby	Morrison	1988
	T	Gun	142 5/8	Mason Fischer	Manchester	1979
	T	Bow	122 3/8	Doyle Shettleworth	Wartrace	1991
Cove Creek WMA	T	Bow	139 6/8	Harold D. Tackett	Caryville	1985
Crockett	NT	Gun	168 4/8	Kenny Bivens	Bells	1999
	T	Gun	146 2/8	Jamie Moore	Alamo	2000
	T	Gun	144 4/8	Jeffery Burress	Alamo	1999
Cumb.	T	Gun	186 1/8	W. A. Foster	Rockwood	1959
	NT	Gun	168 3/8	Jackie Davis	Ooltewah	1972
	T	Gun	162 5/8	George Eller	Crossville	1998
	T	Gun	154 2/8	Scott Houston	Crossville	1990
	T	Gun	152 2/8	James Davis	Crossville	1988
	T	Gun	151 7/8	Billy Hopper, Jr	Crossville	1989
	T	Gun	150 3/8	Billy D Swafford	Crossville	1985
	T	Gun	150 4/8	Bob Fickey	Rockwood	1988
	T	Gun	150 2/8	William Hall	Monterey	1990
	T	Gun	150 1/8	Gene Hall	Crossville	1994
	T	Gun	150 6/8	Adam Hild	Crossville	1995
	T	Gun	149 0/8	Gene Hall	Rockwood	1994

Area	Antler Type	Weapon	Score	Name	City	Year
	T	Gun	148 7/8	James Zachary	Allons	1961
	T	Gun	147 4/8	Joey Whittenburg	Crossville	2001
	T	Gun	147 0/8	Charles S Reed	Grandview	1972
	T	Gun	147 0/8	Kenneth Hemphill	Decatur	1991
	T	Gun	146 7/8	Fred Nelson	Rockwood	1957
	T	Gun	146 6/8	Keith Woody	Crossville	1987
	T	Gun	145 2/8	Randy Vanzant	Knoxville	1999
	T	Gun	145 7/8	Brian Smith	Knoxville	1984
	T	Gun	144 6/8	Bill Collins	Oak Ridge	1983
	T	Gun	144 5/8	Drew Davis	Crossville	1992
	T	Gun	144 6/8	Anthony Vanlandingham	Crossville	1990
	T	Gun	144 3/8	Gary Coffey	Rockwood	1998
	T	Gun	143 3/8	William B Lewis	Crossville	1990
	T	Gun	143 6/8	Robert Orme	Crossville	1990
	T	Gun	143 1/8	Toney Vanlandingham	Crossville	1990
	T	Gun	143 4/8	William G. Wilson	Crossville	1978
	T	Gun	142 4/8	Jonas P. Holloway	Spring City	2000
	T	Gun	142 2/8	Ricky Smith	Crab Orchard	1997
	T	Gun	141 3/8	Earl Bowling	Rockwood	1978
	T	Gun	141 4/8	Taylor T Emery	Cross Plains	1968
	T	Gun	141 7/8	Ike Warner	Crossville	1988
	T	Bow	140 5/8	Frank H Williams	Lenoir City	1981
	T	Gun	140 2/8	Jackie Tollett	Crab Orchard	1985
	T	Gun	140 0/8	Keith Frazier	Crossville	1988
	T	Bow	139 1/8	Ronnie Campbell	Crossville	1987
	T	Gun	139 7/8	Brian Bargoss	Crossville	1993
	T	Bow	134 4/8	Roger Jones	Crossville	2001
	T	Bow	116 5/8	Patrick Garrison	Crossville	1990
Davidson	NT	Gun	184 6/8	Willie D Hallum	Gdltsville.	2001
	T	Bow	175 2/8	W.W. Young	Nashville	1997
	T	Gun	166 7/8	James T Ward	Joelton	1991
	T	Gun	166 7/8	Wade Daugherty	Nashville	1997
	NT	Bow	156 0/8	Will Jones	Franklin	1999
	T	Gun	156 4/8	Gary Bates	Gdltsville.	1998
	T	Gun	154 6/8	Ross Hudson	Nashville	1995
	T	Gun	154 5/8	Wayen Davis	Nashville	1998
	T	Gun	153 0/8	Michael Joyner	Nashville	1992
	T	Gun	153 6/8	Craig Geesaman	Hender'ville	1998
	T	Gun	152 4/8	Lucas Norman	Springfield	1995
	T	Gun	151 2/8	Pat Floyd	Monterey	1990
	T	Gun	150 2/8	King M. Ayers, III	Smyrna	1992
	T	Gun	150 4/8	Mark A. Musel	Cottontown	1997
	T	Gun	150 7/8	James E Stubblefield	Springfield	1998
	T	Gun	150 1/8	Joe Shelton	Joelton	1999
	T	Gun	149 0/8	William Smith	Gdltsville.	1999
	T	Gun	149 1/8	Scott Kimberly	Nashville	2001
	T	Gun	149 2/8	Mike Hendrickson	Ashland City	1975
	T	Bow	147 4/8	Matt Burton	Nashville	1998
	T	Gun	147 4/8	Richard Kieffer	Antioch	1988
	T	Gun	147 2/8	Larry Hudgins	Whites Creek	1987
	T	Gun	146 0/8	William Smith	Gdltsville.	1998
	T	Gun	146 7/8	David Corley	Old Hickory	1999
	T	Gun	146 0/8	Mike Burkey	Joelton	1980
	T	Gun	146 5/8	Ryan Metrick	Nashville	1997
	T	Bow	145 3/8	William Flair Jr	Nashville	1998
	T	Bow	144 4/8	Steve Teague	Nashville	2001
	T	Bow	143 0/8	Jeremy Head	Brentwood	2002
	T	Gun	143 1/8	King M. Ayers, III	Smyrna	1993
	T	Gun	142 3/8	Kevin Yarbrough	Greenbrier	1997
	T	Bow	141 2/8	Gary Morris	Nashville	2000
	T	Gun	141 0/8	Bryan Biggers	Joelton	2000
	T	Bow	132 2/8	Jeffery B Nidiffer	Joelton	1998
	T	Bow	131 2/8	Joe Draper	Nashville	1997
	T	Bow	130 3/8	Billy Johnson	Nashville	1984
	T	Bow	129 5/8	Scottie Hanvy	Nashville	1996
	T	Bow	126 2/8	John Edde	Mt.Juliet	1989
	T	Bow	126 5/8	Matt Burton	Nashville	1998
	T	Bow	125 6/8	Jack Whitson	Laverne	1998
	T	Bow	124 5/8	Larry Faircloth	Hermitage	1998
	T	Bow	123 3/8	Tommy Goodgame	Franklin	1992
	T	Bow	123 4/8	Ricky J. Johnson	Gdltsville.	1993
	T	Bow	119 2/8	Jim Brown	Franklin	1991
	T	Bow	118 2/8	Ronald Kendall, Jr	Mt. Juliet	1990
	T	Bow	117 3/8	Norman Speck	Old Hickory	1989
	T	Bow	117 5/8	Kenneth Biggs	Joelton	1989
	T	Bow	117 3/8	Tim Brown	Nashville	1998
	T	Bow	116 7/8	Don Spain	Madison	1989
Decatur	NT	Gun	182 3/8	Ronnie West	Decaturville	1996
	T	Gun	173 2/8	G D Odle	Parsons	1972
	T	Gun	172 3/8	Danny Pope	Bath Springs	1982
	T	Gun	162 2/8	Dale Brasher	Parsons	1983
	T	Gun	158 2/8	Robert Alexander	Brentwood	1996
	T	Gun	157 4/8	Larry Finley	Saltillo	1980
	T	Gun	156 1/8	Kendall Thompson	Scotts Hill	1996
	T	Gun	155 0/8	Eugene Redden	Decaturville	1976
	T	Gun	150 3/8	Freddie Kennedy	Sardis	1987
	T	Gun	148 2/8	William L. Smart	Bath Springs	1984
	T	Gun	145 5/8	Tommy Adkisson	Brownsville	1976
	T	Gun	143 6/8	J. A. Carrington	Parsons	1975
	T	Gun	142 1/8	Tommy Scott	Scotts Hill	1989
	T	Gun	140 7/8	Colby Gilliam	Lexington	2000
	T	Gun	140 3/8	Mark Stout	Decaturville	1986
	T	Gun	140 5/8	Ralph Barnett	Decaturville	1995
	T	Bow	129 6/8	David Wyatt	Bath Springs	1995
	T	Bow	118 6/8	Joe Paul Myracle	Parsons	1983
Dekalb	T	Gun	156 6/8	Steve Bakaletz	Cookeville	1985
	T	Gun	145 1/8	Byron Poss	Smithville	1983
	T	Gun	144 4/8	Lynn Ayers	Mcminnville	1986
	T	Gun	142 1/8	Paul Gerringer	Smithville	1987
	T	Bow	128 1/8	Gregory Medlin	Cookeville	1994
	T	Bow	125 3/8	Stephen D Ayers	Murfreesboro	1985
	T	Bow	118 6/8	Kenneth Johnson	Smithville	1984
Dickson	T	Gun	162 1/8	Eric Ramsey	Cumb.Furnace	1990
	T	Gun	161 0/8	Chad Lane	Dickson	1992
	T	Gun	160 3/8	Ronnie Morgan	Lawrenceburg	1976
	T	Gun	156 7/8	Wallace M Dewalt	Charlotte	1990
	T	Gun	154 2/8	J.C. Brown, Jr.	White Bluff	1988
	T	Gun	153 3/8	Steve Christy	Clarksville	1985
	T	Gun	149 4/8	Eddie Deaton	Charlotte	1985

Area	Antler Type	Weapon	Score		Name	City	Year
	T	Gun	149	2/8	Chad Lane	Dickson	1998
	NT	Bow	148	6/8	Marlin Perry	Ashland City	2000
	T	Gun	148	6/8	Kerry Davidson	Bon Aqua	1988
	NT	Bow	147	1/8	Jeffrey Hightower	Harrison	1999
	T	Gun	146	5/8	Alan Danley	Charlotte	1987
	T	Gun	145	6/8	Larry Draper	Hendersonville	1987
	T	Gun	145	2/8	Roy Goodwin	Ashland City	1995
	T	Gun	143	6/8	Danny Parchman	McEwen	1998
	T	Gun	143	7/8	Charles Hassell	New John'ville	1986
	T	Gun	143	3/8	Gary R. Trotter	Cumb.Furnace	1987
	T	Gun	142	4/8	Wilson Christy	Cumb.Furnace	2000
	T	Gun	142	7/8	Ronnie Cathey	White Bluff	1989
	T	Gun	142	1/8	Jerry Williams	Bon Aqua	1993
	T	Gun	142	2/8	Dan Hicks	Charlotte	1994
	T	Gun	141	0/8	Wilbur Mangrum	Fairview	1981
	T	Gun	141	6/8	Steve Hughes	Erin	1982
	T	Gun	141	4/8	David Morrow	Hender'ville	1989
	T	Gun	141	6/8	Jewell Loggins	Burns	1993
	T	Gun	140	2/8	James Gamel	Cumb.Furnace	1995
	T	Bow	135	0/8	Bronson Callis	Ashland City	2001
	T	Bow	127	1/8	Walter Morton	Pegram	1999
	T	Bow	126	5/8	Jamie Graves	Chapsboro.	1999
	T	Bow	126	5/8	Troy Gates	White Bluff	1990
	T	Bow	124	6/8	William Spann	White Bluff	1987
	T	Bow	121	1/8	Adam Choate	Dickson	1994
	T	Bow	121	6/8	Ronnie D. Bearden	Dickson	1997
	T	Bow	116	4/8	Gary Wayne Love	Nashville	1993
	T	Bow	116	5/8	Johnny Logan	Vanleer	1998
	T	Bow	115	5/8	Adam Choate	Dickson	1991
Dyer	NT	Gun	175	6/8	Rick Grabe	Dyersburg	1992
	T	Gun	156	1/8	Jamie Gordon	Trimble	2000
	T	Gun	140	4/8	Ronnie Campbell	Dyersburg	1990
	T	Gun	140	7/8	John C Castellaw	Dyersburg	1999
	T	Bow	123	0/8	Al Bradshaw	Dyersburg	1993
Eagle Ck	T	Gun	157	0/8	Keith Staggs	Hohenwald	1992
WMA	T	Gun	146	3/8	Mike Mcgahan	Brentwood	1984
	T	Gun	141	7/8	Tony Creasy	Waynesboro	1989
	T	Gun	140	3/8	Robert A. Dixon	Lawrenceburg	1986
Fall Ck	NT	Gun	176	3/8	J. C. Bradford	Winchester	1955
Falls	T	Gun	148	3/8	J. C. Myers	Jackson	1954
	T	Bow	141	0/8	Dwight Bottoms	Mc Minnville	1995
Fayette	NT	Gun	189	0/8	Boyd Arthur	Gtown.	2000
	NT	Gun	186	7/8	William Powers	Sumerville	1999
	NT	Gun	185	4/8	Crook Jeffrey	Arlington	2000
	T	Gun	184	4/8	Benny Johnson	Col.ville	1979
	NT	Gun	177	1/8	John Markle	Arlington	1978
	NT	Gun	171	4/8	Gene DeFoor	Mason	2000
	NT	Gun	169	3/8	Calvin Hillin	Mphs.	1994
	NT	Gun	167	0/8	Danny Bishop	Whitevile	1998
	T	Gun	165	3/8	Mark Kelly	Oakland	1979
	T	Gun	165	0/8	Harold Elder	Rossville	1985
	T	Gun	161	3/8	Barry Barron	Williston	1979
	T	Gun	160	7/8	Ed Barnett	Brighton	1978
	T	Gun	159	3/8	William Barron	Williston	1986
	T	Gun	156	6/8	Jim Key	Williston	1998

Area	Antler Type	Weapon	Score		Name	City	Year
	T	Gun	154	0/8	David Johnson	S.ville	1985
	T	Gun	152	5/8	David Thompson	Oakland	1986
	T	Gun	152	0/8	R.H. Pulliam	Rossville	1994
	T	Gun	151	7/8	Sam Murrey	Mphs.	2001
	T	Gun	151	6/8	Aaron Tegethoff	Col.ville	1983
	T	Gun	151	0/8	Jamie Cole	Arlington	1997
	T	Gun	150	2/8	Mike Ferguson	Oakland	2001
	T	Gun	150	3/8	Jeff Mcclure	Moscow	1983
	T	Gun	150	4/8	Micheal T Elrod	S.ville	1998
	T	Gun	149	2/8	John Sweeton	S.ville	1984
	T	Gun	148	2/8	Lee Hill	Col.ville	1997
	T	Gun	147	7/8	Eddie C Biggs	Mason	1998
	T	Gun	147	5/8	Bryant Tapp	S.ville	1993
	T	Gun	146	3/8	B. C. Yager Jr	Moscow	1975
	T	Gun	146	0/8	Howell Moore	S.ville	1987
	T	Gun	145	2/8	Richard Goddard	S.ville	1984
	T	Gun	145	1/8	Ralph Myers	S.ville	1986
	T	Gun	145	2/8	Sonny Thompson	Arlington	1989
	T	Gun	145	5/8	Bryant Tapp	S.ville	1993
	T	Gun	145	0/8	Max Boone	Arlington	1999
	T	Gun	144	0/8	Jimmy Stanford	Col.ville	1983
	T	Gun	144	7/8	Gary Cannon	Rossville	1996
	T	Gun	144	1/8	Tommy Day	S.ville	1996
	T	Gun	143	7/8	Cliff Robinson	Mphs.	1984
	T	Gun	143	6/8	Billy J. Wright	Mphs.	1982
	T	Gun	142	0/8	Randy Lucas	Mason	1989
	T	Gun	142	2/8	Paul Blankenship	Rossville	1990
	T	Gun	141	5/8	Jackie Hill	Williston	2000
	T	Gun	141	1/8	Franklin Tapp	S.ville	1996
	T	Gun	140	3/8	Johnny Key	Williston	2000
	T	Bow	118	2/8	Brian Sparks	G.town	1999
Fentress	NT	Gun	190	1/8	Ted Harvey	J.town	2000
	NT	Gun	185	1/8	Bill Thompson	Oneida	1999
	NT	Gun	176	3/8	Thomas T. Smith	J.town	1997
	NT	Gun	175	4/8	Mark Stephens	J.town	1996
	T	Gun	165	1/8	Roger Moon	Byrdstown	1998
	T	Gun	161	6/8	Gerald Crabtree	Allardt	1996
	T	Gun	158	1/8	Delbert Garrett	J.town	1967
	T	Gun	158	7/8	Brandon Holt	J.town	1991
	T	Gun	157	6/8	Danny Campbell	J.town	1984
	T	Gun	157	1/8	Jason Meadows	J.town	1998
	T	Gun	155	0/8	Mark Stewart	J.town	1997
	T	Gun	153	6/8	Jody Bridges	Grimsley	1993
	T	Gun	153	4/8	Johnny Thompson	Monterey	1996
	T	Gun	151	6/8	Ronnie Pyle	J.town	1985
	T	Gun	151	6/8	Cliff Cravens	J.town	1992
	T	Gun	151	5/8	Jody Bridges	Grimsley	1994
	T	Gun	151	2/8	Scott Chambers	Allardt	1998
	T	Gun	150	0/8	Tom Downey	Allardt	1986
	T	Gun	150	0/8	Carl S. Sparks	J.town	1993
	T	Gun	148	0/8	Buddie Conaster	J.town	1989
	T	Gun	148	5/8	Anthony Anderson	Grimsley	1987
	T	Gun	147	2/8	Bill Wheeler	J.town	1986
	T	Gun	146	4/8	Ronnie Pyle	J.town	1999
	T	Gun	146	5/8	Douglas Cobb	J.town	1999
	T	Gun	146	0/8	Benny M Hughes	J.town	1988
	T	Gun	146	4/8	Franklin J. Bledsoe	J.town	1996
	T	Gun	146	6/8	Rusty Leffew	J.town	1998

Area	Antler Type	Weapon	Score	Name	City	Year
	T	Gun	145 3/8	Rusty Leffew	J.town	1999
	T	Gun	145 5/8	Ted Harvey	J.town	1999
	T	Gun	145 5/8	Jeff Robbins	J.town	1993
	T	Gun	145 5/8	Jeffery Hancock	Allardt	1991
	T	Gun	144 1/8	Adam Ramsey	Clarkrange	1998
	T	Gun	144 5/8	Ronnie Crabtree	Pall Mall	1991
	T	Bow	143 5/8	Edgar Parker III	J.town	1996
	T	Bow	142 5/8	Franklin J Bledsoe	J.town	1995
	T	Bow	142 2/8	Ronnie Pyle	J.town	1992
	T	Gun	141 0/8	Bjorn Robinson	Sevierville	1998
	T	Gun	141 2/8	Anthony Anderson	Grimsley	1989
	T	Gun	140 7/8	Anthony Anderson	J.town	1989
Fentress cont.	T	Gun	140 3/8	Douglas	J.town	1994
	T	Gun	140 1/8	Kevin Garrett	Clarkrange	1995
	T	Bow	134 2/8	Donald Winningham	J.town	1994
	T	Bow	132 4/8	Steve Crabtree	J.town	1992
	T	Bow	131 5/8	Brian French	J.town	1994
	T	Bow	123 5/8	William A Threet	Clarkrange	1995
	T	Bow	118 1/8	Donald Winningham	J.town	1994
Franklin	NT	Bow	171 0/8	Steven Layne	Manchester	1981
	T	Bow	158 6/8	Lee Prince	Winchester	1989
	T	Gun	149 2/8	Johnny R. Garner	Cowan	1992
	T	Gun	148 3/8	Phillip Ledbetter	Lynchburg	2001
	T	Gun	148 7/8	David Johnson	Estill Fork	1986
	T	Gun	143 5/8	Paul Crabtree	Decherd	1983
	T	Gun	143 4/8	Phil Robertson	Tullahoma	1987
	T	Gun	143 7/8	Carlton Staples	Castiln. Spgs	1992
	T	Gun	141 2/8	James Mayers Jr.	Saulsbury	1984
	T	Gun	141 2/8	Johnny Baggett	Belvidere	1975
	T	Gun	140 3/8	David Baker	Belvidere	1981
	T	Gun	140 1/8	James L. Syler	Huntland	1978
	T	Bow	132 3/8	Sandy K. Gilliam	Sewanee	1997
	T	Bow	126 1/8	Jeff Morris	Manchester	1994
Ft Campbell	NT	Gun	198 3/8	Clarence McElhaney	Crossville	1978
	NT	Gun	181 1/8	Bobby Grishorn	Mt. Juliet	1976
	NT	Gun	180 4/8	Melvin L. Nichols	Holladay	1978
	T	Gun	180 1/8	Lonnie Hulse	Lebanon	1995
	NT	Gun	179 5/8	Jim Bale	Gdltsvlle.	2000
	NT	Gun	179 7/8	Mark Hulse	Castiln. Spgs	1994
	T	Gun	172 3/8	Cecil Booth	Paris	1990
	NT	Gun	169 4/8	David Byard	Clarksville	1987
	T	Bow	167 0/8	Larry Lee Murphy	Clarksville	1989
	NT	Gun	166 6/8	William Faulkner	Humbolt	1981
	NT	Gun	166 1/8	Darren Holt	Ashland City	1986
	NT	Gun	166 1/8	Aaron Daniels	Woodlawn	1996
	T	Gun	162 5/8	Stanley Thompson	Buchanan	1968
	T	Gun	159 2/8	Ricky Booth	Dover	1990
	T	Gun	159 0/8	A J Ward, Jr	Mt Juliet	1969
	T	Gun	157 3/8	Russell Sneller	Bartlett	1978
	T	Gun	155 5/8	Dana Walker	Dover	1997
	T	Gun	155 0/8	Walter Harden	Portland	1988
	T	Gun	155 1/8	Arnold Henson	Clarksville	1988
	T	Gun	153 1/8	Jim Bale	Gdltsvlle.	1989
	T	Gun	153 4/8	Joe Britt	Clarksville	1975
	T	Gun	152 1/8	William A. Owings	Cordova	1981
	T	Gun	151 6/8	Jimmy Blankinship	Cleveland	1983

Area	Antler Type	Weapon	Score	Name	City	Year
	T	Gun	151 5/8	George Reno	Corryton	1994
	T	Gun	149 1/8	Jeffrey Matthews	Estill Springs	1994
	T	Gun	148 4/8	Wilson Christy	Cumb.Furnace	2000
	T	Gun	148 6/8	Howard Capps	Cumb.Furnace	1987
	T	Gun	148 3/8	Nelson Wallace	Dover	1979
	T	Gun	148 2/8	William Yount	Greenbrier	1996
	T	Gun	147 4/8	Bill Leech	Dickson	1964
	T	Gun	147 5/8	William Heflin	Cumb.Furnace	1980
	T	Gun	147 2/8	Roger Short	Celina	1979
	T	Gun	145 4/8	George A Hazel	Clarksville	1984
	T	Gun	145 5/8	Chad Pickens	Albany	1990
	T	Gun	144 3/8	Robert Spurgeon	Erin	1977
	T	Gun	144 5/8	Sam Chaffin	Hendersonville	1986
	T	Gun	143 1/8	James R Chandler	Humbolt	1975
	T	Gun	141 0/8	Tommy Reagan	Louisville	1997
	T	Gun	140 4/8	Jerry York	Hermitage	1966
	T	Gun	140 7/8	William Rogers	Dyersburg	1977
	T	Gun	140 1/8	Tony Young	Talbot	1996
	T	Bow	139 6/8	Jim Asbury	Morristown	1986
	T	Bow	134 0/8	Jerry Suiter	Clarksville	1985
	T	Bow	125 2/8	Clyde England	Talbott	1983
	T	Bow	121 4/8	Clyde England	Bean Station	1989
	T	Bow	119 4/8	Gary Johnson	Bean Station	1989
	T	Bow	118 5/8	Clayton England	Bean Station	1987
	T	Bow	117 5/8	David T Settlers	Clarksville	1984
	T	Bow	117 3/8	Clyde England	Talbott	1982
	T	Bow	117 0/8	Brad Austin	Crossville	1997
	T	Bow	115 4/8	Randall Brooks	Bean Station	1989
Gibson	T	Gun	153 0/8	Chris Cherry	Gibson	1997
	T	Gun	147 2/8	Lee Vanover	Humboldt	1999
	T	Gun	144 2/8	William Longmire	Bradford	1991
	T	Gun	141 0/8	Stephen Fuller	Milan	1997
Giles	T	Gun	165 0/8	Marcus Colbert	Fayetteville	1988
	T	Bow	160 0/8	Johnny Neal	Pulaski	1984
	T	Gun	157 1/8	Gerald Armstrong	Nashville	1983
	T	Gun	155 5/8	Dennis Walls	Bellevue	1969
	T	Gun	149 0/8	A. B. Cleming	Prospect	1980
	T	Bow	148 5/8	Roger Johnson	Ethridge	1985
	T	Gun	148 2/8	Ned Sullivan	Elkton	1988
	T	Gun	147 3/8	David Alexander	Brentwood	1982
	T	Gun	146 7/8	David Woodward	Huntsville	2000
	T	Gun	145 3/8	Marshall Thornton	Ardmore	1979
	T	Gun	145 5/8	Randy Smith	Burns	1984
	T	Gun	144 5/8	Charles Daniel	Pulaski	1972
	T	Gun	144 2/8	Glynn Newell	Summertown	1978
	T	Gun	142 6/8	Robert Erwin Jr.	Pulaski	1982
	T	Gun	142 2/8	Bobby Bue	Ardmore	1985
	T	Gun	141 6/8	Jeff Slayton	Prostect	1985
	T	Gun	141 7/8	Lawrence Toone	Pulaski	1981
	T	Gun	140 2/8	Bob Wade Curtis	Ardmore	1982
	T	Gun	140 2/8	Don Hinkle	Pulaski	1985
	T	Gun	140 7/8	Steve Clark	Pulaski	1986
	T	Bow	135 2/8	Ronnie Beddingfield	Nashville	1997
	T	Bow	133 1/8	Dennis James	Pulaski	1998
	T	Bow	119 2/8	Wayne E Foster	Pulaski	1970
	T	Bow	115 2/8	Bobby Butler	Ardmore	1988
Grainger	T	Bow	131 4/8	Thomas Greenlee	Blaine	1975

Area	Antler Type	Weapon	Score	Name	City	Year
Greene	T	Gun	149 4/8	Gary Sams	Afton	1987
	T	Gun	146 2/8	Delbert Ottinger	Greeneville	1989
	T	Gun	143 2/8	J.R. Snapes	Midway	1997
	T	Bow	139 7/8	Ricky Thornburg	Chuckey	1987
	T	Bow	135 2/8	Huston Malone	Greeneville	1990
	T	Bow	125 1/8	Kyle Scott Smith	Mohawk	1987
	T	Bow	120 0/8	Gary A Douthat	Midway	2000
Grundy	NT	Gun	192 6/8	Mickey Bush	Murfreesboro	1988
	T	Gun	172 4/8	David Duvall	Manchester	1992
	T	Gun	171 7/8	Wilson W Weaver	Laager	1987
	T	Gun	152 1/8	Ricky Scott	Hixon	1988
	T	Gun	148 2/8	Ronnie Preston	Altamont	1986
	T	Gun	146 2/8	Scott Rummel	Athens	1989
	T	Gun	143 5/8	Robin Smartt	Beersheba Sprgs	1998
	T	Gun	142 2/8	Ricky Simons	McMinnville	1991
	T	Gun	142 6/8	Tommy L. Ferrell	McMinnville	1989
	T	Gun	141 5/8	Chris Fults	McMinnville	1998
	T	Bow	129 2/8	Johnny Wanamaker	Mc Minnville	1999
	T	Bow	123 4/8	Tim Wanamaker	McMinnville	1991
	T	Bow	116 0/8	Anthony Wanamaker	McMinnville	1992
Hamblen	T	Gun	141 5/8	Norman Patterson	Talbott	1983
Hamilton	T	Gun	152 6/8	William Perry	Mcminnville	1989
	T	Gun	151 0/8	Jeff L Kerby	Hixon	1984
	T	Gun	148 7/8	Tommy Andrews	Soddy Daisy	1989
	T	Bow	133 3/8	Robert L Moon Jr	Signal Mtn	1989
Hancock	NT	Gun	179 6/8	Jason Delph	Sneedville	1995
	T	Gun	142 6/8	Willis Mcclain	New Market	1986
	T	Gun	141 6/8	Homer O Johnson	Sneedville	1987
	T	Bow	116 3/8	Robert Vandergriff	Corryton	1987
Hardeman	NT	Gun	175 4/8	William Shelby	Col.ville	1998
	NT	Gun	170 1/8	Ronnie Frederick	Corinth	1985
	NT	Gun	169 6/8	Roger Callahan	Saulsbury	1999
	T	Gun	165 6/8	Bond Stewart	Arlington	1995
	T	Gun	164 0/8	Larry Kimery	Trenton	1974
	T	Gun	162 1/8	Keith Deming	Bolivar	1987
	T	Gun	158 5/8	Zachary Deberry	Hornsby	1999
	T	Gun	157 4/8	Charles Blackburn	Mphs.	1980
	T	Gun	157 4/8	Richard Howell II	Mphs.	1987
	T	Gun	156 0/8	Fred Hinkel	Oakland	1979
	T	Gun	154 6/8	Robert Crowley	Middleton	2000
	T	Gun	154 0/8	Paul Blankenship	Mphs.	1988
	T	Gun	153 5/8	Michael Cullens	Brighton	1993
	T	Gun	150 2/8	Milton James	Eads	1985
	T	Gun	150 2/8	Mike Phillips	S.ville	1997
	T	Gun	147 1/8	Philip Easterling	Mphs.	1977
	T	Gun	147 3/8	Bobby Stewart	Middleton	1987
	T	Gun	146 0/8	Bobby Shepherd	Mphs.	1980
	T	Gun	146 4/8	Chris Deming	Hickory Valley	1997
	T	Bow	145 6/8	Bill English	Middleton	1984
	T	Gun	145 6/8	Terry Wharton	Hornsby	1990
	T	Gun	143 0/8	Dale Ervin	Bolivar	1985
	T	Gun	141 3/8	Carl King	Toone	2000
	T	Gun	141 5/8	Dana Blanton	Whiteville	1985
	T	Gun	141 1/8	Keith Marcum	Bolivar	1994
	T	Gun	140 4/8	Larry Ross	Bartlett	1989
	T	Gun	140 7/8	Jack Crowley	Bolivar	1967
	T	Gun	140 2/8	David Wooten	Whiteville	1989
	T	Bow	138 2/8	Tim Mcalpin	Grd Junction	2000
	T	Bow	126 4/8	Paul Blankenship	Rossville	1991
	T	Bow	116 4/8	Allen Lufcy	Eads	2000
	T	Bow	115 6/8	Stan Howell	Bolivar	1990
Hardin	NT	Gun	189 7/8	Bobby Sullins, Jr	Millington	1995
	NT	Gun	183 2/8	Tommy Willcuti	Michie	1999
	NT	Gun	175 3/8	David Willis	Saltillo	1994
	NT	Gun	165 5/8	Rodney Austin	Savannah	1998
	T	Gun	165 2/8	Scott Conaway	Dacula	1999
	T	Gun	155 7/8	Jada Melson	Olive Hill	1963
	T	Gun	154 7/8	Harold Gray	Savannah	1968
	T	Gun	154 4/8	Don Gass	Saltillo	1990
	T	Gun	153 0/8	Tim Huggins	Rienzi	1992
	T	Gun	152 2/8	Jeffery White	Savannah	1996
	T	Gun	150 5/8	Willie M. Blanton	Counce	1977
	T	Gun	148 5/8	Wesley Short		2000
	T	Gun	148 0/8	Shannon Baugus	Savannah	1996
	T	Gun	146 2/8	Wayne Babb	Sardis	1986
	T	Gun	143 5/8	Rodney Hosea	Savannah	2000
	T	Gun	142 5/8	David Scott	Savannah	2001
	T	Gun	142 4/8	Stan Smith	Savannah	1978
	T	Gun	142 3/8	David Smith	Savannah	1980
	T	Gun	142 7/8	Ronald Brown	Savannah	1998
	T	Gun	141 2/8	Bud Stang	Savannah	1984
	T	Bow	127 1/8	Tommy Delaney	Morris Chapel	1996
	T	Bow	126 3/8	Tom Oaks	Corinth	1988
	T	Bow	125 0/8	Terry Knox	Col.ville	1994
	T	Bow	125 5/8	Bryan Thomas	Savannah	1997
	T	Bow	123 0/8	Randy Gray	Savannah	1986
	T	Bow	121 0/8	Chris Beckham	Clifton	1991
	T	Bow	117 7/8	Philip Blackwelder	Savannah	1999
	T	Bow	116 3/8	Todd Reynolds	Springville	1998
Hatchie NWR	T	Bow	123 0/8	Gary Haynes	Troy	1978
Hawkins	NT	Gun	223 0/8	Luther Fuller	Kingsport	1984
	NT	Gun	181 4/8	Terry Burns	Rogersville	1983
	T	Gun	148 4/8	Mark Duval	Greeneville	1986
	T	Gun	148 3/8	Jerry Dean Holt	Sneedville	1989
	T	Bow	141 4/8	Mark S. Rogers	Church Hill	1993
	T	Gun	141 3/8	Johnny Ford	Kingsport	1987
	T	Gun	140 1/8	Marvin Mathews	Rogersville	1989
	T	Bow	130 4/8	Johnny Ford	Kingsport	1985
	T	Bow	125 3/8	Darrel K. Bailey	Rogersville	1989
	T	Bow	121 7/8	Mitchell Mclain	Rogersville	1996
	T	Bow	116 0/8	R. C. Wilder	Morristown	1985
	T	Bow	116 5/8	Jimmy Duncan	Kingsport	1986
Haywood	NT	Gun	232 7/8	Justin Samples	Jackson	2001
	NT	Gun	185 2/8	Bobby Baggett	Humbolt	1980
	NT	Gun	181 1/8	Kim Hall	Maury City	1991
	T	Gun	172 4/8	Mark Powell	Brownsville	1999

Area	Antler Type	Weapon	Score	Name	City	Year
	T	Gun	155 6/8	Ralph Cochran	Brownsville	1982
	T	Gun	151 1/8	Charles Crockett	Trenton	1997
	T	Gun	149 5/8	Lester Blaylock	Brownsville	1979
	T	Gun	148 0/8	Eddie Mize	Munford	1981
	T	Gun	146 2/8	Aaron Wiggins	Halls	1988
	T	Gun	146 1/8	Jason Byrd	Brownsville	1997
	T	Gun	144 0/8	Paul Marlar	Brownsville	1966
	T	Gun	143 5/8	James Howard	Brownsville	1998
	T	Gun	141 3/8	Richard Chunn	Munford	1981
	T	Gun	140 5/8	Terry Hooper	Brownsville	1995
	T	Gun	140 4/8	Steve Anzini	Drummonds	1997
Henderson	NT	Gun	175 6/8	Danny Phillips	Clinton	1998
	T	Gun	157 3/8	Guy Walker Jr.	Wildersville	1988
	T	Gun	153 3/8	Kevin Petty	Reagan	2000
	T	Gun	150 2/8	Marty Swindle	Reagan	1995
	T	Gun	144 6/8	Mike Clenney	Reagan	2001
	T	Bow	142 3/8	Pat Davis	Lexington	1990
	T	Gun	142 4/8	Randall Wallace	Lexington	1988
	T	Gun	140 1/8	Dale Moser	Jackson	1999
	T	Bow	135 2/8	Greg Hopper	Lexington	1989
	T	Bow	125 7/8	Russell Hepperly	Townsend	1992
	T	Bow	123 0/8	Billy Moody	Lexington	1997
Henry	NT	Gun	175 6/8	H. Earl Mealer Jr.	Puryear	1978
	NT	Gun	166 7/8	Curtis D. Neal	Mansfeild	1995
	NT	Gun	166 4/8	Jeffery Lindsey	Big Sandy	1994
	T	Gun	157 1/8	Ricky Owen	Paris	1987
	T	Gun	152 6/8	Brenda Valentine	Buchannan	1993
	T	Gun	152 1/8	Phillip Harris	Newbern	1994
	T	Gun	151 2/8	Keith Lindsey	Humbolt	1994
	T	Gun	149 0/8	John Rusty Farmer	Springville	2000
	T	Gun	149 2/8	Marty Tyler	Puryear	1994
	T	Gun	148 3/8	Darius Hastings	Mansfield	1996
	T	Gun	148 1/8	Chris Fletcher	Paris	2000
	T	Gun	148 6/8	Kenith Louden	Springville	1980
	T	Gun	147 1/8	Douglas Overton	Paris	1979
	T	Gun	145 3/8	James Matheny	Paris	1989
	T	Gun	143 0/8	Eddie Vandyke	Puryear	2000
	T	Gun	143 6/8	Barbara Coleman	Paris	1990
	T	Gun	143 3/8	Tommy Crane	Paris	1994
	T	Gun	142 4/8	Curtis D. Neal	Mansfield	1994
	T	Gun	141 2/8	Ronnie Howard	Springville	1986
	T	Gun	140 0/8	David Clendenin	Paris	2000
	T	Gun	140 4/8	Jim Napier, Sr	Springville	1991
	T	Gun	140 2/8	Jim Forrest	Puryear	1982
	T	Gun	140 5/8	Jeffery Lindsey	Big Sandy	1995
	T	Bow	132 7/8	Brent Owen	Paris	2000
	T	Bow	124 2/8	Christopher Whitten	Knoxville	2000
	T	Bow	119 2/8	John Bomar	Paris	1997
	T	Bow	119 2/8	Russ Buffington	Paris	2000
Hickman	NT	Gun	176 7/8	Kenny Ambrose	Clinton	1987
	T	Bow	167 3/8	Tony Savage	Nashville	1994
	T	Gun	165 1/8	Ernest Shelby	Franklin	1999
	T	Gun	161 6/8	Harold R. Caughron	Sevierville	1996
	T	Gun	158 3/8	George A. Daniel	Drummonds	1985
	T	Gun	151 4/8	Kelly Webb	Mphs.	1980
	T	Gun	149 1/8	Billy Flowers	Centerville	1969
	T	Gun	149 5/8	Kenneth Chandler	Centerville	1974
	T	Gun	147 0/8	Mickey Brown	Greenville	1995
	T	Gun	146 4/8	Marty England	Duck River	1995
	T	Gun	144 6/8	Jim Kilpatrick	Lobelville	1979
	T	Gun	144 7/8	Matthew Tice	Bristol	1997
	T	Gun	142 5/8	John Wallace	Mcewen	1989
	T	Gun	142 6/8	Carl Simmons	Centerville	1973
	T	Gun	142 2/8	Bill West	Nunnelly	1981
	T	Gun	142 1/8	Gary Mealer	Lenoir City	1991
	T	Gun	141 5/8	Michael Williams	Nashville	1994
	T	Gun	140 5/8	Joe Vaughn	Centerville	1979
	T	Gun	139 7/8	Stephen G Lewis	Hermitage	1995
	T	Bow	135 2/8	Rusty Chivers	Kingston Spgs	1995
	T	Bow	134 4/8	Gerald A Hobbs	Hoenwald	2000
	T	Bow	134 4/8	Stanley Hunt	Hendersonville	1985
	T	Bow	123 2/8	Donald Ray Weaver	Dickson	1987
	T	Bow	123 1/8	Richard Howell	Thompson Sta	1993
	T	Bow	121 4/8	Bob Vaden	Arriagton	1989
Holston Army Ammo Plant	NT	Bow	186 6/8	Mark Phillips	Kingsport	1983
	T	Bow	146 4/8	John P Danko	Church Hill	1983
	T	Bow	146 5/8	Harold Gilliam	Kingsport	1983
	T	Bow	145 7/8	Ronnie Inman	Russelville	1983
	NT	Bow	144 7/8	Timothy Calhoun	Kingsport	1987
	T	Bow	136 2/8	Don Wagner	Oliver Springs	1985
	T	Bow	134 6/8	Mark Marshall	Church Hill	1986
	T	Bow	131 4/8	Kenneth H. Carey	Greenback	1983
	T	Bow	129 7/8	Clarence H Tabor	Bristol	1984
	T	Bow	127 2/8	Johnny Russell	Lafollette	1983
	T	Bow	125 5/8	Thomas H. Russell	Rogersville	1984
	T	Bow	123 6/8	Daniel W. Chase	Kingsport	1983
	T	Bow	123 0/8	Gene Atkins Jr	Bean Station	1984
Houston	NT	Gun	171 0/8	Charles Mathis	Erin	1987
	T	Gun	171 2/8	Pat Clark	Erin	1985
	NT	Gun	168 3/8	Greg Mc Askill	Cumb. City	2001
	NT	Gun	166 1/8	Chuck Lair	Erin	1989
	T	Gun	162 5/8	Nelson Nichols	Erin	1978
	T	Gun	154 3/8	Leonard Hooper	Tn Ridge	1988
	T	Gun	152 0/8	Travis Tidwell	Bon Aqua	2000
	T	Gun	151 7/8	Brian Metcalf	Waverly	1989
	T	Gun	150 1/8	William Dennis	Tenn Ridge	2000
	T	Gun	150 1/8	Joel G Nolen	Erin	1987
	T	Bow	148 4/8	Joey Rouse	Tn Ridge	1999
	T	Bow	148 4/8	Joey Rouse	Tenn. Ridge	1999
	T	Gun	147 6/8	Garner Bailey	Erin	1996
	T	Gun	147 7/8	Paul Martin	Erin	1985
	T	Gun	145 5/8	Harry Day	Tn Ridge	1985
	T	Gun	145 2/8	Clay Mills	Erin	1998
	T	Gun	143 1/8	Randy Hinson	Erin	1984
	T	Bow	136 5/8	Michael Bryant	Nashville	1999
	T	Bow	135 5/8	Robert Hazel	Clinton	2001
	T	Bow	116 0/8	Calvin Rougemont	Erin	1984
Humphreys	NT	Gun	178 2/8	Jimmy Patterson	Waverly	1980
	T	Gun	165 1/8	Clyde Cooley	Waverly	1989

Area	Antler Type	Weapon	Score		Name	City	Year
	T	Gun	160	6/8	Chris Davis	Waverly	1979
	T	Bow	159	0/8	Bill Littleton	Dickson	1988
	T	Gun	159	0/8	R. Scott Stewart	Brentwood	1997
	T	Gun	157	3/8	David Jones	Waverly	2000
	T	Gun	154	5/8	Alden Poyner	New J.ville	1989
	T	Gun	154	3/8	Kenneth N. Gibbs	Cottontown	1997
	T	Gun	153	4/8	Randy Hooper	Mcewen	1989
	T	Gun	152	4/8	Roger George	Waverly	1982
	T	Gun	151	6/8	Jeff Thompson	Centerville	1984
	T	Gun	151	3/8	David Kirby	Madison	1975
	T	Gun	150	5/8	Greg Winstead	Mcewen	1989
	T	Gun	150	2/8	R. Scott Stewart Jr	Brentwood	1998
	T	Gun	149	0/8	Donnie Marrs	Waverly	1985
	T	Gun	149	1/8	Bryan Kinkel	Nashville	1995
	T	Gun	148	6/8	Evan Gaskin	Eva	2001
	T	Gun	147	6/8	George E Pickard	Gallatin	1973
	T	Gun	147	4/8	David Oliphant	Mcewen	1990
	T	Gun	147	5/8	David Nance	Hermitage	1995
	T	Gun	146	4/8	Hubert Curtis Jr.	Waverly	1980
	T	Gun	146	7/8	Darrell Patterson	Waverly	1987
	T	Gun	145	6/8	David Stoever	Smyrna	1975
	T	Gun	145	4/8	William E. Henson	New J.ville	1982
	T	Gun	145	5/8	Charles Brake	Mcewen	1995
	T	Gun	144	7/8	William M Barrett	Antioch	1989
Humphreys	T	Gun	144	3/8	James Lovelady	Erin	1989
cont.	T	Gun	143	1/8	Dwight Davis	Waverly	1988
	T	Gun	143	5/8	Billy A. Tummins	Mcewen	1990
	T	Gun	143	7/8	Donnie Stover	Gallatin	1998
	T	Gun	143	3/8	Phillip Warfield	Mc Ewen	1994
	T	Gun	142	4/8	Eddie Scott	Waverly	1989
	T	Gun	141	2/8	Ronald K. Harris	Columbia	2000
	T	Gun	141	2/8	John Work	Waverly	1985
	T	Gun	141	6/8	James Deakins	Kingsport	1982
	T	Gun	141	3/8	Lloyd Lemaster	Murfreesboro	1989
	T	Gun	141	5/8	Mark Parchman	Dickson	1990
	T	Gun	141	2/8	Johnny Kilburn	Waverly	1990
	T	Gun	141	0/8	Billy Tummis	Mcewen	1990
	T	Gun	141	0/8	Dennis Turner	Waverly	1995
	T	Bow	140	0/8	Ralph Bohannon	Waverly	1992
	T	Gun	140	2/8	Alden Poyner	New J.ville	1988
	T	Gun	140	5/8	John Warden Jr	Waverly	1989
	T	Gun	140	5/8	Junior Smith	Waverly	1990
	T	Gun	140	6/8	Scott Melton	New J.ville	1992
	T	Bow	132	0/8	Tom Hutson	Gdltsville.	1986
	T	Bow	130	0/8	Roger Bohannon	Mcewen	1992
	T	Bow	130	5/8	Clarence Maness	Covington	1996
	T	Bow	126	6/8	Wayne Lambdin	Waverly	1997
	T	Bow	123	0/8	Jacen Davidson	Waverly	1987
	T	Bow	120	4/8	Eric Fuller	Waverly	1999
	T	Bow	119	6/8	Darrell Beeler	Corryton	1988
	T	Bow	118	4/8	Jeff Duncan	New J.ville	1990
	T	Bow	116	4/8	Chris Collingsworth	Ashland City	1990
Jackson	T	Gun	163	7/8	Larry Holt	J.town	1987
	T	Gun	160	0/8	Kipp Holt	J.town	1989
	T	Bow	158	3/8	Larry Holt	J.town	1990
	T	Gun	140	3/8	W.S. Ragland Jr	Livingston	1962
	T	Bow	139	3/8	Michael Mitchell	Cookeville	1983
	T	Bow	136	2/8	Philip E. Lawrence	Lenior City	1998

Area	Antler Type	Weapon	Score		Name	City	Year
	T	Bow	132	1/8	Danny Hall	Loudon	1998
	T	Bow	126	6/8	Steve Draper	Whitleyville	1997
	T	Bow	124	2/8	Larry Holt	J.town	1990
	T	Bow	123	4/8	David Garrett	Lebanon	1992
Jefferson	T	Bow	118	2/8	Kenneth Corum Jr	Knoxville	1980
	T	Bow	121	4/8	Kenneth Corum Jr	Knoxville	1980
Johnson	T	Gun	141	2/8	Caleb Smith Jr.	Elizabethton	1967
Kingston							
Stm Plant	T	Bow	117	0/8	Randy D. Woodell	Harriman	1994
Knox	T	Bow	116	1/8	Mark Gheen	Knoxville	1996
Lake	T	Gun	159	2/8	Johnny Doyle	Tiptonville	1990
	T	Gun	155	0/8	Josh Barnes	Ridgley	1993
	T	Gun	144	3/8	Danny Scott	Tiptonville	1982
	T	Gun	143	2/8	Albert Scott	Tiptonville	1986
Lauderdale	NT	Gun	169	0/8	Mark Rhodes	Cordova	1990
	T	Gun	164	5/8	Glen Arthur	Ripley	1999
	T	Gun	153	5/8	William Sweat	Ripley	1995
	T	Gun	148	0/8	C.D. Heaton III	Mphs.	1997
	T	Gun	145	2/8	Paul Reynolds	Ripley	1999
Laurel Hill	T	Gun	154	5/8	Don Cheatwood	Lawrenceburg	1977
WMA	T	Gun	143	7/8	Audrey Scott	Savannah	1972
Lawrence	NT	Gun	167	1/8	Jimmy Fowler	Loretta	1989
	T	Gun	153	1/8	Woodie Escue	Summertown	1986
	T	Gun	149	7/8	Jason Holloway	Iron City	1991
	T	Gun	148	6/8	Jay Patterson	Lawrenceburg	1969
	T	Gun	147	1/8	Brent Stanford	Loretto	1992
	T	Gun	145	3/8	James Smith	Ethridge	1985
	T	Gun	143	7/8	Robin Street	Hollenwald	2001
	T	Gun	142	1/8	Tim Polk	West Point	1991
	T	Gun	141	7/8	Robert Wunner	Lawrenceburg	1986
	T	Gun	140	6/8	Travis Tidwell	Bon Aqua	2001
	T	Gun	140	6/8	Billy Long	Lawrenceburg	1979
	T	Gun	140	4/8	Ricky Jones	Iron City	1973
	T	Bow	122	1/8	Alan D Shults	Leoma	1990
	T	Bow	121	0/8	Scott Littrell	Lawrenceburg	1994
	T	Bow	119	3/8	Adam Lowery	Lawrenceburg	2000
	T	Bow	117	2/8	Rickie Kizer	Loretto	1992
LBL WMA	NT	Gun	180	4/8	Donald Ragland	Livingston	1974
	T	Gun	176	1/8	Alan Jackson	Humbolt	1996
	T	Gun	172	2/8	Joe K Sanders	Goodlettsville	1984
	T	Gun	172	5/8	Michael Bowers	Whitebluff	1992
	NT	Gun	170	5/8	Nathan Mccarter	Mc Donald	1994
	T	Gun	170	5/8	Robert Traylor	Clarksville	1990
	T	Gun	166	2/8	Robert Gilliam	Tullahoma	1980
	T	Gun	157	4/8	Steve Blount	Kingston	1974
	T	Gun	156	6/8	Charles Primm	Nashville	1974
	T	Gun	155	6/8	Calday A Wyrick	Knoxville	1979
	T	Gun	152	1/8	Ronnie Howard	Springville	1986
	T	Gun	151	1/8	David E Champlin	Lexington	1985
	T	Gun	150	4/8	Dudley King Jr	Nashville	1981

Area	Antler Type	Weapon	Score	Name	City	Year
	T	Bow	148 1/8	Randall Wade	Hollow Rock	1995
	T	Gun	148 7/8	Charlie Melton	Ashland City	1980
	T	Gun	148 0/8	Danny R Page	Buchanan	1993
	T	Gun	147 4/8	Donald R. Fuller	Decaturville	1973
	T	Gun	147 2/8	Jerry Whitley	Corinth	1995
	T	Gun	147 6/8	Tim Henderson	Ashland City	1996
	T	Bow	146 3/8	John Hults	Powell	1995
	T	Gun	146 5/8	Danny Wallace	Camden	1988
	T	Gun	146 4/8	James Collins	Murfreesboro	1994
	T	Gun	145 4/8	Bobby Pate	Mckenzie	1978
	T	Gun	145 5/8	Evans Bohannon	Waverly	1973
	T	Gun	145 1/8	Gabe Krantz	Livingston	1997
	T	Gun	144 7/8	Ava Lorene Hinson	Greenbrier	1978
	T	Gun	144 0/8	Odell Frazier	New John'ville	1974
	T	Gun	144 6/8	James V. Brantley	Knoxville	1987
	T	Gun	143 2/8	Ed Melton	Crossville	1984
	T	Gun	143 4/8	Jeff Bailey	Jackson	1978
	T	Gun	143 4/8	Brian Winford	Cookeville	1990
	T	Gun	142 3/8	Woodrow Wilson	Oldfort	1977
	T	Gun	142 0/8	Johnny Henderson	Cottage Grove	1979
	T	Bow	140 1/8	Boley Gilmore	Big Rock	1972
	T	Gun	140 5/8	Ricky Booth	Dover	1986
	T	Bow	135 5/8	John Harrison	Dandridge	1979
	T	Bow	134 2/8	Danny Hendrick	Nashville	1978
	T	Bow	130 0/8	Mark Thompson	Estill Springs	1994
	T	Bow	128 2/8	John Reed	Shelbyville	1998
	T	Bow	127 3/8	T.G. Gregory	Goodlettsville	1987
	T	Bow	123 0/8	Curtis D. Neal	Mansfield	1978
	T	Bow	122 7/8	Hubert Comer	Hermitage	1982
	T	Bow	118 6/8	Thomas Mellett	Nashville	1976
	T	Bow	117 0/8	Billy H Brimer	Maryville	1983
	T	Bow	117 7/8	Randy Hale	Joelton	1989
	T	Bow	115 2/8	Dale Greer	Paris	1983
	T	Bow	115 7/8	Larry Galyon	Knoxville	1986
Lewis	T	Gun	169 7/8	Kenneth Whitehead	Hohenwald	1974
	T	Gun	151 1/8	Charles P Bennett	Nashville	1962
	T	Gun	148 6/8	Dee Quillen	Centerville	1964
	T	Gun	147 2/8	Bobby Baize	Lawrenceburg	1981
	T	Gun	144 5/8	Jimmy Brakeen	Centerville	1990
	T	Gun	143 7/8	Bill Ramey	Linden	1967
	T	Gun	143 4/8	Bobby Bean	Hohenwald	1993
	T	Bow	121 6/8	Joe Anderson	Lavergne	2000
	T	Bow	115 6/8	Jeff Skelton	Howenwald	1998
Lincoln	NT	Gun	175 2/8	Danny Whitt	Toney	1977
	T	Gun	162 4/8	Jeffery G. Johnson	Flintville	1992
	T	Gun	156 1/8	Kevin Steelman	Fayetteville	1991
	T	Bow	151 4/8	Aaron Prince	Winchester	1988
	T	Gun	151 6/8	Danny Moore	Fayetteville	2000
	T	Gun	151 3/8	Derrick Syler	Fayetteville	1982
	T	Gun	147 2/8	Bobby Arnold	Flintville	1982
	T	Gun	146 1/8	Jacky Childress	Fayetteville	1970
	T	Gun	146 2/8	Mike Pitts	Fayetteville	1976
	T	Gun	146 1/8	Bobby Bye	Pulaski	1976
	T	Gun	146 7/8	Steve Lewter	Ardmore	1985
	T	Gun	146 1/8	Bryon Divis	Fayetteville	1996
	T	Gun	145 5/8	Tom S. Bigham III	Fayetteville	1974
	T	Gun	145 4/8	John I Marks Jr	Huntsville	1989
	T	Gun	144 4/8	Lee Gault	Fayetteville	1995
	T	Gun	143 0/8	Airon Lamb	Elora	1987
	T	Gun	141 4/8	Bill Cunningham	Fayetteville	1986
	T	Gun	141 4/8	Mark Flowers	Petersburg	1989
	T	Bow	140 3/8	Chris Twyman	Fayetteville	1987
	T	Gun	140 7/8	Sandra Whitt	Toney	1984
	T	Bow	123 2/8	Richard Lush	Fayetteville	1996
	T	Bow	122 6/8	Steve Marler	Dayton	1998
	T	Bow	115 3/8	William Harris	Fayetteville	1987
Loudon	NT	Bow	176 6/8	Charles Brewster	Madisonville	2001
	T	Gun	140 6/8	Michael Phillips	Clinton	1987
	T	Bow	115 4/8	James Allmon	Lenoir City	1986
Macon	T	Bow	126 5/8	Roger Draper	Whitleyville	1988
	T	Bow	118 0/8	Roger Draper	Whitleyville	1992
Madison	NT	Gun	178 5/8	Stephen Umhoefer	Jackson	1995
	T	Gun	165 1/8	Edwin Cude	Pinson	2000
	T	Gun	148 6/8	Pat Gaines	Bells	1999
	T	Gun	146 3/8	Don Bell	Jackson	1973
	T	Gun	145 6/8	Danny Lee Walker	S.ville	2000
	T	Gun	145 7/8	Jim Mcadams	Oakfield	1990
	T	Gun	142 3/8	Thomas Lott	Bethel Sprgs	2000
	T	Gun	142 3/8	James Robinson	Jackson	2001
	T	Gun	140 7/8	Rodney E Ivy	Medina	1990
	T	Bow	123 6/8	Trey Lawrence	Jackson	1993
	T	Bow	119 1/8	Allen Stanford	Jackson	1998
	T	Bow	118 0/8	Richard B. Smith	Jackson	1994
Marion	T	Gun	165 0/8	Tommy Newsom	Whitwell	1993
	T	Gun	163 2/8	Bay Copelnd	Tracy	1997
	T	Gun	159 3/8	James Cooper	Whitwell	1988
	T	Gun	158 4/8	William L. Dykes	Sewanee	1978
	T	Gun	149 5/8	Gary Cookston	Whitwell	1979
	T	Gun	145 5/8	Carl Taylor	Jasper	1996
	T	Bow	143 2/8	Larry Gravitt	Jasper	1981
	T	Gun	141 1/8	Ricky Layne	Tracy City	1978
	T	Bow	134 5/8	Paul E. Worley	Dunlap	1983
Marshall	NT	Gun	186 1/8	Earl Haynes	Chapel Hill	1975
	T	Gun	158 1/8	Billy Vandergriff	Columbia	1990
	T	Gun	153 7/8	James E Reed	Lewisburg	1978
	T	Gun	147 1/8	Joseph F. Neeley	Knoxville	1986
	T	Gun	144 6/8	Alan Perryman	Chapel Hill	1987
	T	Gun	141 6/8	Max Oliver	Shelbyville	1995
	T	Gun	141 5/8	John Miller	Belfast	1979
	T	Gun	140 0/8	Lynn K. Frye	Culleoka	1977
	T	Gun	140 1/8	Ernie Crick	Unionville	1980
	T	Gun	140 1/8	Alan Perryman	Chapel Hill	1980
	T	Gun	140 0/8	Troy Gibson	Franklin	1984
	T	Gun	140 0/8	Ray Whitaker	Lavergne	1991
	T	Bow	125 5/8	Alan Perryman	Chapel Hill	1985
Maury	NT	Gun	195 1/8	Chris Hagan	Lawrenceburg	2002
	T	Gun	161 5/8	Tony Pratt	Franklin	1990
	T	Gun	154 4/8	Matt Senter	Culleoka	2000
	T	Bow	151 5/8	Everette Martin	Columbia	1989
	T	Gun	149 1/8	Tony Pratt	Franklin	1979

Area	Antler Type	Weapon	Score		Name	City	Year
	T	Gun	147	6/8	Tony Pratt	Franklin	1985
	T	Gun	146	3/8	Leonard Embler	Columbia	1992
	T	Gun	145	7/8	Dean Sewell	Santa Fe	1982
	T	Gun	144	4/8	Johnny Eastep	Mt Pleasant	1978
	T	Gun	144	3/8	Kevin Alderson	Sante Fe	1995
	T	Gun	143	4/8	Danny Henson	Mt Pleasant	1989
	T	Gun	142	4/8	Eddie Yelverton	Spring Hill	1986
	T	Gun	141	3/8	Polly Williams	Springhill	1992
	T	Gun	140	4/8	Wayne Whitt	Springhill	1997
	T	Gun	140	2/8	Jeff Smithson	Culleoka	1995
	T	Bow	139	3/8	Kenneth England	Brentwood	2000
	T	Bow	131	5/8	Thomas E Johnson	Sprg Hill	1983
	T	Bow	131	5/8	Leonard Williams	Columbia	1998
	T	Bow	120	5/8	Everett Martin	Columbia	1989
	T	Bow	118	6/8	Tim Fox	Santa Fe	1988
	T	Bow	117	2/8	Del Perry	Columbia	2001
McMinn	NT	Gun	196	0/8	Bradley S. Koeppel	G.town	1993
	NT	Gun	166	2/8	Scott Duggan	Englewood	2001
	T	Gun	151	3/8	Brian Wells	Niota	1994
	T	Gun	147	4/8	Jay Landers	Athens	1993
	T	Gun	141	0/8	Tom Minnis	Athens	1986
	T	Bow	137	2/8	David Brown	Cleveland	1985
McNairy	T	Bow	124	4/8	Bobby A Clark	Riceville	1984
	T	Gun	168	2/8	Duane Weaver	Selmer	1990
	T	Gun	166	5/8	Charles Frederick	Booneville	1993
	T	Gun	160	6/8	Ronnie Mulder	Selmer	1992
	T	Gun	156	5/8	Howard Younger	Selmer	1999
	T	Gun	150	1/8	James M Shaw	Michie	1990
	T	Gun	146	5/8	Jay Redmon	Selmer	1997
	T	Bow	145	7/8	Arlus Ray Burney	Selmer	1985
McNairy cont.	T	Gun	145	7/8	Fred Johnson	Bartlett	1996
	T	Gun	144	3/8	Anthony Hopkins	Guys	1989
	T	Gun	143	2/8	William B. Hopkins	Bethel Sprgs	1994
	T	Gun	143	4/8	James Moore	Adamsville	1994
	T	Gun	143	1/8	Sam Keen	Ramer	1998
	T	Gun	143	1/8	Ken Whitehead	Finger	1999
	T	Gun	142	4/8	Tim Ross	Michie	1995
	T	Bow	141	6/8	Gregory Coker	Bartlett	1991
	T	Gun	141	2/8	Paul B Searcy	Guys	1990
	T	Gun	141	3/8	Danny Perkins	Ramer	1990
	T	Gun	141	0/8	Tim Isbell	Michie	1997
	T	Gun	140	1/8	Vam Carter	Walnut	1966
	T	Gun	140	0/8	Ronnie Mulder	Selmer	1995
	T	Bow	131	4/8	Howard Russom	Finger	1984
	T	Bow	127	0/8	Paul Steward	Corinth	1988
	T	Bow	126	3/8	Timothy Smith	Finger	1995
	T	Bow	115	1/8	Jeff Landreth	Finger	1989
Meigs	NT	Gun	186	6/8	Barry Toomey	Athens	1994
	T	Gun	171	2/8	James Rose	Decatur	2000
	T	Gun	161	5/8	Charles V. Maddox	Calhoun	1983
	T	Gun	161	7/8	Dwayne Bales	Ten Mile	1989
	T	Gun	143	1/8	Humphrey Renner	Calhoun	1967
	T	Bow	132	0/8	William Mason	Ten Mile	1989
	T	Bow	115	2/8	Kenny Wilson	Athens	1979
Milan Army	T	Gun	149	2/8	Howard Smith	Milan	1987

Area	Antler Type	Weapon	Score		Name	City	Year
Ammo Pt.	T	Gun	142	7/8	Robert Shelton	Trenton	1987
Monroe	T	Gun	144	5/8	Achie Roach	Celina	2000
Montg'ery	NT	Gun	207	1/8	Mike Davis	Adams	2000
	NT	Gun	207	3/8	Todd James	Clarksville	1997
	NT	Gun	192	2/8	John Teeter	Clarksville	1998
	NT	Gun	173	3/8	Ray Herrell	Southside	1986
	NT	Bow	171	6/8	Dennis Morris	Heidrick	1991
	T	Bow	170	3/8	Jimmy Ray Woods	Nashville	1978
	NT	Gun	169	4/8	Dewey Potts	Clarksville	1982
	T	Gun	168	4/8	Kenneth Madden	Cunningham	2001
	T	Gun	165	0/8	Bobby Welker Sr	Palmyra	1998
	T	Gun	163	2/8	Billy Byand	Clarksville	1976
	T	Bow	161	6/8	Zane Mason	Palmyra	1991
	T	Gun	156	5/8	Jesse Powell	Adams	1999
	T	Gun	154	0/8	Harry Goodrum	Clarksville	1977
	T	Gun	154	6/8	Joe Britt	Clarksville	1990
	NT	Bow	153	2/8	Adrien Boudoin	Clarksville	1990
	T	Gun	153	6/8	Mike Heatherly	Cedar Hill	1963
	T	Gun	152	6/8	Chris Collingsworth	Ash. City	1993
	T	Gun	151	6/8	James E Lee	Cumb.Furnace	1983
	T	Gun	151	3/8	Chris Collinsworth	Ash. City	1993
	T	Gun	151	3/8	Thomas Crawford	Cumb. City	1997
	T	Gun	150	6/8	Cliff Nicholson	Clarksville	2000
	T	Gun	150	2/8	Ronald P Holt	Greenbrier	2000
	T	Gun	149	2/8	Kevin Harrison	Adams	1985
	T	Gun	149	4/8	David Thompson	Clarksville	1988
	T	Bow	148	5/8	Gregory Mitchell	Clarksville	1996
	T	Gun	148	3/8	Ron Alvarez	Clarksville	1999
	T	Gun	148	3/8	William D. Henson	Clarksville	1988
	T	Gun	148	3/8	Steve Nelson	Clarksville	1999
	T	Gun	147	1/8	Virgil Denny	Madison	1975
	T	Bow	146	6/8	Julia Davidson	Clarksville	1989
	T	Bow	146	0/8	Jeffery S. Coffman	Clarksville	1993
	T	Bow	146	2/8	Walter Wright	Adams	1998
	T	Gun	146	5/8	Howard Marklin	Clarksville	1987
	T	Gun	146	0/8	Jerry Clemmons	Daisy	1989
	T	Gun	146	6/8	Lonnie Hembree	Clarksville	1977
	T	Gun	145	4/8	Jimmy D.Sheperd	Woodlawn	1972
	T	Gun	145	7/8	Ralph Craig	Woodlawn	1990
	T	Gun	145	3/8	Ron Widner	Knoxville	1984
	T	Gun	145	3/8	Kenneth Evans	Clarksville	1993
	NT	Bow	144	4/8	Christy Wilson	Cumb.Furnace	1999
	T	Gun	144	3/8	Richard Suiter Jr	Clarksville	1989
	T	Gun	144	4/8	Dwight Spicer	Clarksville	1967
	T	Bow	143	2/8	Ronald Holt	Greenbriar	2001
	T	Gun	143	3/8	Landon Dunn	Southside	1978
	T	Gun	143	6/8	Donald C Binkley	Clarksville	1988
	T	Gun	142	6/8	Emment Denton	Clarksville	1976
	T	Gun	142	2/8	Mark Collins	Smithville	1999
	T	Bow	141	4/8	Rob Towner	Clarksville	1997
	T	Gun	141	4/8	William S Smiley	Nashville	1984
	T	Gun	141	6/8	Kevin Harrison	Adams	1985
	T	Gun	141	5/8	Bill Ferguson	Jonesbor'gh	1997
	T	Bow	140	6/8	Tonia Lewis	Southside	2000
	T	Bow	140	3/8	Tim Bellar	Cumb. City	2001
	T	Gun	140	2/8	Molton Sanders	Holladay	1980
	T	Gun	140	6/8	Greg Lamberson	Mt Juliet	1991

Area	Antler Type	Weapon	Score	Name	City	Year
	T	Gun	140 5/8	Roy P. Holt	Clarksville	1994
	T	Gun	140 0/8	Kenny Louden	Springville	1996
	T	Bow	138 4/8	Michael Taylor	Clarksville	1998
	T	Bow	132 0/8	Ronnie Mimms	Ashland City	1976
	T	Bow	131 7/8	John Shadix	Smyrna	1997
	T	Bow	131 2/8	Bryan Doyle	Clarksville	1992
	T	Bow	130 7/8	Mike Helton	Clarksville	1995
	T	Bow	127 4/8	Paul Eden	Adams	1997
	T	Bow	126 0/8	Billy Epps	Southside	1981
	T	Bow	126 2/8	Jeff Winningham	Clarksville	1996
	T	Bow	124 6/8	James T. Poteete	Antioch	1997
	T	Bow	123 1/8	Mark Baggett	Clarksville	1997
	T	Bow	120 3/8	Henry Milby	Dickson	1987
	T	Bow	120 5/8	Terry Lamb	Clarksville	1997
	T	Bow	119 1/8	Tim Adkins	Adams	1998
	T	Bow	116 2/8	Jarrod K Moore	Clarksville	2001
	T	Bow	115 7/8	Ronald Suiter	Clarksville	2001
	T	Bow	115 0/8	Jerry Suiter	Clarksville	1993
	T	Bow	115 0/8	David Taylor	Clarksville	1998
Moore	NT	Gun	189 5/8	Eddie Dean Smith	Lynchburg	1986
	T	Gun	161 6/8	Tim D Stewart	Winchester	1990
	T	Gun	143 3/8	Harold Partin	Tullahoma	1993
	T	Gun	142 6/8	Jeff Sanders	Huntland	1997
	T	Bow	134 3/8	Phil Robertson	Tullohoma	1988
Morgan	NT	Gun	186 2/8	A. T. Bayless	Morristown	1958
	NT	Gun	179 4/8	Stanley Redmon	Rockwood	1973
	T	Gun	164 2/8	Jamie Deaton	J.town	1981
	T	Gun	163 1/8	David Johnson	Knoxville	1994
	T	Gun	162 0/8	Bill Brackett	Oakdale	1987
	T	Gun	158 0/8	John Singleton	Oliver Springs	1988
	T	Gun	157 5/8	Stephen Gregory	Strawb'ry Plns	1996
	T	Gun	155 1/8	Jeff Smith	Deerlodge	2000
	T	Gun	155 4/8	Mark Gentry	Knoxville	1974
	T	Gun	152 1/8	David Parsons	Oak Ridge	1987
Morgan cont.	T	Gun	151 1/8	Norman Cox	Lansing	1989
	T	Gun	149 7/8	Russell Smith	Knoxville	1983
	T	Gun	149 7/8	J.C. Carden	Lake City	1981
	T	Gun	149 6/8	Daniel Norman	Petros	1999
	T	Gun	148 0/8	William H Bales	Oliver Springs	1985
	T	Gun	148 1/8	Shane Wood	Crossville	1993
	T	Gun	147 2/8	Tim Aytes	Knoxville	1987
	T	Gun	146 1/8	Adam Roberts	Lenoir City	1960
	T	Gun	145 3/8	Ray Brown	Oliver Springs	1984
	T	Gun	145 4/8	Tony Cross	Oliver Springs	1986
	T	Gun	144 0/8	Billy G. Barnes	Maynardville	1982
	T	Gun	144 3/8	Virgil Lyle	Knoxville	1973
	T	Gun	143 6/8	Joe Armes	Lancing	2001
	T	Gun	143 1/8	Ed Melton	Crossville	1981
	T	Gun	142 0/8	Ronald Hatmaker	Andersonville	1974
	T	Gun	141 6/8	David Parsons	Wartburg	1997
	T	Gun	141 2/8	Steve Sublett	Morristown	1972
	T	Bow	127 3/8	Randall Shannon	Sunbright	2001
	T	Bow	123 3/8	Randall Shannon	Sunbright	2000
Natchez Tr. WMA	T	Gun	160 2/8	Billy Mays	Darden	1987
	T	Bow	120 4/8	Stephen Dorris	Lexington	1994
NB Forrest WMA	T	Gun	143 2/8	David Goad	Murfreesboro	1984
	T	Gun	140 6/8	Douglas Howell Jr	Dyersburg	1990
	T	Bow	139 5/8	Randy Hardin	Camden	1985
Oak Ridge WMA	T	Gun	164 0/8	Ronnie Riggs	Andersonville	1988
	T	Bow	163 7/8	John Johnson	Arlington	1987
	NT	Bow	160 7/8	Rodney Maynard	Mcminnville	1986
	T	Bow	154 0/8	Larry Cook	Rockwood	1988
	T	Bow	152 7/8	Rod Brown	Gainesboro	1986
	T	Bow	152 4/8	Jonathan Trantham	Grneville	1990
	T	Bow	152 2/8	Wendell Reeves	Maryville	1990
	T	Gun	151 6/8	David Layne	Coalmont	1985
	T	Bow	149 6/8	Daniel W. Chase	Kingsport	1985
	T	Gun	149 2/8	Terry Dalton	Powder Sprgs	1987
	T	Gun	149 3/8	Robert Swabe, Jr	Madisonville	1987
	T	Gun	149 5/8	Stan Murrey	Ooltewah	1987
	T	Gun	146 1/8	James Brooks	Knoxville	1985
	NT	Bow	145 4/8	Terry Miller	Jacksboro	1986
	T	Bow	144 1/8	Curtis Flannagan	Rockwood	1985
	T	Gun	144 5/8	Oneil Gray	Athens	1985
	NT	Bow	142 4/8	Darryl Chapman	Jacksboro	1990
	T	Gun	142 0/8	John Hensley, Jr.	Chatt.	1985
	T	Gun	141 7/8	Jeffery Sisk	Johnson City	1986
	T	Bow	140 3/8	Kenneth Mitchell	Dayton	1999
	T	Bow	137 2/8	Ron Cassell	Church Hill	1985
	T	Bow	133 6/8	Robert Hazel	Clinton	1992
	T	Bow	131 6/8	Danny E Lawson	Cleveland	1985
	T	Bow	130 1/8	Harold D. Tackett	Caryville	1985
	T	Bow	130 6/8	John Brock	Heidrick	1991
	T	Bow	129 1/8	Mack Hicks	Rogersville	1987
	T	Bow	128 7/8	Martin Reed	Spring City	1985
	T	Bow	127 5/8	William A Simms	Knoxville	1985
	T	Bow	127 6/8	Larry Herron	Oak Ridge	1994
	T	Bow	124 3/8	Jerry Shepard	Rockwood	1985
	T	Bow	122 4/8	Tommy Reagan	Louisville	1995
	T	Bow	121 6/8	Mark S Fickey	Harriman	1985
	T	Bow	120 0/8	W.S. Wells	Mohawk	1986
	T	Bow	119 0/8	Ricky Thompson	Cookeville	1985
	T	Bow	119 7/8	Darrell Beeler	Corryton	1987
	T	Bow	119 0/8	Jim Baker	Knoxville	1993
	T	Bow	118 6/8	Jerry Mcnulty	Seymour	1996
	T	Bow	117 3/8	Richard F Smith	Dayton	1985
	T	Bow	117 1/8	Richard Begley	Mooresburg	1985
	T	Bow	117 7/8	Stewart A. Skeen	Coryton	1986
	T	Bow	117 0/8	Claude Carver	Morristown	1985
	T	Bow	117 3/8	Timothy Pendergrass	Rickman	1985
Obion	NT	Gun	185 5/8	Frank Hutchison	Hornbeak	1979
	NT	Gun	185 4/8	Gregory Smith	Union City	1999
	NT	Gun	178 4/8	Gregg Mitchell	Mphs.	1998
	NT	Gun	170 4/8	Mike Reed	Martin	2000
	T	Gun	151 4/8	Doug Richards	Dresden	1993
	T	Gun	148 5/8	Jason T Chandler	Kenton	1990
	T	Gun	147 1/8	Claude Cranford Jr	Hornbeak	1989
	T	Gun	146 5/8	Grant Mcguire	Hornbeak	1992
	T	Gun	145 4/8	Mike Oliver	Union City	1980
	T	Gun	144 0/8	Jeff Huff	Union City	1988

Area	Antler Type	Weapon	Score		Name	City	Year
	T	Gun	142	3/8	Ron Seaton	Dyersburg	1982
	T	Gun	142	1/8	Michael Staggs	Union City	1988
	T	Bow	124	1/8	Gary Haynes	Troy	1988
Overton	T	Gun	159	4/8	Tony Robbins	Monroe	1969
	T	Gun	158	0/8	Robert Lee Ray	Cookeville	1994
	T	Gun	149	3/8	Junior Ledbetter	Livingston	1995
	T	Bow	148	2/8	Gary Jolley	Livingston	1991
	T	Gun	148	6/8	James Kimbrell	J.town	1995
	T	Gun	146	2/8	Kenneth Webb	Livingston	2001
	T	Gun	146	3/8	Tommy Barrett	Cookeville	1997
	T	Gun	145	7/8	Gabe Krantz	Monterey	1993
	T	Bow	143	0/8	James D Lewis	J.town	1999
	T	Gun	143	5/8	Glenn Ledbetter	Alpine	1982
	T	Gun	141	1/8	Anna Brady	Livingston	1982
	T	Gun	140	4/8	Sam Davis	Livingston	1988
	T	Gun	140	6/8	Brian Burgess	Crossville	1993
P Cooper WMA	T	Gun	144	6/8	Denise Snider	Vonore	1987
Perry	NT	Gun	182	7/8	Rodney Edwards	Lobelville	2001
	NT	Gun	170	0/8	Chad Brewer	Hohenwad	2001
	T	Gun	165	3/8	Lindy Wilsdorf	Linden	1975
	T	Gun	158	0/8	Kenneth Parrish	Parsons	1988
	T	Bow	153	3/8	Robert Scott	Lyles	1991
	T	Gun	151	1/8	Dennis White	Linden	1983
	T	Gun	150	7/8	David Cook	Regan	2001
	T	Gun	149	5/8	Willie Osborne	Humbolt	1976
	T	Gun	148	1/8	Eric Mercer	Linden	1995
	T	Gun	146	1/8	Bobby Baize	Lawrencence	1983
	T	Gun	143	3/8	Jimmy Holmes	Scotts Hill	2001
	T	Gun	143	1/8	Mike Strube	Nashville	1988
	T	Gun	143	4/8	Lannie Dedrick	Lobelville	1995
	T	Gun	142	6/8	Ricky Haynes	Nashville	1990
	T	Gun	141	1/8	Yancey Carlton	Lobeville	1992
	T	Bow	120	0/8	James Brown	Lebanon	1991
	T	Bow	116	1/8	James Morris	New J.ville	1985
Pickett	NT	Gun	214	2/8	Ronnie Jr Perry	Brydstown	2001
	T	Gun	166	7/8	Roger Moon	Byrdstown	1998
	T	Gun	154	3/8	Christy Elliott	Lake City	1958
	T	Gun	149	7/8	Danny Frank	Friendsville	1997
	T	Bow	145	0/8	Robert Lee	Brydstown	1993
	T	Bow	145	3/8	Robert Lee	Byrdstown	1993
	T	Gun	144	5/8	Tommy Aaron	Byrdstown	1985
	T	Bow	133	7/8	Robert Lee	Byrdstown	1993
	T	Bow	132	0/8	Fred Elder	Byrdstown	2000
	T	Bow	125	3/8	Eddie Stimon	Pall Mall	1996
	T	Bow	122	1/8	Gary Holt	J.town	1989
	T	Bow	118	3/8	Dowell Amonette	Byrdstown	1986
Polk	T	Gun	168	4/8	Tim Kimsey	Charleston	2000
	T	Gun	163	1/8	Eddie Newman	Englewood	1995
	T	Gun	154	7/8	Terry Day	Old Fort	1985
	T	Gun	148	0/8	George Smith	Spring City	1958
	T	Gun	145	1/8	Oscar Cross	Ducktown	1990
	T	Gun	143	5/8	Harvey Benton	Rogersville	1986
	T	Gun	141	2/8	Gary Bowman	Ocoee	1994
Putnam	T	Gun	156	5/8	John Lonsway	Oak Ridge	1996
	T	Gun	152	3/8	Jeff Hensley	Baxter	1998
	T	Gun	152	5/8	Sid Stafford	Lenoir City	1996
	T	Gun	150	7/8	Fowler Prichard	Cookeville	2000
	T	Gun	148	6/8	Frank W. Hodge	Rockwood	1995
	T	Gun	148	3/8	Eddie Hamby	Robbins	1996
	T	Gun	146	6/8	Jim Reels	Cookeville	1988
	T	Gun	141	3/8	Richard Chaffin	Cookville	1999
	T	Gun	141	1/8	Chester Bush	Crossville	1989
	T	Gun	140	6/8	Jeff Betcher Jr	Mcminnville	1994
	T	Gun	140	1/8	Walter W. Carlen	Cookeville	2000
	T	Gun	140	5/8	Robert Brown	Baxter	1985
	T	Bow	137	1/8	Doyle Wilmoth	Cookeville	1980
	T	Bow	134	1/8	James Hanks	Knoxville	1993
	T	Bow	122	0/8	Jim Ed Austin	Baxter	1984
Reelfoot NWR	NT	Gun	203	2/8	James Cobb	Jackson	1988
Reelfoot WMA	T	Bow	147	2/8	Charles Hayes	Ridgely	1996
Rhea	NT	Gun	167	6/8	Anthony Martin	Madisonville	1991
	NT	Gun	166	7/8	Philip Evenett	Dayton	1995
	T	Gun	149	1/8	Bobby C Tallent	Dayton	1980
	T	Gun	147	5/8	Barry White	Crossville	2000
	T	Bow	146	6/8	John Mccampbell	Spring City	1979
	T	Gun	142	4/8	Larry W Olinger	Dayton	1999
	T	Gun	140	0/8	Jason Roberts	Dayton	1984
	T	Gun	140	3/8	Micky Maynor	Knoxville	1987
	T	Gun	140	6/8	Steven Marler	Dayton	1962
Roane	T	Gun	161	1/8	Bob Black	Oliver Springs	1994
	T	Gun	159	5/8	Tim Earick	Kingston	1990
	T	Bow	157	6/8	Jeff Lamb	Cookville	1995
	T	Gun	156	4/8	Greg Graham	Knoxville	2001
	T	Gun	152	0/8	Willie Hixson	Ten Mile	1984
	T	Bow	150	6/8	Bobby Russell	Lenoir City	2000
	T	Gun	148	5/8	Dallas Clifton	Rockwood	1987
	T	Gun	145	7/8	Jerry Black	Harriman	1995
	T	Bow	140	7/8	Rickey Nelson	Kingston	1989
	T	Bow	126	4/8	Dennis Atkinson	Deerlodge	1991
	T	Bow	119	2/8	Anthony Bivens	Knoxville	1992
	T	Bow	118	1/8	Martin Reed	Spring City	1990
	T	Bow	117	6/8	Rejeau Martin	Knoxville	1993
	T	Bow	117	4/8	Alan Parsons	Oak Ridge	1994
Robertson	T	Gun	175	1/8	Matt Cutrell	Hendville	1988
	T	Gun	160	6/8	Mike Winters	Cedar Hill	1974
	T	Gun	155	6/8	Hank Smith	Cedar Hill	2000
	T	Gun	153	1/8	Scott Williams	Bordeaux	1995
	T	Gun	152	1/8	Bobby Hand	Springfield	1985
	T	Gun	152	7/8	Ricky D West	Springfield	1998
	T	Gun	149	7/8	Bruce Reed	Helenwood	1987
	T	Gun	148	1/8	Ricky Pentecost	Springfield	1988
	T	Gun	148	3/8	Wesley Wilbur	Greenbrier	1989
	T	Bow	144	7/8	Jason Duke	Cedar Hill	1997
	T	Gun	144	6/8	Randy Dorris	Springfield	1986

Tennessee Whitetails

Area	Antler Type	Weapon	Score	Name	City	Year
	T	Gun	144 3/8	Kelly Sneed	Portland	1982
	T	Gun	144 5/8	Bruce W. Tripp	Madison	1992
	T	Gun	143 0/8	Ricky Sneed	Orlinda	1990
	T	Gun	142 6/8	Mark Phillips	Goodlettsville	1984
	T	Gun	141 1/8	Michael Burns	Greenbrier	1998
	T	Gun	140 6/8	Taylor T Emery	Cross Plains	1982
	T	Bow	133 7/8	Anthony S Heatherly	Adams	1995
	T	Bow	132 3/8	Mike Biederman	Springfield	1998
	T	Bow	128 4/8	Howard Jones, Jr	Greenbrier	1993
	T	Bow	128 0/8	Chris Traughber	Cedar Hill	1996
	T	Bow	127 2/8	Terry Carter	Adams	1985
	T	Bow	127 3/8	Adrian Strange	Goodlettsville	1997
	T	Bow	125 5/8	John Rozanski	Elizabethtown	2001
	T	Bow	122 7/8	Barry Voorhies	Pleasant View	1999
	T	Bow	118 1/8	Wade Daugherty	Nashville	1989
	T	Bow	117 7/8	Robert C. Slade	Hendrsnville	1992
	T	Bow	115 5/8	Ricky Hall	Springfield	1997
Rutherford	NT	Gun	187 1/8	Patrick Anderson	Gallatin	1983
	NT	Gun	171 3/8	Mickey Bush	Christiana	1990
	T	Gun	163 2/8	Steve Holden	Bell Buckle	1996
	T	Gun	159 2/8	Greg Estes	Murfreesboro	1987
	T	Gun	154 2/8	Ron Adcock	Smyrna	1994
	T	Gun	149 5/8	Ron Adcock	Smyrna	1994
	T	Gun	147 2/8	Randy Ayers	Smyrna	1991
	T	Gun	146 4/8	Mark Cale	Springfield	1996
	T	Bow	145 5/8	Randall Henderson	Rockvale	2001
	T	Gun	145 4/8	Craig Lynch	Fosterville	1993
	T	Bow	144 4/8	Ray Lane, Sr.	Murfreesboro	1999
	T	Gun	144 7/8	Jason Robinson	Decaturville	2001
	T	Gun	144 4/8	Mickey Bush	Murfreesboro	1987
	T	Gun	140 5/8	Joel Jernigan	Murfreesboro	1988
	T	Bow	126 5/8	Pat Hatclift	Lascassas	2000
	T	Bow	125 3/8	Samuel Tucker	Lavergne	1999
	T	Bow	116 3/8	Robert E. Comer	Mt. Juliet	1996
	T	Bow	115 1/8	Steve Stump	Lavergne	1985
Scott	T	Gun	178 5/8	Charles H. Smith	Mohawk	1978
	T	Gun	168 5/8	Elmer Ledbetter	Jamestowm	1982
	T	Gun	165 6/8	Jeffrey Jeffers	Helenwood	1989
	T	Gun	155 6/8	Donald Brown	Jacksboro	1993
	T	Gun	152 6/8	Chester Byrd	Huntsville	1990
	T	Gun	152 0/8	Jerry L Watson	Oneida	1986
	T	Gun	152 7/8	Billy J Claxton	Helenwood	1995
Scott cont.	T	Bow	151 7/8	Lynn Phillips	Helenwood	1982
	T	Gun	147 6/8	Bryan P King	Oneida	1994
	T	Gun	146 4/8	Kenny Justice	Knoxville	1984
	T	Gun	146 4/8	Wayne Ferguson	Jacksboro	1994
	T	Gun	145 3/8	Mike Baker	Strberry Plain	1982
	T	Gun	144 6/8	John Effler	Maynardville	1986
	T	Gun	144 5/8	Bruce Terry	Helenwood	1994
	T	Gun	144 0/8	Jerry Carson	Helenwood	1993
	T	Gun	143 5/8	Rudy Slaven	J.town	1984
	T	Gun	141 0/8	Ted Cook	Knoxville	1987
	T	Gun	141 3/8	Larry Hancock	Oneida	1981
	T	Gun	141 0/8	Kenny Hedrick	Helenwood	1988
	T	Gun	141 2/8	James Strunk Jr.	Helenwood	1992
	T	Gun	141 1/8	Nicholas Duncan	Clinton	1995
	T	Bow	140 6/8	Jared Terry	Oneida	1994
	T	Gun	140 6/8	Darrel Burke	Oneida	1972
	T	Gun	140 1/8	Sammy Terry	Helenwood	1983
	T	Gun	140 6/8	Mike Babb	Oneida	1984
	T	Bow	129 5/8	Marty Lowe	Huntsville	2000
	T	Bow	129 2/8	Robert Mcgee	Jacksboro	1989
	T	Bow	115 4/8	Bruce Reed	Helenwood	1993
Sequatchie	T	Gun	153 2/8	Philip L Kiper	Dunlap	1999
	T	Bow	125 2/8	Robert Moon Jr	Signal Mtn	1989
	T	Bow	119 4/8	Kenny Slatton	Dunlap	1992
Sevier	T	Bow	123 6/8	Jerry Mcnulty	Seymour	1997
Shelby	NT	Gun	188 6/8	William Crawford	Ripley	1997
	T	Gun	173 4/8	John J. Heirigs	Mphs.	1962
	T	Gun	162 1/8	Charles Simmons	Bartlett	1995
	T	Gun	161 4/8	Nathan W Thomas	Williston	1990
	T	Gun	161 2/8	Robert Mitchell	Col.ville	1997
	T	Gun	160 4/8	Ben Daniel	Mphs.	1998
	T	Gun	156 5/8	Jackie Welch	Col.ville	1998
	T	Gun	156 0/8	Russell Long	Cordova	1990
	T	Gun	154 3/8	James Butler	Mphs.	1994
	T	Gun	150 2/8	Ross Granderson	Arlington	1996
	T	Gun	149 7/8	Joe Coggins	G.town	1982
	T	Gun	146 1/8	Bob Thomas	Mphs.	1915
	T	Gun	146 7/8	Barbara Robinson	Mphs.	1983
	T	Gun	144 1/8	Jackie Welch	Collerville	1999
	T	Gun	143 2/8	Jim Elam	Mphs.	1997
	T	Gun	142 7/8	Gary M Roe	Cordova	1982
	T	Gun	141 4/8	Nathan Thomas	Williston	1998
	T	Gun	140 2/8	Thomas R Hughes	Hernado	1999
	T	Gun	140 0/8	David Irby	West Mphs.	1994
	T	Bow	134 5/8	Jim Baker	Cordova	1990
Stewart	NT	Gun	185 1/8	Galyn Cross	Clarksville	1991
	NT	Gun	166 4/8	Ricky Johnson	Cederhill	2001
	NT	Gun	165 2/8	Jeff Stapleton	Sneedville	1998
	T	Bow	165 0/8	Alan Coope	Maryville	1992
	T	Gun	164 5/8	Tony Nichols	Erin	1990
	T	Bow	160 4/8	John Hults	Powell	1999
	T	Gun	158 6/8	Tony Wirth	Nashville	1987
	T	Gun	158 1/8	Clay Cherry	Dover	1986
	T	Gun	158 2/8	Tony Christy	Cumb. Furnace	1963
	T	Gun	158 2/8	Charles Miller	Bumpus Mills	1994
	T	Gun	157 1/8	James Mathis	Dover	1987
	T	Gun	157 1/8	Danny Heicher	Madison	1994
	T	Gun	157 3/8	Darren Grimes	Indian Mound	1997
	T	Gun	155 7/8	Alrick Fitzbugh	Dover	1975
	T	Gun	155 4/8	Gary Wallace	Dover	1990
	T	Gun	155 6/8	Ricky Booth	Dover	1990
	T	Gun	155 1/8	Charles Miller	Bumpus Mills	1994
	NT	Bow	154 2/8	Ron Widner	Knoxville	1974
	T	Bow	154 5/8	Barry A. Elkins	Heiskell	1994
	T	Gun	154 4/8	Gary Maxwell	Milan	1974
	T	Gun	154 3/8	Thomas Bryant	Antioch	1993
	T	Gun	154 2/8	Daniel Davis	Mcdonald	1998
	NT	Bow	153 6/8	Terry Bowles	Woodlawn	1990
	T	Gun	153 0/8	Stony Odom	Tenn Ridge	1986
	T	Gun	152 4/8	Burris Byrd	Dover	1974

Area	Antler Type	Weapon	Score	Name	City	Year
	T	Gun	152 2/8	Andy Vanzant	Cumb. City	1989
	T	Gun	152 5/8	Curtis Wallace	Dover	1992
	T	Gun	152 6/8	Paul Elliott	Clarksville	1964
	T	Gun	151 2/8	Steve Bennett		1976
	T	Gun	150 7/8	Boley Gilmore	Big Rock	1968
	T	Gun	150 2/8	Stanley Overstreet	Cottontown	1974
	T	Gun	148 5/8	Ricky Booth	Dover	1990
	T	Gun	148 4/8	Tim A. Byrd	Dover	1991
	T	Gun	148 0/8	Jeff Butt	Nashville	1993
	T	Gun	148 2/8	Gerald Gregory	Stewart	1997
	T	Gun	147 4/8	Hugh C. Hall	Clarksville	1969
	T	Gun	147 2/8	Charles Foster	Nashville	1977
	T	Gun	147 4/8	Ricky Booth	Dover	1991
	T	Gun	146 1/8	Greg Reynolds	Stewart	1986
	T	Gun	146 3/8	Neil Mathis	Dover	1963
	T	Gun	145 1/8	Greg Reynolds	Stewart	1971
	T	Gun	144 0/8	Andy Kent	Indian Mound	1990
	T	Gun	143 6/8	Steve Rushing	Pinson	2001
	T	Gun	143 4/8	Jim Tippitt	Goodlettsville	1990
	T	Gun	143 6/8	Joe Brown	Gallatin	1997
	T	Gun	142 3/8	Greg Poole	Martin	2001
	T	Gun	142 5/8	James Hassett	Nashville	1998
	T	Gun	141 3/8	Jeff Quinn	Dover	1989
	T	Gun	141 7/8	Henry Reno	Harrison	1991
	T	Gun	141 0/8	Thomas Vaughan	Indian Mound	1991
	T	Gun	141 5/8	Robert Elliott	Knoxville	1998
	T	Gun	140 5/8	Timmy Keatts	Indian Mound	1990
	T	Gun	140 5/8	David M. Arms	Dover	1990
	T	Gun	140 3/8	Jim Tippitt	Goodlettsville	1994
	T	Gun	140 0/8	Patrick Woodside	Smithville	1995
	T	Gun	140 1/8	Chris Diehl	Knoxville	1995
	T	Bow	139 3/8	Randy Waller	Whites Creek	1987
	T	Bow	134 6/8	Chris Irizarry	Indian Mound	1993
	T	Bow	133 2/8	Aaron Daniels	Woodlawn	1994
	T	Bow	133 5/8	Tim Byrd	Dover	1996
	T	Bow	128 7/8	Mark Greene	Cumb.	1995
	T	Bow	127 0/8	James Keatts	Indian Mound	1998
	T	Bow	123 6/8	Charles Melson	Normandy	1985
	T	Bow	122 3/8	Josh Bradley	Nashville	1996
	T	Bow	121 7/8	Danny Goodrum	Clarksville	1988
	T	Bow	118 7/8	Donny Williams	Old Hickory	1996
Sullivan	T	Bow	173 0/8	C. Alan Altizer	Kingsport	1984
	T	Gun	153 3/8	Michael Church	Blountville	1993
	T	Gun	152 6/8	Douglas Williams	Bluff City	1992
	T	Gun	149 5/8	Danny Spears	Kingsport	1994
	T	Gun	148 2/8	Joe Robinson	Piney Flats	1986
	T	Bow	129 2/8	Robert Morrison	Blountville	1987
Sumner	NT	Gun	244 3/8	David K. Wachtel	Nashville	2000
	T	Gun	173 3/8	Stephen C Jones	Hendville	1990
	NT	Gun	169 7/8	Michael Moss	Gallatin	1990
	T	Gun	162 0/8	Moye Mccullough	Gallatin	1968
	T	Gun	155 2/8	William Mcpherson	Gdlttsville	1995
	T	Gun	152 2/8	Robert Biggers	Castilian Spgs	1993
	T	Gun	148 0/8	George Krulik	Portland	1987
	T	Bow	147 5/8	Henry Estrada	Portland	1998
	T	Gun	146 5/8	Bill Breedlove	Gallatin	1999
	T	Gun	146 3/8	Edward Wulff	Hendrsnville	1994
	T	Bow	144 5/8	Jay Graves	Gallatin	1994

Area	Antler Type	Weapon	Score	Name	City	Year
	T	Gun	143 0/8	Don Rippy	Goodletsville	1999
	T	Gun	140 5/8	Tommy Hutson	Whitehouse	1998
	T	Bow	136 0/8	Parker Batey	Gallatin	2001
	T	Bow	131 7/8	Toby Tate	Goodletsville	2001
	T	Bow	131 5/8	Charles Dale	Gallatin	1995
	T	Bow	130 7/8	Darrell C Hamlett	Gallatin	1989
	T	Bow	130 0/8	Rodney Gross	Adolphus	1995
	T	Bow	128 3/8	Ray Hall	Goodlettsville	1995
	T	Bow	121 7/8	Jack Presley	Greenbrier	2000
	T	Bow	119 6/8	Roger D. Lyle	Hendrsnville	1994
	T	Bow	118 2/8	David Maples	Gallatin	2001
	T	Bow	118 1/8	Don Fox	Lebanon	1985
	T	Bow	117 2/8	Richard Bennet	Hendrsnville	1996
Tellico Lake	T	Gun	144 7/8	Lance Belcher	Madisonville	1989
Tellico WMA	T	Gun	148 7/8	Curtis Johnson	Harrison	1962
	T	Gun	144 7/8	Bobby H Garren	Tellico Plains	1973
	T	Gun	143 2/8	Eddie Walls	Tellico Plains	1983
Tennessee NWR	T	Gun	140 1/8	Mark Smith	Decaturville	1999
Thiefneck Is. SP	T	Bow	144 5/8	Danny Foster	Rockwood	1994
	T	Bow	122 6/8	Robert M Taylor	Etowah	1975
Tipton	NT	Gun	172 0/8	Steve Cook	Brighton	2000
	T	Gun	152 1/8	Vincent L Formon	Mphs.	2000
Trousdale	T	Bow	118 6/8	Greg Tomlinson	Hartsville	1992
Unicoi	T	Gun	146 5/8	Jerry Hopson	Unicoi	1989
Union	T	Gun	140 4/8	Kyle Gentry	Maynardville	1963
	T	Bow	137 6/8	Kyle Gentry	Maynardville	1984
Van Buren	NT	Gun	208 2/8	Duane Hodges	Spencer	1994
	NT	Gun	185 4/8	Joe Sullivan	Spencer	1998
	NT	Gun	176 7/8	Harrison Walling	Pikeville	2001
	T	Gun	160 5/8	Bryan Measles	Spencer	1991
	T	Gun	159 2/8	James C. Panter	Mcminnville	1994
	T	Gun	159 7/8	Danny Dodson	Spencer	1995
	T	Gun	153 0/8	Raymond Bickford	Spencer	1987
	T	Gun	153 0/8	Robert Madewell	Spencer	1993
	T	Gun	147 6/8	Harold Brock	Spencer	1975
	T	Gun	146 1/8	Clifford Sullivan	Rock Island	1995
	T	Gun	145 0/8	George Blevins	Jasper	1990
	T	Gun	144 6/8	Billy Shockley	Spencer	1985
	T	Gun	143 0/8	Brian Cunningham	Spencer	1993
	T	Gun	142 4/8	Bob Crittenden	Spencer	1998
	T	Gun	141 1/8	Ronald Measles	Spencer	1993
	T	Bow	140 5/8	Phillip K. Hedgecough	Spencer	1998
	T	Bow	140 2/8	Ronnie Dodson	Doyle	2000
	T	Gun	140 0/8	Wayne Kress	Doyle	1965
	T	Gun	139 7/8	David Swindell	Spencer	1993
	T	Bow	119 2/8	Tim Wanamaker	McMinnville	1991
Volunteer AAP	T	Bow	119 5/8	James Silver Jr.	Cleveland	1977

Area	Antler Type	Weapon	Score	Name	City	Year
Warren	T	Gun	147 3/8	Larry Smartt	Mcminnville	1993
	T	Gun	145 0/8	Ricky Simons	Mc Minnville	1997
	T	Gun	142 6/8	Jimmy Barnes	Rock Island	1985
	T	Gun	141 0/8	Clarence Bonner	Mcminnville	1984
	T	Gun	141 6/8	Larry Fults	Rock Island	1993
	T	Gun	141 0/8	Larry Fults	Morrison	1994
	T	Gun	140 5/8	Dwayne Finger	Mcminnville	2000
	T	Gun	140 2/8	Tim Wanamaker	Mcminnville	1991
	T	Bow	135 0/8	Lonnie Thaxton	Morrison	2000
	T	Bow	117 3/8	Brent Jones	Mc Minnville	1995
Washington	NT	Gun	197 6/8	Elmer Payne	Jonesboro	1972
	T	Gun	145 2/8	W W Crawford	Gray	1972
	T	Gun	142 1/8	Roy Payne	Jonesboro	1979
	T	Bow	136 4/8	Bobby Davis	Gray	1985
Wayne	NT	Gun	178 5/8	Mark Mosley	Leoma	1997
	T	Gun	157 5/8	James A. Berry	Collinwood	1995
	T	Gun	156 4/8	Ralph Hensley	Collinwood	1993
	T	Gun	156 3/8	James T Brewer	Waynesboro	1998
	T	Gun	153 1/8	Travis Hendrix	Waynesboro	1992
	T	Gun	151 0/8	Paul Searcy	Guys	1986
	T	Gun	151 0/8	Ronald Burks	Waynesboro	1994
	T	Gun	149 5/8	Chris Earnest	Iron City	2000
	T	Gun	148 7/8	Ronnie Roberson	Iron City	1977
	T	Gun	147 0/8	Randy Butler	Collinwood	1988
	T	Gun	146 5/8	Terry Lewis	Powell	1997
	T	Gun	144 1/8	Kenneth Chapman	Nashville	1981
	T	Gun	144 7/8	Michael Angel	Killen	1989
	T	Gun	144 7/8	Richard Kephart	Collinwood	1994
	T	Gun	143 1/8	Nick Tally	Clifton	1990
	T	Gun	143 5/8	Ronnie Burleson	Collinwood	1992
	T	Gun	142 2/8	Bobby Thomas	Mphs.	1984
	T	Gun	142 7/8	Damon Allen	Clifton	1989
	T	Gun	141 3/8	Stoney Lynn	Waynesboro	2000
	T	Gun	141 0/8	Ronnie Burks	Waynesboro	1996
	T	Gun	140 5/8	Andy Long	Waynesboro	1989
	T	Gun	140 3/8	Bennie Briley	Savannah	1990
	T	Bow	138 0/8	Brad May	Savannah	1999
	T	Bow	125 6/8	Randal Richardson	Arrington	1989
	T	Bow	124 3/8	David Nutt	Waynesboro	1980
	T	Bow	123 6/8	David Berry	Cypress Inn	2000
Weakley	T	Gun	151 2/8	Jack Hill	Dyersburg	1985
	T	Gun	151 1/8	Brent Osborne	Dreseden	1994
	T	Gun	150 1/8	Brent Osborne	Dresden	1993
	T	Gun	143 4/8	Dwain Cooper	Cott Grove	1997
	T	Gun	140 5/8	Gerald Caldwell	Sharon	1987
	T	Bow	128 7/8	James Reynolds	Sharon	1986
	T	Bow	127 7/8	Ricky Stutts	Martin	1999
	T	Bow	117 0/8	Brent Osborne	Dresden	1992
	T	Bow	115 0/8	Brent Osborne	Dresden	1993
White	NT	Gun	173 0/8	Jason English	Crossville	1995
	T	Gun	168 3/8	David Guy	Sparta	1990
	T	Gun	163 7/8	Jerry W. Cope	Sparta	1984
	T	Gun	157 4/8	Larry Frady	Pikeville	1991
	T	Gun	153 1/8	Jackie Billings	Doyle	1984
	T	Gun	150 1/8	Michael Isbill	Sparta	1998
	T	Gun	149 7/8	Jerry W Holder	Quebeck	1984
	T	Gun	145 1/8	Hershel Blaylock	Sparta	1975
	T	Gun	143 3/8	Michael Miller	Sparta	1998
	T	Gun	143 1/8	Paul Reeves	Sparta	1990
	T	Gun	141 2/8	Jackie Davis	Ooltewah	1979
	T	Gun	141 2/8	Tom Crawford	Sparta	1982
	T	Gun	141 1/8	Hartford Daniels	Sparta	1986
	T	Gun	140 0/8	Floyd T Cunningham	Sparta	1994
Williamson	NT	Gun	178 2/8	J P Jones	College Grove	1977
	NT	Gun	177 2/8	Jamie Cantrell	Nolensville	1983
	T	Gun	175 6/8	Roger Kelly	Franklin	1984
	T	Gun	169 3/8	William Bozeman	Franklin	1991
	NT	Gun	168 6/8	Hal Adcock	Nashville	1995
	T	Gun	166 5/8	John Beasley	Franklin	1972
	T	Gun	166 6/8	Mark Cothran	Franklin	1990
	T	Gun	164 4/8	Michael Vaughn	Franklin	1994
	T	Gun	161 2/8	Jim Brown	Franklin	2000
	T	Gun	159 3/8	George Sweeney	Thomp Stn	1989
	T	Gun	158 5/8	Harry Eads III	Nashville	1984
	T	Gun	157 7/8	Foster Butts	Madison	1984
	T	Gun	157 0/8	Barney Moore	Ormond Beach	1997
	T	Gun	155 0/8	Tilford Randolph	Brentwood	2000
	T	Gun	155 0/8	Ennis Wallace	Franklin	2000
	NT	Bow	154 6/8	Marvin Stewart	Madison	1998
	T	Gun	153 2/8	Ward Phipps	Crossville	1985
	T	Gun	153 5/8	Robin Mcclure	Nolensville	1994
	T	Gun	152 2/8	John Mccluskey	Nashville	1991
	T	Gun	151 3/8	James H. Smith	Dickson	1996
	T	Gun	150 5/8	Larry Skinner	College Grove	1984
	T	Gun	150 5/8	David Harper	Brentwood	1990
	T	Gun	150 4/8	Wayne Yates	Antioch	1993
	NT	Bow	149 7/8	Vernon Jr Spicer	Nashville	1998
	T	Gun	149 7/8	Ryan Pearman	Franklin	1998
	T	Gun	148 3/8	Carneal Walden	Antioch	1991
	T	Gun	148 3/8	Danny Decker	Fairview	1973
	T	Gun	148 1/8	Jeff Byram	Nashville	1998
	T	Gun	147 4/8	Gregory Mangrum	Fairview	2000
	T	Gun	147 4/8	Mark Cothran	Franklin	1995
	T	Gun	147 6/8	Danny Baggett	Franklin	1998
	T	Gun	146 5/8	Clark Taplin	Franklin	2000
	T	Bow	145 5/8	John Rutledge	Brentwood	1997
	T	Gun	145 3/8	Doug Fields	Mt. Juliet	1989
	T	Gun	144 0/8	Wayne Ketchum	Pegram	1994
	T	Gun	144 3/8	James V. Lackey	Nashville	1996
	T	Gun	143 6/8	William T. Byrd	Mt Juliet	1991
	T	Gun	142 0/8	Kevin High	College Grove	1991
	T	Gun	142 7/8	Kerry Stringer	Fairview	1992
	T	Gun	142 5/8	Tandy Logan	Thompson Statio	1997
	T	Gun	141 7/8	Tim Costello	Franklin	1990
	T	Gun	141 0/8	James A. Dunn	Brentwood	1992
	T	Gun	140 1/8	Frank Perritt	Nashville	1999
	T	Gun	140 1/8	Rich Scott	Franklin	1995
	T	Gun	140 2/8	Buford Fisher	Fairview	1998
	T	Bow	138 6/8	Ronnie Beddingfield	Nashville	1997
	T	Bow	130 2/8	Richard Beard	Franklin	1998
	T	Bow	124 0/8	Dillard Wa Howell	Franklin	2001
	T	Bow	123 7/8	Willard Young III	Nashville	1995
	T	Bow	122 4/8	Scott Weber	Brentwood	1996

Area	Antler Type	Weapon	Score	Name	City	Year
	T	Bow	121 7/8	John Edde	Laverne	1992
	T	Bow	121 3/8	Robert Brownlee	Nashville	1997
	T	Bow	120 2/8	Dalton Garner	Franklin	1999
	T	Bow	120 6/8	James Coleman	Franklin	2001
	T	Bow	118 1/8	Steve Knight	Franklin	1990
	T	Bow	116 7/8	Wa Curtis	Nashville	1993
	T	Bow	115 0/8	Travis Vernon	Spring Hill	1997
	T	Bow	115 4/8	Bobby Hale	Eagleville	1989
Wilson	T	Gun	154 3/8	Kenneth Mace	Mt Juliet	1991
	T	Gun	153 6/8	Joe Duncan	Lebenon	1997

Area	Antler Type	Weapon	Score	Name	City	Year
	T	Gun	149 2/8	Mark Bottom	Lebanon	1987
	T	Gun	147 5/8	John Tramel	Lebanon	1979
	T	Gun	146 7/8	Brad Moss	Lebanon	1999
	T	Gun	145 5/8	Wayne Tramel	Bellwood	1979
	T	Gun	144 7/8	Scott Saunders	Lebanon	1994
	T	Gun	143 2/8	Steve Smith	Mt. Juliet	1992
	T	Bow	142 3/8	Larry Faircloth	Hermitage	1998
	T	Gun	140 2/8	Tommy Payne	Lebanon	1984
	T	Bow	127 0/8	Joshua Moffitt	Mt Juliet	1998
	T	Bow	116 5/8	David Patrick	Bon Aqua	1998

TYPICAL BOW ENTRIES

Rank	Score	Name	Hometown	Area	Year
1	175 2/8	W.W.Young	Nashville	Davidson	1997
2	173 0/8	C. Alan Altizer	Kingsport	Sullivan	1984
3	170 3/8	Jimmy Ray Woods	Nashville	Montgomery	1978
4	167 3/8	Tony Savage	Nashville	Hickman	1994
5	167 0/8	Larry Lee Murphy	Clarksville	Ft Campbell	1989
6	165 0/8	Alan Coope	Maryville	Stewart	1992
7	163 7/8	John Johnson	Arlington	Oak Ridge WMA	1987
8	161 6/8	Zane Mason	Palmyra	Montgomery	1991
9	160 4/8	John Hults	Powell	Stewart	1999
10	160 0/8	Johnny Neal	Pulaski	Giles	1984
11	159 0/8	Bill Littleton	Dickson	Humphreys	1988
12	158 6/8	Lee Prince	Winchester	Franklin	1989
13	158 3/8	Larry Holt	Jamestown	Jackson	1990
14	157 6/8	Jeff Lamb	Cookville	Roane	1995
15	154 6/8	Barry A. Elkins	Heiskell	Stewart	1994
16	154 0/8	Larry Cook	Rockwood	Oak Ridge WMA	1988
17	153 3/8	Robert Scott	Lyles	Perry	1991
18	152 7/8	Rod Brown	Gainesboro	Oak Ridge WMA	1986
19	152 4/8	Jonathan Trantham	Greeneville	Oak Ridge WMA	1990
20	152 2/8	Wendell Reeves	Maryville	Oak Ridge WMA	1990
21	151 7/8	Lynn Phillips	Helenwood	Scott	1982
22	151 5/8	Everette Martin	Columbia	Maury	1989
23	151 4/8	Aaron Prince	Winchester	Lincoln	1988
24	150 6/8	Bobby Russell	Lenoir City	Roane	2000
25	149 6/8	Daniel W. Chase	Kingsport	Oak Ridge WMA	1985
26	148 5/8	Roger Johnson	Ethridge	Giles	1985
27	148 5/8	Gregory Mitchell	Clarksville	Montgomery	1996
28	148 4/8	Joey Rouse	Tn Ridge	Houston	1999
29	148 4/8	Joey Rouse	Tennessee Ridge	Houston	1999
30	148 2/8	Gary Jolley	Livingston	Overton	1991
31	148 1/8	Randall Wade	Hollow Rock	Lbl WMA	1995
32	148 0/8	William Manery	Pikeville	Bledsoe	1986
33	147 5/8	Henry Estrada	Portland	Sumner	1998
34	147 4/8	Matt Burton	Nashville	Davidson	1998
35	147 2/8	Charles Hayes	Ridgely	Reelfoot WMA	1996
36	146 6/8	Julia Davidson	Clarksville	Montgomery	1989
37	146 6/8	John Mccampbell	Spring City	Rhea	1979
38	146 5/8	Harold Gilliam	Kingsport	Holston Aap	1983
39	146 4/8	John P Danko	Church Hill	Holston Aap	1983
40	146 3/8	John Hults	Powell	Lbl WMA	1995
41	146 2/8	Walter Wright	Adams	Montgomery	1998
42	146 0/8	Jeffery S. Coffman	Clarksville	Montgomery	1993
43	145 7/8	Ronnie Inman	Russelville	Holston Aap	1983
44	145 7/8	Arlus Ray Burney	Selmer	Mcnairy	1985
45	145 6/8	Bill English	Middleton	Hardeman	1984
46	145 5/8	Randall F. Henderson	Rockvale	Rutherford	2001
47	145 5/8	John Rutledge	Brentwood	Williamson	1997
48	145 3/8	William Flair Jr	Nashville	Davidson	1998
49	145 3/8	Robert Lee	Byrdstown	Pickett	1993
50	145 0/8	Robert Lee	Brydstown	Pickett	1993
51	144 7/8	Jason Duke	Cedar Hill	Robertson	1997
52	144 5/8	Jay Graves	Gallatin	Sumner	1994
53	144 5/8	Danny Foster	Rockwood	Thiefneck Isl	1994
54	144 4/8	Willard Young III	Nashville	Benton	1995
55	144 4/8	Steve Teague	Nashville	Davidson	2001
56	144 4/8	Ray Lane, Sr.	Murfreesboro	Rutherford	1999
57	144 3/8	Johnny W. Jobe	Lake City	Anderson	1985
58	144 1/8	Curtis Flannagan	Rockwood	Oak Ridge WMA	1985
59	143 5/8	Edgar F. Parker III	Jamestown	Fentress	1996
60	143 2/8	Larry Gravitt	Jasper	Marion	1981
61	143 2/8	Ronald Holt	Greenbriar	Montgomery	2001
62	143 0/8	Jeremy Head	Brentwood	Davidson	2002
63	143 0/8	James D Lewis	Jamestown	Overton	1999
64	142 5/8	Franklin J Bledsoe	Jamestown	Fentress	1995
65	142 4/8	Dewayne Holloway	Louisville	Blount	1992
66	142 3/8	Pat Davis	Lexington	Henderson	1990
67	142 3/8	Larry Faircloth	Hermitage	Wilson	1998
68	141 6/8	Gregory Coker	Bartlett	Mcnairy	1991
69	141 4/8	Mark S. Rogers	Church Hill	Hawkins	1993
70	141 4/8	Rob Towner	Clarksville	Montgomery	1997
71	141 2/8	Gary Morris	Nashville	Davidson	2000
72	141 0/8	Dwight Bottoms	Mc Minnville	Fall Ck Falls	1995
73	140 7/8	Rickey Nelson	Kingston	Roane	1989
74	140 6/8	Tonia Lewis	Southside	Montgomery	2000
75	140 6/8	Jared Terry	Oneida	Scott	1994
76	140 5/8	Frank H Williams	Lenoir City	Cumberland	1981
77	140 5/8	Phillip Hedgecough	Spencer	Van Buren	1998
78	140 3/8	Chris Twyman	Fayetteville	Lincoln	1987
79	140 3/8	Tim Bellar	Cumberland City	Montgomery	2001
80	140 3/8	Kenneth Mitchell	Dayton	Oak Ridge WMA	1999
81	140 2/8	Ronnie Dodson	Doyle	Van Buren	2000
82	140 1/8	Boley Gilmore	Big Rock	Lbl WMA	1972

Rank	Score	Name	Hometown	Area	Year	Rank	Score	Name	Hometown	Area	Year
83	140 0/8	Ralph Bohannon	Waverly	Humphreys	1992	143	133 5/8	Ray Morris	Ashland City	Cheatham	1990
84	139 7/8	Ricky Thornburg	Chuckey	Greene	1987	144	133 5/8	Tim Byrd	Dover	Stewart	1996
85	139 6/8	Harold D. Tackett	Caryville	Cove Creek Wm	1985	145	133 4/8	Daniel Cooper	Camden	Benton	1997
86	139 6/8	Jim Asbury	Morristown	Ft Campbell	1986	146	133 3/8	Robert L Moon Jr	Signal Mtn	Hamilton	1989
87	139 5/8	Randy Hardin	Camden	Nb Forrest Wm	1985	147	133 2/8	Royce Fugate	Calhoun	Bradley	1990
88	139 3/8	Michael Mitchell	Cookeville	Jackson	1983	148	133 2/8	Aaron Daniels	Woodlawn	Stewart	1994
89	139 3/8	Kenneth England	Brentwood	Maury	2000	149	133 1/8	Dennis James	Pulaski	Giles	1998
90	139 3/8	Randy Waller	Whites Creek	Stewart	1987	150	132 7/8	Brent Owen	Paris	Henry	2000
91	139 1/8	Danny Peels	Cleveland	Bradley	2000	151	132 4/8	Steve Crabtree	Jamestown	Fentress	1992
92	139 1/8	Ronnie Campbell	Crossville	Cumberland	1987	152	132 3/8	Sandy K. Gilliam	Sewanee	Franklin	1997
93	139 0/8	Mark Wagner	Ashland City	Cheatham	1999	153	132 3/8	Mike Biederman	Springfield	Robertson	1998
94	138 7/8	Joe Townsend	Kingston Spring	Cheatham	1999	154	132 2/8	Jeffery B Nidiffer	Joelton	Davidson	1998
95	138 6/8	Ronnie Beddingfield	Nashville	Williamson	1997	155	132 1/8	Chuck Elean	Nashville	Cheatham	1987
96	138 4/8	Michael Taylor	Clarksville	Montgomery	1998	156	132 1/8	Danny Hall	Loudon	Jackson	1998
97	138 2/8	Tim Mcalpin	Grand Junction	Hardeman	2000	157	132 0/8	Tom Hutson	Goodletsville	Humphreys	1986
98	138 0/8	Brad May	Savannah	Wayne	1999	158	132 0/8	William Mason	Ten Mile	Meigs	1989
99	137 6/8	Kyle Gentry	Maynardville	Union	1984	159	132 0/8	Ronnie Mimms	Ashland City	Montgomery	1976
100	137 2/8	David Brown	Cleveland	Mcminn	1985	160	132 0/8	Fred Elder	Byrdstown	Pickett	2000
101	137 2/8	Ron Cassell	Church Hill	Oak Ridge WMA	1985	161	131 7/8	Carl Wood	Ashland City	Cheatham	1992
102	137 1/8	Doyle Wilmoth	Cookeville	Putnam	1980	162	131 7/8	John Shadix	Smyrna	Montgomery	1997
103	136 5/8	Michael Bryant	Nashville	Houston	1999	163	131 7/8	Toby Tate	Goodletsville	Sumner	2001
104	136 4/8	Ricky Orange	Ashland City	Cheatham	1999	164	131 6/8	Danny E Lawson	Cleveland	Oak Ridge WMA	1985
105	136 4/8	Bobby Davis	Gray	Washington	1985	165	131 5/8	Brian French	Jamestown	Fentress	1994
106	136 3/8	Monty Bartel	Crossville	Cheatham WMA	1999	166	131 5/8	Thomas E Johnson	Spring Hill	Maury	1983
107	136 2/8	Chris Hunt	Chapmansboro	Cheatham	1993	167	131 5/8	Leonard Williams	Columbia	Maury	1998
108	136 2/8	Junior Smith	Thompkinsville	Clay	1991	168	131 5/8	Charles Dale	Gallatin	Sumner	1995
109	136 2/8	Don Wagner	Oliver Springs	Holston Aap	1985	169	131 4/8	Thomas E Greenlee	Blaine	Grainger	1975
110	136 2/8	Philip E. Lawrence	Lenior City	Jackson	1998	170	131 4/8	Kenneth H. Carey	Greenback	Holston Aap	1983
111	136 0/8	Chris Hunt	Chapmansboro	Cheatham	1993	171	131 4/8	Howard Russom	Finger	Mcnairy	1984
112	136 0/8	Parker Batey	Gallatin	Sumner	2001	172	131 2/8	Joe Draper	Nashville	Davidson	1997
113	135 5/8	Robert Hazel	Clinton	Houston	2001	173	131 2/8	Bryan Doyle	Clarksville	Montgomery	1992
114	135 5/8	John Harrison	Dandridge	Lbl WMA	1979	174	130 7/8	Donald Urnstead	Camden	Benton	1978
115	135 4/8	Michael Pruett	Nashville	Benton	1999	175	130 7/8	Mike Helton	Clarksville	Montgomery	1995
116	135 2/8	Ronnie Beddingfield	Nashville	Giles	1997	176	130 7/8	Darrell C Hamlett	Gallatin	Sumner	1989
117	135 2/8	Huston Malone	Greeneville	Greene	1990	177	130 6/8	John Brock	Heidrick	Oak Ridge WMA	1991
118	135 2/8	Greg Hopper	Lexington	Henderson	1989	178	130 5/8	Clarence Maness	Covington	Humphreys	1996
119	135 2/8	Rusty Chivers	Kingston Spgs	Hickman	1995	179	130 4/8	Johnny Ford	Kingsport	Hawkins	1985
120	135 0/8	Bronson Callis	Ashland City	Dickson	2001	180	130 3/8	Billy Johnson	Nashville	Davidson	1984
121	135 0/8	Lonnie Thaxton	Morrison	Warren	2000	181	130 2/8	Richard Beard	Franklin	Williamson	1998
122	134 7/8	Robert Hendren	Clinton	Anderson	1987	182	130 1/8	Roy Haun	Knox	Blount	1996
123	134 6/8	Mark Marshall	Church Hill	Holston Aap	1986	183	130 1/8	Harold D. Tackett	Caryville	Oak Ridge WMA	1985
124	134 6/8	Chris Irizarry	Indian Mound	Stewart	1993	184	130 0/8	Roger Bohannon	Mcewen	Humphreys	1992
125	134 5/8	Scott Stamps	Pleasant View	Cheatham	1996	185	130 0/8	Mark Thompson	Estill Springs	Lbl WMA	1994
126	134 5/8	David A Allred	Celina	Clay	1993	186	130 0/8	Rodney Gross	Adolphus	Sumner	1995
127	134 5/8	Paul E. Worley	Dunlap	Marion	1983	187	129 7/8	Clarence H Tabor	Bristol	Holston Aap	1984
128	134 5/8	David M. Arms	Dover	Montgomery	0	188	129 6/8	David Wyatt	Bath Springs	Decatur	1995
129	134 5/8	Jim Baker	Cordova	Shelby	1990	189	129 5/8	Scottie Hanvy	Nashville	Davidson	1996
130	134 4/8	Roger Jones	Crossville	Cumberland	2001	190	129 5/8	Marty Lowe	Huntsville	Scott	2000
131	134 4/8	Gerald A Hobbs	Hoenwald	Hickman	2000	191	129 2/8	Chris Ferguson	Ashland City	Cheatham	2000
132	134 4/8	Stanley Hunt	Hendersonville	Hickman	1985	192	129 2/8	Johnny Wanamaker	Mc Minnville	Grundy	1999
133	134 3/8	Phil Robertson	Tullohoma	Moore	1988	193	129 2/8	Robert Mcgee	Jacksboro	Scott	1989
134	134 2/8	Troy Cable	Alcoa	Blount	1999	194	129 2/8	Robert Morrison	Blountville	Sullivan	1987
135	134 2/8	Donald Winningham	Jamestown	Fentress	1994	195	129 1/8	Mack Hicks	Rogersville	Oak Ridge WMA	1987
136	134 2/8	Danny Hendrick	Nashville	Lbl WMA	1978	196	129 0/8	Bill Herbert	Kingston Spring	Cheatham	1994
137	134 1/8	Robert Fann	Evensville	Bledsoe	1994	197	128 7/8	Martin Reed	Spring City	Oak Ridge WMA	1985
138	134 1/8	James Hanks	Knoxville	Putnam	1993	198	128 7/8	Mark Greene	Cumberland	Stewart	1995
139	134 0/8	Jerry Suiter	Clarksville	Ft Campbell	1985	199	128 7/8	James R. Reynolds	Sharon	Weakley	1986
140	133 7/8	Robert Lee	Byrdstown	Pickett	1993	200	128 4/8	Howard R. Jones, Jr	Greenbrier	Robertson	1993
141	133 7/8	Anthony Heatherly	Adams	Robertson	1995	201	128 3/8	Ray Hall	Goodlettsville	Sumner	1995
142	133 6/8	Robert Hazel	Clinton	Oak Ridge WMA	1992	202	128 2/8	John Reed	Shelbyville	Lbl	1998

Rank	Score	Name	Hometown	Area	Year
203	128 1/8	Gregory Medlin	Cookeville	Dekalb	1994
204	128 0/8	Chris Traughber	Cedar Hill	Robertson	1996
205	127 7/8	Ricky Stutts	Martin	Weakley	1999
206	127 6/8	Larry Herron	Oak Ridge	Oak Ridge WMA	1994
207	127 5/8	William A Simms	Knoxville	Oak Ridge WMA	1985
208	127 4/8	Paul Eden	Adams	Montgomery	1997
209	127 3/8	T.G. Gregory	Goodlettsville	Lbl WMA	1987
210	127 3/8	Randall	Sunbright	Morgan	2001
211	127 3/8	Adrian Strange	Goodletsville	Robertson	1997
212	127 2/8	Johnny Russell	Lafollette	Holston Aap	1983
213	127 2/8	Terry Carter	Adams	Robertson	1985
214	127 1/8	Walter Morton	Pegram	Dickson	1999
215	127 1/8	Tommy Delaney	Morris Chapel	Hardin	1996
216	127 0/8	Paul Steward	Corinth	Mcnairy	1988
217	127 0/8	James Keatts	Indian Mound	Stewart	1998
218	127 0/8	Joshua Moffitt	Mt Juliet	Wilson	1998
219	126 6/8	Wayne Lambdin	Waverly	Humphreys	1997
220	126 6/8	Steve Draper	Whitleyville	Jackson	1997
221	126 5/8	Matt Burton	Nashville	Davidson	1998
222	126 5/8	Jamie Graves	Chapmansboro	Dickson	1999
223	126 5/8	Troy Gates	White Bluff	Dickson	1990
224	126 5/8	Roger Draper	Whitleyville	Macon	1988
225	126 5/8	Pat Hatclift	Lascassas	Rutherford	2000
226	126 4/8	Paul Blankenship	Rossville	Hardeman	1991
227	126 4/8	Dennis Atkinson	Deerlodge	Roane	1991
228	126 3/8	Tom Oaks	Corinth	Hardin	1988
229	126 3/8	Timothy Smith	Finger	Mcnairy	1995
230	126 2/8	John Edde	Mt.Juliet	Davidson	1989
231	126 2/8	Jeff Winningham	Clarksville	Montgomery	1996
232	126 1/8	Jeff Morris	Manchester	Franklin	1994
233	126 0/8	Billy Epps	Southside	Montgomery	1981
234	125 7/8	Russell Hepperly	Townsend	Henderson	1992
235	125 6/8	Jack Whitson	Laverne	Davidson	1998
236	125 6/8	Randal Richardson	Arrington	Wayne	1989
237	125 5/8	Bryan Thomas	Savannah	Hardin	1997
238	125 5/8	Thomas H. Russell	Rogersville	Holston Aap	1984
239	125 5/8	Alan Perryman	Chapel Hill	Marshall	1985
240	125 5/8	John Rozanski	Elizabethtown	Robertson	2001
241	125 3/8	Stephen D Ayers	Murfreesboro	Dekalb	1985
242	125 3/8	Darrel K. Bailey	Rogersville	Hawkins	1989
243	125 3/8	Eddie Stimon	Pall Mall	Pickett	1996
244	125 3/8	Samuel Tucker	Lavergne	Rutherford	1999
245	125 2/8	Clyde England	Talbott	Ft Campbell	1983
246	125 2/8	Robert Moon Jr	Signal Mtn	Sequatchie	1989
247	125 1/8	John Mckeon	Chapel Hill	Bedford	1999
248	125 1/8	Truman Wilson	Caryville	Campbell	1987
249	125 1/8	Kyle Scott Smith	Mohawk	Greene	1987
250	125 0/8	Phil Ware	Old Hickory	Cheatham	1999
251	125 0/8	Terry Knox	Collierville	Hardin	1994
252	124 6/8	William Spann	White Bluff	Dickson	1987
253	124 6/8	James T. Poteete	Antioch	Montgomery	1997
254	124 5/8	Larry Faircloth	Hermitage	Davidson	1998
255	124 4/8	Bobby A Clark	Riceville	Mcminn	1984
256	124 3/8	Jerry Shepard	Rockwood	Oak Ridge WMA	1985
257	124 3/8	David Nutt	Waynesboro	Wayne	1980
258	124 3/8	Christopher Whitten	Knoxville	Henry	2000
259	124 2/8	Larry Holt	Jamestown	Jackson	1990
260	124 1/8	Gary Haynes	Troy	Obion	1988
261	124 0/8	Dillard Wa Howell	Franklin	Williamson	2001
262	123 7/8	Kevin Carney	Clarksville	Cheatham	1997

Rank	Score	Name	Hometown	Area	Year
263	123 7/8	Randall Epperson	Washburn	Chuck Swan WMA	1987
264	123 7/8	Willard Young III	Nashville	Williamson	1995
265	123 6/8	Daniel W. Chase	Kingsport	Holston Aap	1983
266	123 6/8	Trey Lawrence	Jackson	Madison	1993
267	123 6/8	Jerry Mcnulty	Seymour	Sevier	1997
268	123 6/8	Charles M Melson	Normandy	Stewart	1985
269	123 6/8	David Berry	Cypress Inn	Wayne	2000
270	123 5/8	William A Threet	Clarkrange	Fentress	1995
271	123 4/8	Ricky J. Johnson	Goodlettsville	Davidson	1993
272	123 4/8	Tim Wanamaker	Mcminnville	Grundy	1991
273	123 4/8	David Garrett	Lebanon	Jackson	1992
274	123 3/8	Dwayne Archer	Knoxville	Chuck Swan WMA	1988
275	123 3/8	Tommy Goodgame	Franklin	Davidson	1992
276	123 3/8	Randall K Shannon	Sunbright	Morgan	2000
277	123 2/8	Donald Ray Weaver	Dickson	Hickman	1987
278	123 2/8	Richard Lush	Fayetteville	Lincoln	1996
279	123 1/8	Richard Howell	Thompson Sta	Hickman	1993
280	123 1/8	Mark Baggett	Clarksville	Montgomery	1997
281	123 0/8	Al Bradshaw	Dyersburg	Dyer	1993
282	123 0/8	Randy Gray	Savannah	Hardin	1986
283	123 0/8	Gary Haynes	Troy	Hatchie Nwr	1978
284	123 0/8	Billy Moody	Lexington	Henderson	1997
285	123 0/8	Gene Atkins Jr	Bean Station	Holston Aap	1984
286	123 0/8	Jacen Davidson	Waverly	Humphreys	1987
287	123 0/8	Curtis D. Neal	Mansfield	Lbl WMA	1978
288	122 7/8	James Bibee	Pegram	Cheatham	1990
289	122 7/8	Hubert Comer	Hermitage	Lbl WMA	1982
290	122 7/8	Barry Voorhies	Pleasant View	Robertson	1999
291	122 6/8	Bobby Cunningham	Shelbyville	Bedford	1991
292	122 6/8	David Hughes	Bradyville	Cannon	1998
293	122 6/8	Steve Marler	Dayton	Lincoln	1998
294	122 6/8	Rodney Sullivan		Robertson	1993
295	122 6/8	Robert M Taylor	Etowah	Thiefneck Isl	1975
296	122 4/8	Tommy Reagan	Louisville	Oak Ridge WMA	1995
297	122 4/8	Scott Weber	Brentwood	Williamson	1996
298	122 3/8	Doyle Shettleworth	Wartrace	Coffee	1991
299	122 3/8	Josh Bradley	Nashville	Stewart	1996
300	122 1/8	Robert Coker	Murrayville	Cheatham	1997
301	122 1/8	Alan D Shults	Leoma	Lawrence	1990
302	122 1/8	Gary Holt	Jamestown	Pickett	1989
303	122 0/8	Jim Ed Austin	Baxter	Putnam	1984
304	121 7/8	Mitchell Mclain	Rogersville	Hawkins	1996
305	121 7/8	Danny Goodrum	Clarksville	Stewart	1988
306	121 7/8	Jack Presley	Greenbrier	Sumner	2000
307	121 7/8	John Edde	Laverne	Williamson	1992
308	121 6/8	Ronnie D. Bearden	Dickson	Dickson	1997
309	121 6/8	Joe Anderson	Lavergne	Lewis	2000
310	121 6/8	Mark S Fickey	Harriman	Oak Ridge WMA	1985
311	121 4/8	Clyde England	Bean Station	Ft Campbell	1989
312	121 4/8	Bob Vaden	Arriagton	Hickman	1989
313	121 4/8	Kenneth Corum Jr	Knoxville	Jefferson	1980
314	121 3/8	Robert Brownlee	Nashville	Williamson	1997
315	121 1/8	Chris Sharp	Powell	Campbell	1986
316	121 1/8	Adam Choate	Dickson	Dickson	1994
317	121 0/8	Chris Beckham	Clifton	Hardin	1991
318	121 0/8	Scott Littrell	Lawrenceburg	Lawrence	1994
319	120 7/8	Chris Collingsworth	Ashland City	Cheatham	1997
320	120 6/8	James Coleman	Franklin	Williamson	2001
321	120 5/8	Everett Martin	Columbia	Maury	1989
322	120 5/8	Terry Lamb	Clarksville	Montgomery	1997

Rank	Score	Name	Hometown	Area	Year
323	120 4/8	Eric Fuller	Waverly	Humphreys	1999
324	120 4/8	Stephen Dorris	Lexington	Natchez T WMA	1994
325	120 3/8	Henry Milby	Dickson	Montgomery	1987
326	120 2/8	Dalton Garner	Franklin	Williamson	1999
327	120 0/8	Gary A Douthat	Midway	Greene	2000
328	120 0/8	W.S. Wells	Mohawk	Oak Ridge WMA	1986
329	120 0/8	James Brown	Lebanon	Perry	1991
330	119 7/8	Darrell Beeler	Corryton	Oak Ridge WMA	1987
331	119 6/8	Darrell Beeler	Corryton	Humphreys	1988
332	119 6/8	Roger D. Lyle	Hendersonville	Sumner	1994
333	119 5/8	James D Silver Jr.	Cleveland	Volunteer Aap	1977
334	119 4/8	Gary Johnson	Bean Station	Ft Campbell	1989
335	119 4/8	Kenny Slatton	Dunlap	Sequatchie	1992
336	119 3/8	Bobby Shepard	Bon Aqua	Cheatham	1999
337	119 3/8	Adam Lowery	Lawrenceburg Dr	Lawrence	2000
338	119 2/8	Jim Brown	Franklin	Davidson	1991
339	119 2/8	Wayne E Foster	Pulaski	Giles	1970
340	119 2/8	John Bomar	Paris	Henry	1997
341	119 2/8	Russ Buffington	Paris	Henry	2000
342	119 2/8	Anthony Bivens	Knoxville	Roane	1992
343	119 2/8	Tim Wanamaker	Mcminnville	Van Buren	1991
344	119 1/8	Allen Stanford	Jackson	Madison	1998
345	119 1/8	Tim Adkins	Adams	Montgomery	1998
346	119 0/8	Ricky Thompson	Cookeville	Oak Ridge WMA	1985
347	119 0/8	Jim Baker	Knoxville	Oak Ridge WMA	1993
348	118 7/8	Donny E. Williams	Old Hickory	Stewart	1996
349	118 6/8	Joe Paul Myracle	Parsons	Decatur	1983
350	118 6/8	Kenneth Johnson	Smithville	Dekalb	1984
351	118 6/8	Thomas Mellett, Sr	Nashville	Lbl WMA	1976
352	118 6/8	Tim Fox	Santa Fe	Maury	1988
353	118 6/8	Jerry Mcnulty	Seymour	Oak Ridge WMA	1996
354	118 6/8	Greg Tomlinson	Hartsville	Trousdale	1992
355	118 5/8	Clayton England	Bean Station	Ft Campbell	1987
356	118 4/8	Jeff Duncan	New Johnsonvill	Humphreys	1990
357	118 3/8	Dowell Amonette	Byrdstown	Pickett	1986
358	118 2/8	Ronald Kendall, Jr	Mt. Juliet	Davidson	1990
359	118 2/8	Brian Sparks	Germantown	Fayette	1999
360	118 2/8	Kenneth Corum Jr	Knoxville	Jefferson	1980
361	118 2/8	David Maples	Gallatin	Sumner	2001
362	118 1/8	Larry Moore	Shelbyville	Bedford	1998
363	118 1/8	Donald Winningham	Jamestown	Fentress	1994
364	118 1/8	Martin Reed	Spring City	Roane	1990
365	118 1/8	Wade Daugherty	Nashville	Robertson	1989
366	118 1/8	Don Fox	Lebanon	Sumner	1985
367	118 1/8	Steve Knight	Franklin	Williamson	1990
368	118 0/8	Roger Draper	Whitleyville	Macon	1992
369	118 0/8	Richard B. Smith	Jackson	Madison	1994
370	117 7/8	Philip Blackwelder	Savannah	Hardin	1999
371	117 7/8	Randy Hale	Joelton	Lbl WMA	1989
372	117 7/8	Stewart A. Skeen	Coryton	Oak Ridge WMA	1986
373	117 7/8	Robert C. Slade	Hendersonville	Robertson	1992
374	117 6/8	Rejeau Martin	Knoxville	Roane	1993
375	117 5/8	Kenneth Biggs	Joelton	Davidson	1989
376	117 5/8	David T Settlers	Clarksville	Ft Campbell	1984
377	117 4/8	Alan Parsons	Oak Ridge	Roane	1994
378	117 3/8	Norman Speck	Old Hickory	Davidson	1989
379	117 3/8	Tim Brown	Nashville	Davidson	1998
380	117 3/8	Clyde England	Talbott	Ft Campbell	1982
381	117 3/8	Richard F Smith	Dayton	Oak Ridge WMA	1985
382	117 3/8	Timothy Pendergrass	Rickman	Oak Ridge WMA	1985
383	117 3/8	Brent Jones	Mc Minnville	Warren	1995
384	117 2/8	Dana Keeble	Maryville	Blount	1991
385	117 2/8	Michael Brooks	Parrottsville	Cocke	1995
386	117 2/8	Rickie Kizer	Loretto	Lawrence	1992
387	117 2/8	Del Perry	Columbia	Maury	2001
388	117 2/8	Richard Bennet Jr	Hendersonville	Sumner	1996
389	117 1/8	Richard Begley	Mooresburg	Oak Ridge WMA	1985
390	117 0/8	Brad Austin	Crossville	Ft Campbell	1997
391	117 0/8	Randy D. Woodell	Harriman	Kingston Stm P	1994
392	117 0/8	Billy H Brimer	Maryville	Lbl WMA	1983
393	117 0/8	Claude Carver	Morristown	Oak Ridge WMA	1985
394	117 0/8	Brent Osborne	Dresden	Weakley	1992
395	116 7/8	Don Spain	Madison	Davidson	1989
396	116 7/8	Wa Curtis	Nashville	Williamson	1993
397	116 5/8	Patrick Garrison	Crossville	Cumberland	1990
398	116 5/8	Johnny Logan	Vanleer	Dickson	1998
399	116 5/8	Jimmy Duncan	Kingsport	Hawkins	1986
400	116 5/8	David Patrick	Bon Aqua	Wilson	1998
401	116 4/8	Gary Wayne Love	Nashville	Dickson	1993
402	116 4/8	Allen Lufcy	Eads	Hardeman	2000
403	116 4/8	Chris Collingsworth	Ashland City	Humphreys	1990
404	116 3/8	Robert Vandergriff	Corryton	Hancock	1987
405	116 3/8	Todd Reynolds	Springville	Hardin	1998
406	116 3/8	Robert E. Comer	Mt. Juliet	Rutherford	1996
407	116 2/8	Scott Earls	Russellville	Bledsoe	2001
408	116 2/8	Jarrod K Moore	Clarksville	Montgomery	2001
409	116 1/8	Mark Gheen	Knoxville	Knox	1996
410	116 1/8	James Morris	New Johnsonvill	Perry	1985
411	116 0/8	Anthony Wanamaker	Mcminnville	Grundy	1992
412	116 0/8	R. C. Wilder	Morristown	Hawkins	1985
413	116 0/8	Calvin Rougemont	Erin	Houston	1984
414	115 7/8	Charles Cobb	Jackson	Benton	1987
415	115 7/8	John Fudge	Madison	Cheatham	1994
416	115 7/8	Larry Galyon	Knoxville	Lbl WMA	1986
417	115 7/8	Ronald Suiter	Clarksville	Montgomery	2001
418	115 6/8	Terry Skeen	Seymour	Blount	1995
419	115 6/8	Doug Cameron	Newport	Cocke	1985
420	115 6/8	Stan Howell	Bolivar	Hardeman	1990
421	115 6/8	Jeff Skelton	Howenwald	Lewis	1998
422	115 5/8	Adam Choate	Dickson	Dickson	1991
423	115 5/8	Ricky Hall	Springfield	Robertson	1997
424	115 4/8	Randall Brooks	Bean Station	Ft Campbell	1989
425	115 4/8	James Allmon	Lenoir City	Loudon	1986
426	115 4/8	Bruce Reed	Helenwood	Scott	1993
427	115 4/8	Bobby Hale	Eagleville	Williamson	1989
428	115 3/8	William Harris	Fayetteville	Lincoln	1987
429	115 2/8	Bobby Butler	Ardmore	Giles	1988
430	115 2/8	Dale Greer	Paris	Lbl WMA	1983
431	115 2/8	Kenny Wilson	Athens	Meigs	1979
432	115 1/8	Charles Tipton	Townsend	Blount	1997
433	115 1/8	Tim Carlton	Huntingdon	Carroll	1995
434	115 1/8	Jeff Landreth	Finger	Mcnairy	1989
435	115 1/8	Steve Stump	Lavergne	Rutherford	1985
436	115 0/8	Brian Collingsworth	Pleasant View	Cheatham	1991
437	115 0/8	Jerry Suiter	Clarksville	Montgomery	1993
438	115 0/8	David Taylor	Clarksville	Montgomery	1998
439	115 0/8	Brent Osborne	Dresden	Weakley	1993
440	115 0/8	Travis Vernon	Spring Hill	Williamson	1997

TYPICAL GUN ENTRIES

Rank	Score	Name	Hometown	Area Killed	Year	Rank	Score	Name	Hometown	Area Killed	Year
1	186 1/8	W. A. Foster	Rockwood	Cumberland	1959	61	163 7/8	Jerry W. Cope	Sparta	White	1984
2	184 4/8	Benny Johnson	Collierville	Fayette	1979	62	163 2/8	Bay Copelnd	Tracy	Marion	1997
3	180 1/8	Lonnie Hulse	Lebanon	Ft Campbell	1995	63	163 2/8	Billy Byand	Clarksville	Montgomery	1976
4	178 5/8	Charles H. Smith	Mohawk	Scott	1978	64	163 2/8	Steve Holden	Bell Buckle	Rutherford	1996
5	176 1/8	Alan Jackson	Humbolt	LBL WMA	1996	65	163 1/8	David Johnson	Knoxville	Morgan	1994
6	175 6/8	Roger Kelly	Franklin	Williamson	1984	66	163 1/8	Eddie Newman	Englewood	Polk	1995
7	175 1/8	Matt Cutrell	Hendersonville	Robertson	1988	67	162 5/8	George Eller	Crossville	Cumberland	1998
8	173 4/8	John J. Heirigs	Memphis	Shelby	1962	68	162 5/8	Stanley Thompson	Buchanan	Ft Campbell	1968
9	173 3/8	Stephen C Jones	Hendersonville	Sumner	1990	69	162 5/8	Nelson Nichols	Erin	Houston	1978
10	173 2/8	G D Odle	Parsons	Decatur	1972	70	162 4/8	Col. Edgar Snodgrass	Oak Ridge	Catoosa WMA	1955
11	172 5/8	Michael Bowers	Whitebluff	LBL WMA	1992	71	162 4/8	Jeffery G. Johnson	Flintville	Lincoln	1992
12	172 4/8	David Duvall	Manchester	Grundy	1992	72	162 2/8	Dale Brasher	Parsons	Decatur	1983
13	172 4/8	Mark Powell	Brownsville	Haywood	1999	73	162 1/8	Eric Ramsey	Cumb'land Furnace	Dickson	1990
14	172 3/8	Danny Pope	Bath Springs	Decatur	1982	74	162 1/8	Keith Deming	Bolivar	Hardeman	1987
15	172 3/8	Cecil Booth	Paris	Ft Campbell	1990	75	162 1/8	Charles Simmons	Bartlett	Shelby	1995
16	172 2/8	Joe K Sanders	Goodlettsville	LBL WMA	1984	76	162 0/8	Bill Brackett	Oakdale	Morgan	1987
17	171 7/8	Wilson W Weaver	Laager	Grundy	1987	77	162 0/8	Moye Mccullough	Gallatin	Sumner	1968
18	171 2/8	Pat Clark	Erin	Houston	1985	78	161 7/8	Andrew Gleaves	Ashland City	Cheatham	1963
19	171 2/8	James Rose	Decatur	Meigs	2000	79	161 7/8	Dwayne Bales	Ten Mile	Meigs	1989
20	170 5/8	Robert Traylor	Clarksville	LBL WMA	1990	80	161 6/8	Gerald Crabtree	Allardt	Fentress	1996
21	169 7/8	Kenneth Whitehead	Hohenwald	Lewis	1974	81	161 6/8	Harold R. Caughron	Sevierville	Hickman	1996
22	169 3/8	William Bozeman	Franklin	Williamson	1991	82	161 6/8	Tim D Stewart	Winchester	Moore	1990
23	168 5/8	Elmer Ledbetter	Jamestown	Scott	1982	83	161 5/8	Tony Pratt	Franklin	Maury	1990
24	168 4/8	Kenneth Madden	Cunningham	Montgomery	2001	84	161 5/8	Charles V. Maddox	Calhoun	Meigs	1983
25	168 4/8	Tim Kimsey	Charleston	Polk	2000	85	161 4/8	Nathan W Thomas	Williston	Shelby	1990
26	168 3/8	David Guy	Sparta	White	1990	86	161 3/8	Don Bell	Jackson	Benton	1971
27	168 2/8	Duane Weaver	Selmer	Mcnairy	1990	87	161 3/8	Barry Barron	Williston	Fayette	1979
28	168 1/8	Richard Edmons	Pikeville	Bledsoe	1996	88	161 2/8	Gene Currin	Tullahoma	AEDC WMA	1966
29	167 3/8	James B Mercer	Clarksville	Cheatham WMA	1959	89	161 2/8	Robert Mitchell	Collierville	Shelby	1997
30	166 7/8	Sam Bible	Kodak	Catoosa WMA	1995	90	161 2/8	Jim Brown	Franklin	Williamson	2000
31	166 7/8	James T Ward	Joelton	Davidson	1991	91	161 1/8	Bob Black	Oliver Springs	Roane	1994
32	166 7/8	Wade Daugherty	Nashville	Davidson	1997	92	161 0/8	Chad Lane	Dickson	Dickson	1997
33	166 7/8	Roger Moon	Byrdstown	Pickett	1998	93	160 7/8	Ed Barnett	Brighton	Fayette	1978
34	166 6/8	Mark Cothran	Franklin	Williamson	1990	94	160 6/8	W. A. Campbell	Athens	Catoosa WMA	1958
35	166 5/8	Roy Pulley	Chapmansboro	Cheatham	1993	95	160 6/8	Chris Davis	Waverly	Humphreys	1979
36	166 5/8	Charles Frederick	Booneville	Mcnairy	1993	96	160 6/8	Ronnie Mulder	Selmer	Mcnairy	1992
37	166 5/8	John Beasley	Franklin	Williamson	1972	97	160 6/8	Mike Winters	Cedar Hill	Robertson	1974
38	166 2/8	Robert Gilliam	Tullahoma	LBL WMA	1980	98	160 5/8	Bryan Measles	Spencer	Van Buren	1991
39	166 1/8	Bond Stewart	Arlington	Hardeman	1995	99	160 4/8	Ben Daniel	Memphis	Shelby	1998
40	165 6/8	Jeffrey Jeffers	Helenwood	Scott	1989	100	160 3/8	Marvin R Lord	Lexington	Carroll	2001
41	165 5/8	Keith Matlock	Camden	Benton	1987	101	160 3/8	Ronnie Morgan	Lawrenceburg	Dickson	1976
42	165 3/8	Mark Kelly	Oakland	Fayette	1979	102	160 2/8	Billy Mays	Darden	Natchez T WMA	1987
43	165 3/8	Lindy Wilsdorf	Linden	Perry	1975	103	160 0/8	Kipp Holt	Jamestown	Jackson	1989
44	165 2/8	Scott Conaway	Dacula	Hardin	1999	104	159 7/8	Danny Dodson	Spencer	Van Buren	1995
45	165 1/8	Roger Moon	Byrdstown	Fentress	1998	105	159 5/8	Jerry Windle	Livingston	Catoosa WMA	1965
46	165 1/8	Ernest Shelby	Franklin	Hickman	1999	106	159 5/8	Walter A. Turner	Smyrna	Catoosa WMA	1958
47	165 1/8	Clyde Cooley	Waverly	Humphreys	1989	107	159 5/8	Tim Earick	Kingston	Roane	1990
48	165 1/8	Edwin Cude	Pinson	Madison	2000	108	159 4/8	Tony Robbins	Monroe	Overton	1969
49	165 0/8	Harold Elder	Rossville	Fayette	1985	109	159 3/8	William Barron, Jr.	Williston	Fayette	1986
50	165 0/8	Marcus Colbert	Fayetteville	Giles	1988	110	159 3/8	James Cooper	Whitwell	Marion	1988
51	165 0/8	Tommy Newsom	Whitwell	Marion	1993	111	159 3/8	George Sweeney	Thompsons Stn	Williamson	1989
52	165 0/8	Bobby Welker Sr	Palmyra	Montgomery	1998	112	159 2/8	Ricky Booth	Dover	Ft Campbell	1990
53	164 5/8	Glen Arthur	Ripley	Lauderdale	1999	113	159 2/8	Johnny Doyle	Tiptonville	Lake	1990
54	164 5/8	Tony Nichols	Erin	Stewart	1990	114	159 2/8	Greg Estes	Murfreesboro	Rutherford	1987
55	164 4/8	Rex Allen Berry	Huntington	Carroll	1990	115	159 2/8	James C. Panter	Mcminnville	Van Buren	1994
56	164 4/8	Michael Vaughn	Franklin	Williamson	1994	116	159 0/8	Charles M Green	Caryville	Campbell	1998
57	164 2/8	Jamie Deaton	Jamestown	Morgan	1981	117	159 0/8	A J Ward, Jr	Mt Juliet	Ft Campbell	1969
58	164 0/8	Larry Kimery	Trenton	Hardeman	1974	118	159 0/8	R. Scott Stewart	Brentwood	Humphreys	1997
59	164 0/8	Ronnie Riggs	Andersonville	Oak Ridge WMA	1988	119	158 7/8	Brandon Holt	Jamestown	Fentress	1991
60	163 7/8	Larry Holt	Jamestown	Jackson	1987	120	158 6/8	James Maiden	Harrogate	Claiborne	1994

Rank	Score	Name	Hometown	Area Killed	Year	Rank	Score	Name	Hometown	Area Killed	Year
121	158 6/8	Tony Wirth	Nashville	Stewart	1987	181	155 6/8	Donald Brown	Jacksboro	Scott	1993
122	158 5/8	Zachary Deberry	Hornsby	Hardeman	1999	182	155 6/8	Ricky Booth	Dover	Stewart	1990
123	158 5/8	Harry Eads III	Nashville	Williamson	1984	183	155 5/8	Dana Walker	Dover	Ft Campbell	1997
124	158 4/8	William L. Dykes	Sewanee	Marion	1978	184	155 5/8	Dennis Walls	Bellevue	Giles	1969
125	158 3/8	George A. Daniel	Drummonds	Hickman	1985	185	155 4/8	Robert Childs	Memphis	And-Tully WMA	1964
126	158 2/8	Robert Alexander	Brentwood	Decatur	1996	186	155 4/8	Mark Gentry	Knoxville	Morgan	1974
127	158 2/8	Tony Christy	Cum'land Furnace	Stewart	1963	187	155 4/8	Gary Wallace	Dover	Stewart	1990
128	158 2/8	Charles Miller	Bumpus Mills	Stewart	1994	188	155 2/8	William Mcpherson	Goodlettsville	Sumner	1995
129	158 1/8	Delbert Garrett	Jamestown	Fentress	1967	189	155 1/8	Arnold Henson	Clarksville	Ft Campbell	1988
130	158 1/8	Billy Vandergriff	Columbia	Marshall	1990	190	155 1/8	Jeff Smith	Deerlodge	Morgan	2000
131	158 1/8	Clay Cherry	Dover	Stewart	1986	191	155 1/8	Charles Miller	Bumpus Mills	Stewart	1994
132	158 0/8	John Singleton	Oliver Springs	Morgan	1988	192	155 0/8	Kenneth E Parker	Bell Buckle	Bedford	1990
133	158 0/8	Robert Lee Ray	Cookeville	Overton	1994	193	155 0/8	Eugene Redden	Decaturville	Decatur	1976
134	158 0/8	Kenneth Parrish	Parsons	Perry	1988	194	155 0/8	Mark Stewart	Jamestown	Fentress	1997
135	157 7/8	Foster Butts	Madison	Williamson	1984	195	155 0/8	Walter Harden	Portland	Ft Campbell	1988
136	157 6/8	Rick Parsons	Shelbyville	Bedford	1976	196	155 0/8	Josh Barnes	Ridgley	Lake	1993
137	157 6/8	Danny Campbell	Jamestown	Fentress	1984	197	155 0/8	Tilford Randolph	Brentwood	Williamson	2000
138	157 5/8	Stephen Gregory	Strawberry Plns	Morgan	1996	198	155 0/8	Ennis C Jr Wallace	Franklin	Williamson	2000
139	157 5/8	James A. Berry	Collinwood	Wayne	1995	199	154 7/8	Harold Gray	Savannah	Hardin	1968
140	157 4/8	Larry Finley	Saltillo	Decatur	1980	200	154 7/8	Terry Day	Old Fort	Polk	1985
141	157 4/8	Charles Blackburn	Memphis	Hardeman	1980	201	154 6/8	Ross Hudson	Nashville	Davidson	1995
142	157 4/8	Richard Howell II	Memphis	Hardeman	1987	202	154 6/8	Robert Crowley	Middleton	Hardeman	2000
143	157 4/8	Steve Blount	Kingston	LBL WMA	1974	203	154 6/8	Joe Britt	Clarksville	Montgomery	1990
144	157 4/8	Larry Frady	Pikeville	White	1991	204	154 5/8	J. V. Mcalexander	Milan	Carroll	1975
145	157 3/8	Russell Sneller	Bartlett	Ft Campbell	1978	205	154 5/8	Harold Bolden	Tazewell	Claiborne	1984
146	157 3/8	Guy Walker Jr.	Wildersville	Henderson	1988	206	154 5/8	Wayen Davis	Nashville	Davidson	1998
147	157 3/8	David Jones	Waverly	Humphreys	2000	207	154 5/8	Alden Poyner	New Johnsonvill	Humphreys	1989
148	157 3/8	Darren Grimes	Indian Mound	Stewart	1997	208	154 5/8	Don Cheatwood	Lawrenceburg	Laurel Hill WMA	1977
149	157 1/8	Jason Meadows	Jamestown	Fentress	1998	209	154 4/8	Eugene King	Ashland City	Cheatham	1989
150	157 1/8	Gerald Armstrong	Nashville	Giles	1983	210	154 4/8	Don Gass	Saltillo	Hardin	1990
151	157 1/8	Ricky Owen	Paris	Henry	1987	211	154 4/8	Matt Senter	Culleoka	Maury	2000
152	157 1/8	James Mathis	Dover	Stewart	1987	212	154 4/8	Gary Maxwell	Milan	Stewart	1974
153	157 1/8	Danny Heicher	Madison	Stewart	1994	213	154 3/8	Ken Butcher	Knoxville	Catoosa WMA	1992
154	157 0/8	Keith Staggs	Hohenwald	Eagle Ck WMA	1992	214	154 3/8	Leonard Hooper	Tn Ridge	Houston	1988
155	157 0/8	Barney Moore	Ormond Beach	Williamson	1997	215	154 3/8	Kenneth N. Gibbs	Cottontown	Humphreys	1997
156	156 7/8	Kenneth Pinson	Clarksville	Cheatham	2000	216	154 3/8	Christy Elliott	Lake City	Pickett	1958
157	156 7/8	Wallace M Dewalt	Charlotte	Dickson	1990	217	154 3/8	James Butler	Memphis	Shelby	1994
158	156 6/8	Steve Bakaletz	Cookeville	Dekalb	1985	218	154 3/8	Thomas Bryant	Antioch	Stewart	1993
159	156 6/8	Jim Key	Williston	Fayette	1998	219	154 3/8	Kenneth Mace	Mt Juliet	Wilson	1991
160	156 6/8	Charles Primm	Nashville	LBL WMA	1974	220	154 2/8	Scott Houston	Crossville	Cumberland	1990
161	156 5/8	Howard Younger	Selmer	Mcnairy	1999	221	154 2/8	J.C. Brown, Jr.	White Bluff	Dickson	1988
162	156 5/8	Jesse Powell	Adams	Montgomery	1999	222	154 2/8	Ron Adcock	Smyrna	Rutherford	1994
163	156 5/8	John Lonsway	Oak Ridge	Putnam	1996	223	154 2/8	Daniel Davis	Mcdonald	Stewart	1998
164	156 5/8	Jackie Welch	Collierville	Shelby	1998	224	154 0/8	David Johnson	Somerville	Fayette	1985
165	156 4/8	Gary Bates	Goodlettsville	Davidson	1998	225	154 0/8	Paul Blankenship	Memphis	Hardeman	1988
166	156 4/8	Greg Graham	Knoxville	Roane	2001	226	154 0/8	Harry Goodrum	Clarksville	Montgomery	1977
167	156 4/8	Ralph Hensley	Collinwood	Wayne	1993	227	153 7/8	James E Reed	Lewisburg	Marshall	1978
168	156 3/8	James T Brewer	Waynesboro	Wayne	1998	228	153 6/8	Harry Wilkerson	Athens	Catoosa WMA	1971
169	156 2/8	Freddy E Griffith	Petros	Anderson	1990	229	153 6/8	Craig Geesaman	Hendersonville	Davidson	1998
170	156 1/8	Kendall Thompson	Scotts Hill	Decatur	1996	230	153 6/8	Jody Bridges	Grimsley	Fentress	1993
171	156 1/8	Jamie Gordon	Trimble	Dyer	2000	231	153 6/8	Steve Thompson		Ft Campbell	1994
172	156 1/8	Kevin Steelman	Fayetteville	Lincoln	1991	232	153 6/8	Mike Heatherly	Cedar Hill	Montgomery	1963
173	156 0/8	Fred Hinkel	Oakland	Hardeman	1979	233	153 6/8	Joe Duncan	Lebenon	Wilson	1997
174	156 0/8	Russell Long	Cordova	Shelby	1990	234	153 5/8	Michael Cullens	Brighton	Hardeman	1993
175	155 7/8	James Likens	Red Boiling Spg	Clay	1983	235	153 5/8	William Sweat	Ripley	Lauderdale	1995
176	155 7/8	Jada Melson	Olive Hill	Hardin	1963	236	153 5/8	Robin Mcclure	Nolensville	Williamson	1994
177	155 7/8	Alrick Fitzbugh	Dover	Stewart	1975	237	153 4/8	Johnny Thompson	Monterey	Fentress	1996
178	155 6/8	Ralph Cochran	Brownsville	Haywood	1982	238	153 4/8	Joe Britt	Clarksville	Ft Campbell	1975
179	155 6/8	Calday A Wyrick	Knoxville	LBL WMA	1979	239	153 4/8	Randy Hooper	Mcewen	Humphreys	1989
180	155 6/8	Hank Smith	Cedar Hill	Robertson	2000	240	153 3/8	Steve Christy	Clarksville	Dickson	1985

Rank	Score	Name	Hometown	Area Killed	Year	Rank	Score	Name	Hometown	Area Killed	Year
241	153 3/8	Kevin Petty	Reagan	Henderson	2000	301	151 6/8	Jimmy Blankinship	Cleveland	Ft Campbell	1983
242	153 3/8	Michael A. Church	Blountville	Sullivan	1993	302	151 6/8	Jeff Thompson	Centerville	Humphreys	1984
243	153 2/8	Philip L Kiper	Dunlap	Sequatchie	1999	303	151 6/8	Danny Moore	Fayetteville	Lincoln	2000
244	153 2/8	Ward Phipps	Crossville	Williamson	1985	304	151 6/8	James E Lee	Cum'land Furnace	Montgomery	1983
245	153 1/8	Jim Bale	Goodlettsville	Ft Campbell	1989	305	151 6/8	David Layne	Coalmont	Oak Ridge WMA	1985
246	153 1/8	Woodie Escue	Summertown	Lawrence	1986	306	151 5/8	R E Stoudt	Chattanooga	AEDC WMA	1966
247	153 1/8	Scott Williams	Bordeaux	Robertson	1995	307	151 5/8	Jody Bridges	Grimsley	Fentress	1994
248	153 1/8	Travis Hendrix	Waynesboro	Wayne	1992	308	151 5/8	George Reno	Corryton	Ft Campbell	1994
249	153 1/8	Jackie Billings	Doyle	White	1984	309	151 4/8	Kelly Webb	Memphis	Hickman	1980
250	153 0/8	Michael Joyner	Nashville	Davidson	1992	310	151 3/8	Frank Phillips	Knoxville	Anderson	1993
251	153 0/8	Chris Cherry	Gibson	Gibson	1997	311	151 3/8	Harold D Douglas	Holladay	Benton	1976
252	153 0/8	Tim Huggins	Rienzi	Hardin	1992	312	151 3/8	David Kirby	Madison	Humphreys	1975
253	153 0/8	Stony Odom	Tennessee Ridge	Stewart	1986	313	151 3/8	Derrick Syler	Fayetteville	Lincoln	1982
254	153 0/8	Raymond Bickford	Spencer	Van Buren	1987	314	151 3/8	Brian Wells	Niota	Mcminn	1994
255	153 0/8	Robert Madewell	Spencer	Van Buren	1993	315	151 3/8	Chris Collinsworth	Ashland City	Montgomery	1993
256	152 7/8	Joe Townsend	Kingston Spring	Cheatham	2000	316	151 3/8	Thomas Crawford	Cumberland City	Montgomery	1997
257	152 7/8	Ricky D West	Springfield	Robertson	1998	317	151 3/8	James H. Smith	Dickson	Williamson	1996
258	152 7/8	Billy J Claxton	Helenwood	Scott	1995	318	151 2/8	Pat Floyd	Monterey	Davidson	1990
259	152 6/8	William Perry	Mcminnville	Hamilton	1989	319	151 2/8	Scott Chambers	Allardt	Fentress	1998
260	152 6/8	Brenda Valentine	Buchannan	Henry	1993	320	151 2/8	Keith Lindsey	Humbolt	Henry	1994
261	152 6/8	Chris Collingsworth	Ashland City	Montgomery	1993	321	151 2/8	Steve Bennett		Stewart	1976
262	152 6/8	Chester Byrd	Huntsville	Scott	1990	322	151 2/8	Jack Hill	Dyersburg	Weakley	1985
263	152 6/8	Paul Elliott	Clarksville	Stewart	1964	323	151 1/8	Charles Crockett	Trenton	Haywood	1997
264	152 6/8	Douglas Williams	Bluff City	Sullivan	1992	324	151 1/8	David E Champlin	Lexington	LBL WMA	1985
265	152 5/8	Paul Watson	Ashland City	Cheatham	1979	325	151 1/8	Charles P Bennett	Nashville	Lewis	1962
266	152 5/8	David Thompson	Oakland	Fayette	1986	326	151 1/8	Norman Cox	Lansing	Morgan	1989
267	152 5/8	Sid Stafford	Lenoir City	Putnam	1996	327	151 1/8	Doug Richards	Dresden	Obion	1993
268	152 5/8	Curtis Wallace	Dover	Stewart	1992	328	151 1/8	Dennis White	Linden	Perry	1983
269	152 4/8	Lucas Norman	Springfield	Davidson	1995	329	151 1/8	Brent Osborne	Dreseden	Weakley	1994
270	152 4/8	Roger George	Waverly	Humphreys	1982	330	151 0/8	Marshall Hicks	Camden	Benton	1976
271	152 4/8	Burris Byrd	Dover	Stewart	1974	331	151 0/8	L.C. Dykes	Pikeville	Bledsoe	1991
272	152 3/8	Jeff Hensley	Baxter	Putnam	1998	332	151 0/8	Gabe Brown	Louisville	Blount	1997
273	152 2/8	Tim Cunningham	Soddy-Daisy	Bledsoe	1985	333	151 0/8	Jamie Cole	Arlington	Fayette	1997
274	152 2/8	James Davis	Crossville	Cumberland	1988	334	151 0/8	Jeff L Kerby	Hixon	Hamilton	1984
275	152 2/8	Jeffery White	Savannah	Hardin	1996	335	151 0/8	Paul Searcy	Guys	Wayne	1986
276	152 2/8	Andy Vanzant	Cumberland City	Stewart	1989	336	151 0/8	Ronald Burks	Waynesboro	Wayne	1994
277	152 2/8	Robert Biggers	Castilian Spgs	Sumner	1993	337	150 7/8	James E Stubblefield	Springfield	Davidson	1998
278	152 2/8	John Mccluskey	Nashville	Williamson	1991	338	150 7/8	David Cook	Regan	Perry	2001
279	152 1/8	Cantrell Phifer	Eva	Benton	1978	339	150 7/8	Fowler Prichard	Cookeville	Putnam	2000
280	152 1/8	Michael Sweezy	Moss	Clay	1995	340	150 7/8	Boley Gilmore	Big Rock	Stewart	1968
281	152 1/8	William A. Owings	Cordova	Ft Campbell	1981	341	150 6/8	Adam Hild	Crossville	Cumberland	1995
282	152 1/8	Ricky Scott	Hixon	Grundy	1988	342	150 6/8	Cliff Nicholson	Clarksville	Montgomery	2000
283	152 1/8	Phillip Harris	Newbern	Henry	1994	343	150 5/8	Dick Besancenez	Winchester	AEDC WMA	1971
284	152 1/8	Ronnie Howard	Springville	LBL WMA	1986	344	150 5/8	Willie M. Blanton	Counce	Hardin	1977
285	152 1/8	David Parsons	Oak Ridge	Morgan	1987	345	150 5/8	Greg Winstead	Mcewen	Humphreys	1989
286	152 1/8	Bobby Hand	Springfield	Robertson	1985	346	150 5/8	Larry Skinner	College Grove	Williamson	1984
287	152 1/8	Vincent L Formon	Memphis	Tipton	2000	347	150 5/8	David Harper	Brentwood	Williamson	1990
288	152 0/8	Jack Southard	Clinton	Anderson	1993	348	150 4/8	Bob Fickey	Rockwood	Cumberland	1988
289	152 0/8	Rick Acosta	Memphis	Benton	1978	349	150 4/8	Mark A. Musel	Cottontown	Davidson	1997
290	152 0/8	R.H. Pulliam	Rossville	Fayette	1994	350	150 4/8	Micheal T Elrod	Somerville	Fayette	1998
291	152 0/8	Travis Tidwell	Bon Aqua	Houston	2000	351	150 4/8	Dudley King Jr	Nashville	LBL WMA	1981
292	152 0/8	Willie Hixson	Ten Mile	Roane	1984	352	150 4/8	Wayne Yates	Antioch	Williamson	1993
293	152 0/8	Jerry L Watson	Oneida	Scott	1986	353	150 3/8	Billy D Swafford	Crossville	Cumberland	1985
294	151 7/8	Billy Hopper, Jr	Crossville	Cumberland	1989	354	150 3/8	Freddie Kennedy	Sardis	Decatur	1987
295	151 7/8	Sam Murrey	Memphis	Fayette	2001	355	150 3/8	Jeff Mcclure	Moscow	Fayette	1983
296	151 7/8	Brian Metcalf	Waverly	Houston	1989	356	150 3/8	Bill Mccreary	Jacksboro	Campbell	1992
297	151 6/8	Joe Setser	Knoxville	Catoosa WMA	1962	357	150 2/8	William Hall	Monterey	Cumberland	1990
298	151 6/8	Aaron Tegethoff	Collierville	Fayette	1983	358	150 2/8	King M. Ayers, III	Smyrna	Davidson	1992
299	151 6/8	Ronnie Pyle	Jamestown	Fentress	1985	359	150 2/8	Mike Ferguson	Oakland	Fayette	2001
300	151 6/8	Cliff Cravens	Jamestown	Fentress	1992	360	150 2/8	Milton James	Eads	Hardeman	1985

Rank	Score	Name	Hometown	Area Killed	Year
361	150 2/8	Mike Phillips	Somerville	Hardeman	1997
362	150 2/8	Marty Swindle	Reagan	Henderson	1995
363	150 2/8	R. Scott Stewart Jr	Brentwood	Humphreys	1998
364	150 2/8	Ronald P Holt	Greenbrier	Montgomery	2000
365	150 2/8	Ross Granderson	Arlington	Shelby	1996
366	150 2/8	Stanley Overstreet	Cottontown	Stewart	1974
367	150 1/8	Gene Hall	Crossville	Cumberland	1994
368	150 1/8	Joe Shelton	Joelton	Davidson	1999
369	150 1/8	William Dennis	Tenn Ridge	Houston	2000
370	150 1/8	Joel G Nolen	Erin	Houston	1987
371	150 1/8	James M Shaw	Michie	Mcnairy	1990
372	150 1/8	Brent Osborne	Dresden	Weakley	1993
373	150 1/8	Michael Isbill	Sparta	White	1998
374	150 0/8	Johnny Allen	Hilham	Clay	2001
375	150 0/8	Tom Downey	Allardt	Fentress	1986
376	150 0/8	Carl S. Sparks	Jamestown	Fentress	1993
377	149 7/8	Jason Holloway	Iron City	Lawrence	1991
378	149 7/8	Russell Smith	Knoxville	Morgan	1983
379	149 7/8	J.C. Carden	Lake City	Morgan	1981
380	149 7/8	Danny Frank	Friendsville	Pickett	1997
381	149 7/8	Bruce Reed	Helenwood	Robertson	1987
382	149 7/8	Joe Coggins	Germantown	Shelby	1982
383	149 7/8	Jerry W Holder	Quebeck	White	1984
384	149 7/8	Ryan Pearman	Franklin	Williamson	1998
385	149 6/8	James R. Brewer	Pikeville	Bledsoe	1984
386	149 6/8	Daniel Norman	Petros	Morgan	1999
387	149 5/8	Kenny Summers	Hollow Rock	Carroll	1988
388	149 5/8	Chris Williams	Lexington	Carroll	1999
389	149 5/8	Darryl R Hall	Heiskell	Catoosa WMA	1982
390	149 5/8	Chris Collingsworth	Ashland City	Cheatham	2000
391	149 5/8	Lester Blaylock	Brownsville	Haywood	1979
392	149 5/8	Kenneth Chandler	Centerville	Hickman	1974
393	149 5/8	Gary Cookston	Whitwell	Marion	1979
394	149 5/8	Stan Murrey	Ooltewah	Oak Ridge WMA	1987
395	149 5/8	Willie Osborne	Humbolt	Perry	1976
396	149 5/8	Ron Adcock	Smyrna	Rutherford	1994
397	149 5/8	Danny Spears	Kingsport	Sullivan	1994
398	149 5/8	Chris Earnest	Iron City	Wayne	2000
399	149 4/8	Eddie Deaton	Charlotte	Dickson	1985
400	149 4/8	Gary Sams	Afton	Greene	1987
401	149 4/8	David Thompson	Clarksville	Montgomery	1988
402	149 3/8	Dwayne Porterfield	White Pine	Catoosa WMA	1982
403	149 3/8	Robert Swabe, Jr	Madisonville	Oak Ridge WMA	1987
404	149 3/8	Junior Ledbetter	Livingston	Overton	1995
405	149 2/8	Mike Hendrickson	Ashland City	Davidson	1975
406	149 2/8	Chad Lane	Dickson	Dickson	1998
407	149 2/8	John Sweeton	Somerville	Fayette	1984
408	149 2/8	Johnny R. Garner	Cowan	Franklin	1992
409	149 2/8	Marty Tyler	Puryear	Henry	1994
410	149 2/8	Howard Smith	Milan	Milan Aap	1987
411	149 2/8	Kevin Harrison	Adams	Montgomery	1985
412	149 2/8	Terry Dalton	Powder Springs	Oak Ridge WMA	1987
413	149 2/8	Mark Bottom	Lebanon	Wilson	1987
414	149 1/8	Scott Kimberly	Nashville	Davidson	2001
415	149 1/8	Jeffrey Matthews	Estill Springs	Ft Campbell	1994
416	149 1/8	Billy Flowers	Centerville	Hickman	1969
417	149 1/8	Bryan Kinkel	Nashville	Humphreys	1995
418	149 1/8	Tony Pratt	Franklin	Maury	1979
419	149 1/8	Bobby C Tallent	Dayton	Rhea	1980
420	149 0/8	Bill Young	Lake City	Anderson	2000
421	149 0/8	Gene Hall	Rockwood	Cumberland	1994
422	149 0/8	William Smith	Goodlettsville	Davidson	1999
423	149 0/8	A. B. Cleming	Prospect	Giles	1980
424	149 0/8	John Rusty Farmer	Springville	Henry	2000
425	149 0/8	Donnie Marrs	Waverly	Humphreys	1985
426	148 7/8	James Zachary	Allons	Cumberland	1961
427	148 7/8	David Johnson	Estill Fork	Franklin	1986
428	148 7/8	Tommy Andrews	Soddy Daisy	Hamilton	1989
429	148 7/8	Charlie Melton	Ashland City	LBL WMA	1980
430	148 7/8	Curtis Johnson	Harrison	Tellico WMA	1962
431	148 7/8	Ronnie Roberson	Iron City	Wayne	1977
432	148 6/8	Kerry Davidson	Bon Aqua	Dickson	1988
433	148 6/8	Howard Capps	Cum'land Furnace	Ft Campbell	1987
434	148 6/8	Kenith Louden	Springville	Henry	1980
435	148 6/8	Evan Gaskin	Eva	Humphreys	2001
436	148 6/8	Jay Patterson	Lawrenceburg	Lawrence	1969
437	148 6/8	Dee Quillen	Centerville	Lewis	1964
438	148 6/8	Pat Gaines	Bells	Madison	1999
439	148 6/8	James Kimbrell	Jamestown	Overton	1995
440	148 6/8	Frank W. Hodge	Rockwood	Putnam	1995
441	148 5/8	Vic Harrison	Elizabethton	Carter	1986
442	148 5/8	Anthony Anderson	Grimsley	Fentress	1987
443	148 5/8	Wesley Short		Hardin	2000
444	148 5/8	Jason Todd Chandler	Kenton	Obion	1990
445	148 5/8	Dallas Clifton	Rockwood	Roane	1987
446	148 5/8	Ricky Booth	Dover	Stewart	1990
447	148 4/8	Johnny W Tucker	Huntington	Carroll	1978
448	148 4/8	Tim Mcdonald	Livingston	Clay	2000
449	148 4/8	Wilson Christy	Cum'land Furnace	Ft Campbell	2000
450	148 4/8	Mark Duval	Greeneville	Hawkins	1986
451	148 4/8	Tim A. Byrd	Dover	Stewart	1991
452	148 3/8	J. C. Myers	Jackson	Fall Ck Falls	1954
453	148 3/8	Phillip Ledbetter	Lynchburg	Franklin	2001
454	148 3/8	Nelson Wallace	Dover	Ft Campbell	1979
455	148 3/8	Jerry Dean Holt	Sneedville	Hawkins	1989
456	148 3/8	Darius Hastings	Mansfield	Henry	1996
457	148 3/8	Ron Alvarez	Clarksville	Montgomery	1999
458	148 3/8	William D. Henson	Clarksville	Montgomery	1988
459	148 3/8	Steve Nelson	Clarksville	Montgomery	1999
460	148 3/8	Eddie Hamby	Robbins	Putnam	1996
461	148 3/8	Wesley Wilbur	Greenbrier	Robertson	1989
462	148 3/8	Carneal Walden	Antioch	Williamson	1991
463	148 3/8	Danny Decker	Fairview	Williamson	1973
464	148 2/8	William L. Smart	Bath Springs	Decatur	1984
465	148 2/8	Lee Hill	Collierville	Fayette	1997
466	148 2/8	William Yount	Greenbrier	Ft Campbell	1996
467	148 2/8	Ned Sullivan	Elkton	Giles	1988
468	148 2/8	Ronnie Preston	Altamont	Grundy	1986
469	148 2/8	Gerald Gregory	Stewart	Stewart	1997
470	148 2/8	Joe Robinson	Piney Flats	Sullivan	1986
471	148 1/8	Larry Hollingswort	Bruceton	Benton	1983
472	148 1/8	Randy Vanzant	Knoxville	Catoosa WMA	1999
473	148 1/8	Chris Fletcher	Paris	Henry	2000
474	148 1/8	Shane Wood	Crossville	Morgan	1993
475	148 1/8	Eric Mercer	Linden	Perry	1995
476	148 1/8	Ricky Pentecost	Springfield	Robertson	1988
477	148 1/8	Jeff Byram	Nashville	Williamson	1998
478	148 0/8	David Patty	Camden	Benton	1988
479	148 0/8	Buddie H. Conaster	Jamestown	Fentress	1989
480	148 0/8	Shannon Baugus	Savannah	Hardin	1996

Rank	Score	Name	Hometown	Area Killed	Year	Rank	Score	Name	Hometown	Area Killed	Year
481	148 0/8	Eddie Mize	Munford	Haywood	1981	541	147 0/8	Randy Butler	Collinwood	Wayne	1988
482	148 0/8	C.D. Heaton III	Memphis	Lauderdale	1997	542	146 7/8	James Songer	Dunlap	Bledsoe	1976
483	148 0/8	Danny R Page	Buchanan	LBL WMA	1993	543	146 7/8	David Brown	Clarksville	Cheatham	1984
484	148 0/8	William H Bales	Oliver Springs	Morgan	1985	544	146 7/8	Fred Nelson	Rockwood	Cumberland	1957
485	148 0/8	George Smith	Spring City	Polk	1958	545	146 7/8	David Corley	Old Hickory	Davidson	1999
486	148 0/8	Jeff Butt	Nashville	Stewart	1993	546	146 7/8	David Woodward	Huntsville	Giles	2000
487	148 0/8	George Krulik	Portland	Sumner	1987	547	146 7/8	Darrell Patterson	Waverly	Humphreys	1987
488	147 7/8	Larry Busby	Henderson	Chester	1990	548	146 7/8	Steve Lewter	Ardmore	Lincoln	1985
489	147 7/8	Eddie C Biggs	Mason	Fayette	1998	549	146 7/8	Barbara Robinson	Memphis	Shelby	1983
490	147 7/8	Paul Martin	Erin	Houston	1985	550	146 7/8	Brad Moss	Lebanon	Wilson	1999
491	147 6/8	Randall M Clarke	Cedar Grove	Carroll	1982	551	146 6/8	Keith Woody	Crossville	Cumberland	1987
492	147 6/8	Allen Fowler	White Pine	Cocke	1987	552	146 6/8	Rusty Leffew	Jamestown	Fentress	1998
493	147 6/8	Garner Bailey	Erin	Houston	1996	553	146 6/8	Lonnie Hembree	Clarksville	Montgomery	1977
494	147 6/8	George E Pickard	Gallatin	Humphreys	1973	554	146 6/8	Jim Reels	Cookeville	Putnam	1988
495	147 6/8	Tim Henderson	Ashland City	LBL WMA	1996	555	146 5/8	Eldridge Murphy	Pegram	Cheatham	1968
496	147 6/8	Tony Pratt	Franklin	Maury	1985	556	146 5/8	Pat W. Spangler	Manchester	Coffee	1987
497	147 6/8	Bryan P King	Oneida	Scott	1994	557	146 5/8	Ryan Metrick	Nashville	Davidson	1997
498	147 6/8	Harold Brock	Spencer	Van Buren	1975	558	146 5/8	Alan Danley	Charlotte	Dickson	1987
499	147 6/8	Danny Baggett	Franklin	Williamson	1998	559	146 5/8	Douglas Cobb	Jamestown	Fentress	1999
500	147 5/8	Brian A. Chester	Nashville	Cheatham	1994	560	146 5/8	Danny Wallace	Camden	LBL WMA	1988
501	147 5/8	Bryant Tapp	Somerville	Fayette	1993	561	146 5/8	Jay Redmon	Selmer	Mcnairy	1997
502	147 5/8	William Heflin	Cum'land Furnace	Ft Campbell	1980	562	146 5/8	Howard Marklin	Clarksville	Montgomery	1987
503	147 5/8	David Nance	Hermitage	Humphreys	1995	563	146 5/8	Grant Mcguire	Hornbeak	Obion	1992
504	147 5/8	Barry White	Crossville	Rhea	2000	564	146 5/8	Bill Breedlove	Gallatin	Sumner	1999
505	147 5/8	John Tramel	Lebanon	Wilson	1979	565	146 5/8	Jerry Hopson	Unicoi	Unicoi	1989
506	147 4/8	David Mcbride	Jackson	Chester	1996	566	146 5/8	Terry Lewis	Powell	Wayne	1997
507	147 4/8	Joey Whittenburg	Crossville	Cumberland	2001	567	146 5/8	Clark Taplin	Franklin	Williamson	2000
508	147 4/8	Richard Kieffer	Antioch	Davidson	1988	568	146 4/8	Daniel D Jones II	Oliver Springs	Anderson	1990
509	147 4/8	Bill Leech	Dickson	Ft Campbell	1964	569	146 4/8	Jerry Ward	Camden	Benton	1990
510	147 4/8	David Oliphant	Mcewen	Humphreys	1990	570	146 4/8	Darren Holt	Ashland City	Cheatham	1971
511	147 4/8	Donald R. Fuller	Decaturville	LBL WMA	1973	571	146 4/8	Ronnie Pyle	Jamestown	Fentress	1999
512	147 4/8	Jay Landers	Athens	Mcminn	1993	572	146 4/8	Franklin J. Bledsoe	Jamestown	Fentress	1996
513	147 4/8	Hugh C. Hall	Clarksville	Stewart	1969	573	146 4/8	Chris Deming	Hickory Valley	Hardeman	1997
514	147 4/8	Ricky Booth	Dover	Stewart	1991	574	146 4/8	Marty England	Duck River	Hickman	1995
515	147 4/8	Gregory Mangrum	Fairview	Williamson	2000	575	146 4/8	Hubert Curtis Jr.	Waverly	Humphreys	1980
516	147 4/8	Mark Cothran	Franklin	Williamson	1995	576	146 4/8	James Collins	Murfreesboro	LBL WMA	1994
517	147 3/8	David L. Alexander	Brentwood	Giles	1982	577	146 4/8	Mark Cale	Springfield	Rutherford	1996
518	147 3/8	Bobby Stewart	Middleton	Hardeman	1987	578	146 4/8	Kenny Justice	Knoxville	Scott	1984
519	147 3/8	Larry Smartt	Mcminnville	Warren	1993	579	146 4/8	Wayne Ferguson	Jacksboro	Scott	1994
520	147 2/8	Poole Hillous	Ashland City	Cheatham	1978	580	146 3/8	Mike Mcgahan	Brentwood	Eagle Ck WMA	1984
521	147 2/8	Larry Hudgins	Whites Creek	Davidson	1987	581	146 3/8	B. C. Yager Jr	Moscow	Fayette	1975
522	147 2/8	Bill Wheeler	Jamestown	Fentress	1986	582	146 3/8	Don Bell	Jackson	Madison	1973
523	147 2/8	Roger Short	Celina	Ft Campbell	1979	583	146 3/8	Leonard Embler	Columbia	Maury	1992
524	147 2/8	Lee Vanover	Humboldt	Gibson	1999	584	146 3/8	Tommy Barrett	Cookeville	Overton	1997
525	147 2/8	Jerry Whitley	Corinth	LBL WMA	1995	585	146 3/8	Neil Mathis	Dover	Stewart	1963
526	147 2/8	Bobby Baize	Lawrenceburg	Lewis	1981	586	146 3/8	Edward Wulff	Hendersonville	Sumner	1994
527	147 2/8	Bobby Arnold	Flintville	Lincoln	1982	587	146 2/8	Philip T Walker	Crossville	Bledsoe	1989
528	147 2/8	Tim Aytes	Knoxville	Morgan	1987	588	146 2/8	Jamie Moore	Alamo	Crockett	2000
529	147 2/8	Randy Ayers	Smyrna	Rutherford	1991	589	146 2/8	Delbert Ottinger	Greeneville	Greene	1989
530	147 2/8	Charles Foster	Nashville	Stewart	1977	590	146 2/8	Scott Rummel	Athens	Grundy	1989
531	147 1/8	Harley D. Swafford II	Dayton	Anderson	1996	591	146 2/8	Wayne Babb	Sardis	Hardin	1986
532	147 1/8	Philip Easterling	Memphis	Hardeman	1977	592	146 2/8	Aaron Wiggins	Halls	Haywood	1988
533	147 1/8	Douglas Overton	Paris	Henry	1979	593	146 2/8	Mike Pitts	Fayetteville	Lincoln	1976
534	147 1/8	Brent Stanford	Loretto	Lawrence	1992	594	146 2/8	Kenneth Webb	Livingston	Overton	2001
535	147 1/8	Joseph F. Neeley	Knoxville	Marshall	1986	595	146 1/8	Calvin Bell	Ashland City	Cheatham	2000
536	147 1/8	Virgil Denny	Madison	Montgomery	1975	596	146 1/8	Jason Byrd	Brownsville	Haywood	1997
537	147 1/8	Claude Cranford Jr	Hornbeak	Obion	1989	597	146 1/8	Jacky Childress	Fayetteville	Lincoln	1970
538	147 0/8	Charles S Reed	Grandview	Cumberland	1972	598	146 1/8	Bobby Bye	Pulaski	Lincoln	1976
539	147 0/8	Kenneth Hemphill	Decatur	Cumberland	1991	599	146 1/8	Bryon Divis	Fayetteville	Lincoln	1996
540	147 0/8	Mickey Brown	Greenville	Hickman	1995	600	146 1/8	Adam Roberts	Lenoir City	Morgan	1960

293

Rank	Score	Name	Hometown	Area Killed	Year
601	146 1/8	James Brooks	Knoxville	Oak Ridge WMA	1985
602	146 1/8	Bobby Baize	Lawrencence	Perry	1983
603	146 1/8	Bob Thomas	Memphis	Shelby	1915
604	146 1/8	Greg Reynolds	Stewart	Stewart	1986
605	146 1/8	Clifford E. Sullivan Jr	Rock Island	Van Buren	1995
606	146 0/8	William Smith	Goodlettsville	Davidson	1998
607	146 0/8	Mike Burkey	Joelton	Davidson	1980
608	146 0/8	Howell Moore	Somerville	Fayette	1987
609	146 0/8	Benny M Hughes	Jamestown	Fentress	1988
610	146 0/8	Bobby Shepherd	Memphis	Hardeman	1980
611	146 0/8	Jerry Clemmons	Daisy	Montgomery	1989
612	145 7/8	Brian Smith	Knoxville	Cumberland	1984
613	145 7/8	Jim Mcadams	Oakfield	Madison	1990
614	145 7/8	Dean Sewell	Santa Fe	Maury	1982
615	145 7/8	Fred Johnson	Bartlett	Mcnairy	1996
616	145 7/8	Ralph Craig	Woodlawn	Montgomery	1990
617	145 7/8	Gabe Krantz	Monterey	Overton	1993
618	145 7/8	Jerry Black	Harriman	Roane	1995
619	145 6/8	Larry Frady	Pikeville	Bledsoe	1995
620	145 6/8	Larry Draper	Hendersonville	Dickson	1987
621	145 6/8	Terry Wharton	Hornsby	Hardeman	1990
622	145 6/8	David Stoever	Smyrna	Humphreys	1975
623	145 6/8	Danny Lee Walker	Somerville	Madison	2000
624	145 5/8	Eddie Harris	Atwood	Carroll	1990
625	145 5/8	Robert Akin	Madison	Cheatham	1980
626	145 5/8	Tommy Adkisson	Brownsville	Decatur	1976
627	145 5/8	Bryant Tapp	Somerville	Fayette	1993
628	145 5/8	Ted Harvey	Jamestown	Fentress	1999
629	145 5/8	Jeff Robbins	Jamestown	Fentress	1993
630	145 5/8	Jeffery Hancock	Allardt	Fentress	1991
631	145 5/8	Chad Pickens	Albany	Ft Campbell	1990
632	145 5/8	Randy Smith	Burns	Giles	1984
633	145 5/8	Harry Day	Tn Ridge	Houston	1985
634	145 5/8	Charles Brake	Mcewen	Humphreys	1995
635	145 5/8	Evans Bohannon	Waverly	LBL WMA	1973
636	145 5/8	Tom S. Bigham III	Fayetteville	Lincoln	1974
637	145 5/8	Carl Taylor	Jasper	Marion	1996
638	145 5/8	Wayne Tramel	Bellwood	Wilson	1979
639	145 4/8	Tim Boyd	Huntingdon	Carroll	1998
640	145 4/8	George A Hazel	Clarksville	Ft Campbell	1984
641	145 4/8	William E. Henson	New John'ville	Humphreys	1982
642	145 4/8	Bobby Pate	Mckenzie	LBL WMA	1978
643	145 4/8	John I Marks Jr	Huntsville	Lincoln	1989
644	145 4/8	Jimmy D. Sheperd	Woodlawn	Montgomery	1972
645	145 4/8	Tony Cross	Oliver Springs	Morgan	1986
646	145 4/8	Mike Oliver	Union City	Obion	1980
647	145 4/8	Craig Lynch	Fosterville	Rutherford	1993
648	145 3/8	Donny Shelby	Duff	Campbell	1998
649	145 3/8	Rusty Leffew	Jamestown	Fentress	1999
650	145 3/8	Marshall Thornton	Ardmore	Giles	1979
651	145 3/8	James Matheny	Paris	Henry	1989
652	145 3/8	James Smith	Ethridge	Lawrence	1985
653	145 3/8	Ron Widner	Knoxville	Montgomery	1984
654	145 3/8	Kenneth Evans	Clarksville	Montgomery	1993
655	145 3/8	Ray Ryan	Oliver Springs	Morgan	1984
656	145 3/8	Mike Baker	Strawberry Plain	Scott	1982
657	145 3/8	Doug Fields	Mt. Juliet	Williamson	1989
658	145 3/8	Thomas Allen	Trezevant	Carroll	1989
659	145 2/8	Jeff Brown	Maynardville	Claiborne	1995
660	145 2/8	Randy Vanzant	Knoxville	Cumberland	1999
661	145 2/8	Roy Goodwin	Ashland City	Dickson	1995
662	145 2/8	Richard N Goddard	Somerville	Fayette	1984
663	145 2/8	Sonny Thompson	Arlington	Fayette	1989
664	145 2/8	Clay Mills	Erin	Houston	1998
665	145 2/8	Paul Reynolds	Ripley	Lauderdale	1999
666	145 2/8	W W Crawford	Gray	Washington	1972
667	145 1/8	Danny Hudson	Big Sandy	Benton	1989
668	145 1/8	Byron Poss	Smithville	Dekalb	1983
669	145 1/8	Ralph Myers	Somerville	Fayette	1986
670	145 1/8	Gabe Krantz	Livingston	LBL WMA	1997
671	145 1/8	Oscar Cross	Ducktown	Polk	1990
672	145 1/8	Greg Reynolds	Stewart	Stewart	1971
673	145 1/8	Hershel Blaylock	Sparta	White	1975
674	145 0/8	Anthony Spradlin	Knoxville	Campbell	1991
675	145 0/8	Max Boone	Arlington	Fayette	1999
676	145 0/8	George Blevins	Jasper	Van Buren	1990
677	145 0/8	Ricky Simons	Mc Minnville	Warren	1997
678	144 7/8	Larry E Frazier	New John'ville	Benton	1981
679	144 7/8	Gary Cannon	Rossville	Fayette	1996
680	144 7/8	Matthew Tice	Bristol	Hickman	1997
681	144 7/8	William M Barrett	Antioch	Humphreys	1989
682	144 7/8	Ava Lorene Hinson	Greenbrier	LBL WMA	1978
683	144 7/8	Jason Robinson	Decaturville	Rutherford	2001
684	144 7/8	Lance Belcher	Madisonville	Tellico Lake	1989
685	144 7/8	Bobby H Garren	Tellico Plains	Tellico WMA	1973
686	144 7/8	Michael Angel	Killen	Wayne	1989
687	144 7/8	Richard Kephart	Collinwood	Wayne	1994
688	144 7/8	Scott Saunders	Lebanon	Wilson	1994
689	144 6/8	Ed Tubbs	Parsons	Carroll	1984
690	144 6/8	Bill Collins	Oak Ridge	Cumberland	1983
691	144 6/8	A.Vanlandingham	Crossville	Cumberland	1990
692	144 6/8	Mike Clenney	Reagan	Henderson	2001
693	144 6/8	Jim Kilpatrick	Lobelville	Hickman	1979
694	144 6/8	James V. Brantley	Knoxville	LBL WMA	1987
695	144 6/8	Alan Perryman	Chapel Hill	Marshall	1987
696	144 6/8	Denise Snider	Vonore	P Cooper WMA	1987
697	144 6/8	Randy Dorris	Springfield	Robertson	1986
698	144 6/8	John Effler	Maynardville	Scott	1986
699	144 6/8	Billy Shockley	Spencer	Van Buren	1985
700	144 5/8	Drew Davis	Crossville	Cumberland	1992
701	144 5/8	Ronnie Crabtree	Pall Mall	Fentress	1991
702	144 5/8	Sam Chaffin	Hendersonville	Ft Campbell	1986
703	144 5/8	Charles Daniel	Pulaski	Giles	1972
704	144 5/8	Jimmy Brakeen	Centerville	Lewis	1990
705	144 5/8	Achie Roach	Celina	Monroe	2000
706	144 5/8	Oneil Gray	Athens	Oak Ridge WMA	1985
707	144 5/8	Tommy Aaron	Byrdstown	Pickett	1985
708	144 5/8	Bruce W. Tripp	Madison	Robertson	1992
709	144 5/8	Bruce Terry	Helenwood	Scott	1994
710	144 4/8	Jeffery Burress	Alamo	Crockett	1999
711	144 4/8	Lynn Ayers	Mcminnville	Dekalb	1986
712	144 4/8	Lee Gault	Fayetteville	Lincoln	1995
713	144 4/8	Johnny Eastep	Mt Pleasant	Maury	1978
714	144 4/8	Dwight Spicer	Clarksville	Montgomery	1967
715	144 4/8	Mickey Bush	Murfreesboro	Rutherford	1987
716	144 3/8	Fred Foster	Knoxville	Catoosa WMA	1956
717	144 3/8	Gary Coffey	Rockwood	Cumberland	1998
718	144 3/8	Robert Spurgeon	Erin	Ft Campbell	1977
719	144 3/8	James Lovelady	Erin	Humphreys	1989
720	144 3/8	Danny Scott	Tiptonville	Lake	1982
721	144 3/8	Kevin Alderson	Sante Fe	Maury	1995
722	144 3/8	Anthony Hopkins	Guys	Mcnairy	1989

Tennessee Deer Registry - 2002
TYPICAL GUN ENTRIES

Rank	Score	Name	Hometown	Area Killed	Year	Rank	Score	Name	Hometown	Area Killed	Year
723	144 3/8	Richard Suiter Jr	Clarksville	Montgomery	1989	784	143 3/8	Tommy Crane	Paris	Henry	1994
724	144 3/8	Virgil Lyle	Knoxville	Morgan	1973	785	143 3/8	Phillip Warfield	Mc Ewen	Humphreys	1994
725	144 3/8	Kelly Sneed	Portland	Robertson	1982	786	143 3/8	Landon Dunn	Southside	Montgomery	1978
726	144 3/8	James V. Lackey	Nashville	Williamson	1996	787	143 3/8	Harold Partin	Tullahoma	Moore	1993
727	144 2/8	Randy Foster	Petros	Anderson	1994	788	143 3/8	Jimmy Holmes	Scotts Hill	Perry	2001
728	144 2/8	Eddie Stinnet	Ft Oglethorpe	Coffee	1995	789	143 3/8	Michael Miller	Sparta	White	1998
729	144 2/8	William Longmire	Bradford	Gibson	1991	790	143 2/8	J.R. Snapes	Midway	Greene	1997
730	144 2/8	Glynn Newell	Summertown	Giles	1978	791	143 2/8	Albert Scott	Tiptonville	Lake	1986
731	144 1/8	Tommy Day	Somerville	Fayette	1996	792	143 2/8	Ed Melton	Crossville	LBL WMA	1984
732	144 1/8	Adam Ramsey	Clarkrange	Fentress	1998	793	143 2/8	William B. Hopkins	Bethel Springs	Mcnairy	1994
733	144 1/8	Jackie Welch	Collerville	Shelby	1999	794	143 2/8	David Goad	Murfreesboro	Nb Forrest Wm	1984
734	144 1/8	Kenneth Chapman	Nashville	Wayne	1981	795	143 2/8	Jim Elam	Memphis	Shelby	1997
735	144 0/8	David Stoltzfus	Bethel Springs	Chester	1994	796	143 2/8	Eddie Walls	Tellico Plains	Tellico WMA	1983
736	144 0/8	Jimmy Stanford	Collierville	Fayette	1983	797	143 2/8	Steve Smith	Mt. Juliet	Wilson	1992
737	144 0/8	Paul Marlar	Brownsville	Haywood	1966	798	143 1/8	Wayne Simons	Shelbyville	Bedford	1987
738	144 0/8	Odell Frazier	New John'ville	LBL WMA	1974	799	143 1/8	Clarence Smith	Charleston	Bradley	1985
739	144 0/8	Billy G. Barnes	Maynardville	Morgan	1982	800	143 1/8	Randall Pierce	Lafollette	Campbell	1984
740	144 0/8	Jeff Huff	Union City	Obion	1988	801	143 1/8	Ralph Alexander	Reagan	Chester	1992
741	144 0/8	Jerry Carson	Helenwood	Scott	1993	802	143 1/8	Mark Kirby	Morrison	Coffee	1988
742	144 0/8	Andy Kent	Indian Mound	Stewart	1990	803	143 1/8	T. Vanlandingham	Crossville	Cumberland	1990
743	144 0/8	Wayne Ketchum	Pegram	Williamson	1994	804	143 1/8	King M. Ayers, III	Smyrna	Davidson	1993
744	143 7/8	Charles Hassell	New Johnsnville	Dickson	1986	805	143 1/8	James R Chandler	Humbolt	Ft Campbell	1975
745	143 7/8	Cliff Robinson	Memphis	Fayette	1984	806	143 1/8	Randy Hinson	Erin	Houston	1984
746	143 7/8	Carlton Staples	Castilian Spgs	Franklin	1992	807	143 1/8	Dwight Davis	Waverly	Humphreys	1988
747	143 7/8	Donnie Stover	Gallatin	Humphreys	1998	808	143 1/8	Sam Keen	Ramer	Mcnairy	1998
748	143 7/8	Audrey Scott	Savannah	Laurel Hill WMA	1972	809	143 1/8	Ken Whitehead	Finger	Mcnairy	1999
749	143 7/8	Robin Street	Hollenwald	Lawrence	2001	810	143 1/8	Humphrey C Renner	Calhoun	Meigs	1967
750	143 7/8	Bill Ramey	Linden	Lewis	1967	811	143 1/8	Ed Melton	Crossville	Morgan	1981
751	143 7/8	Darryl Lynn		Maury	1995	812	143 1/8	Mike Strube	Nashville	Perry	1988
752	143 6/8	Robert Orme	Crossville	Cumberland	1990	813	143 1/8	Nick Tally	Clifton	Wayne	1990
753	143 6/8	J. A. Carrington	Parsons	Decatur	1975	814	143 1/8	Paul Reeves	Sparta	White	1990
754	143 6/8	Danny Parchman	Mcewen	Dickson	1998	815	143 0/8	Dale Ervin	Bolivar	Hardeman	1985
755	143 6/8	Billy J. Wright	Memphis	Fayette	1982	816	143 0/8	Eddie Vandyke	Puryear	Henry	2000
756	143 6/8	Barbara Coleman	Paris	Henry	1990	817	143 0/8	Airon Lamb	Elora	Lincoln	1987
757	143 6/8	Donald C Binkley	Clarksville	Montgomery	1988	818	143 0/8	Ricky Sneed	Orlinda	Robertson	1990
758	143 6/8	Joe Armes	Lancing	Morgan	2001	819	143 0/8	Don Rippy	Goodletsville	Sumner	1999
759	143 6/8	Steve Rushing	Pinson	Stewart	2001	820	143 0/8	Brian Cunningham	Sparta	Van Buren	1993
760	143 6/8	Joe Brown	Gallatin	Stewart	1997	821	142 7/8	Ronnie Cathey	White Bluff	Dickson	1989
761	143 6/8	William T. Byrd	Mt Juliet	Williamson	1991	822	142 7/8	Ronald Brown	Savannah	Hardin	1998
762	143 5/8	Joe Townsend	Kingston Spring	Cheatham	2000	823	142 7/8	Robert Shelton	Trenton	Milan Aap	1987
763	143 5/8	Paul Graham	Decherd	Franklin	1983	824	142 7/8	Gary M Roe	Cordova	Shelby	1982
764	143 5/8	Robin Smartt	Beersheba Sprgs	Grundy	1998	825	142 7/8	Damon Allen	Clifton	Wayne	1989
765	143 5/8	Rodney Hosea	Savannah	Hardin	2000	826	142 7/8	Kerry Stringer	Fairview	Williamson	1992
766	143 5/8	James Howard	Brownsville	Haywood	1998	827	142 6/8	Brad Pendegrass	Pikeville	Bledsoe	1994
767	143 5/8	Billy A. Tummins	Mcewen	Humphreys	1990	828	142 6/8	Maynard Wallace	Lafollette	Campbell	1997
768	143 5/8	Glenn Ledbetter	Alpine	Overton	1982	829	142 6/8	T W Meadows	Ashland City	Cheatham	1989
769	143 5/8	Harvey Benton	Rogersville	Polk	1986	830	142 6/8	Ronald Carney	Joelton	Cheatham	1996
770	143 5/8	Rudy Slaven	Jamestown	Scott	1984	831	142 6/8	Danny Jobe	Cornith	Chester	1999
771	143 5/8	Ronnie Burleson	Collinwood	Wayne	1992	832	142 6/8	Robert Erwin Jr.	Pulaski	Giles	1982
772	143 4/8	William G. Wilson	Crossville	Cumberland	1978	833	142 6/8	Tommy L. Ferrell	Mcminnville	Grundy	1989
773	143 4/8	Phil Robertson	Tullahoma	Franklin	1987	834	142 6/8	Willis Mcclain	New Market	Hancock	1986
774	143 4/8	Jeff Bailey	Jackson	LBL WMA	1978	835	142 6/8	Carl Simmons	Centerville	Hickman	1973
775	143 4/8	Brian Winford	Cookeville	LBL WMA	1990	836	142 6/8	Emment Denton	Clarksville	Montgomery	1976
776	143 4/8	Bobby Bean	Hohenwald	Lewis	1993	837	142 6/8	Jeff Sanders	Huntland	Moore	1997
777	143 4/8	Danny Henson	Mt Pleasant	Maury	1989	838	142 6/8	Ricky Haynes	Nashville	Perry	1990
778	143 4/8	James Moore	Adamsville	Mcnairy	1994	839	142 6/8	Mark Phillips	Goodlettsville	Robertson	1984
779	143 4/8	Lannie Dedrick	Lobelville	Perry	1995	840	142 6/8	Jimmy Barnes	Rock Island	Warren	1985
780	143 4/8	Jim Tippitt	Goodlettsville	Stewart	1990	841	142 5/8	Randy Butts	Gallatin	Cheatham WMA	1973
781	143 4/8	Dwain Cooper	Cottage Grove	Weakley	1997	842	142 5/8	Mason Fischer	Manchester	Coffee	1979
782	143 3/8	William B Lewis	Crossville	Cumberland	1990	843	142 5/8	David Scott	Savannah	Hardin	2001
783	143 3/8	Gary R. Trotter	Cum'land Furnace	Dickson	1987	844	142 5/8	John Wallace	Mcewen	Hickman	1989

Rank	Score	Name	Hometown	Area Killed	Year	Rank	Score	Name	Hometown	Area Killed	Year
845	142 5/8	James Hassett	Nashville	Stewart	1998	906	141 6/8	Larry Fults	Rock Island	Warren	1993
846	142 5/8	Tandy Logan	Thompson Statio	Williamson	1997	907	141 5/8	Jackie Hill	Williston	Fayette	2000
847	142 4/8	Kevin Butts	Bell Buckle	Bedford	1986	908	141 5/8	Chris Fults	Mcminnville	Grundy	1998
848	142 4/8	Ray Nelson Boles	Celina	Clay	1993	909	141 5/8	Norman Patterson	Talbott	Hamblen	1983
849	142 4/8	Jonas P. Holloway	Spring City	Cumberland	2000	910	141 5/8	Dana Blanton	Whiteville	Hardeman	1985
850	142 4/8	Wilson Christy	Cum'land Furnace	Dickson	2000	911	141 5/8	Michael Williams	Nashville	Hickman	1994
851	142 4/8	Stan Smith	Savannah	Hardin	1978	912	141 5/8	Mark Parchman	Dickson	Humphreys	1990
852	142 4/8	Randall Wallace	Lexington	Henderson	1988	913	141 5/8	John Miller	Belfast	Marshall	1979
853	142 4/8	Curtis D. Neal	Mansfield	Henry	1994	914	141 5/8	Bill Ferguson	Jonesborough	Montgomery	1997
854	142 4/8	Eddie Scott	Waverly	Humphreys	1989	915	141 5/8	Robert Elliott	Knoxville	Stewart	1998
855	142 4/8	Eddie Yelverton	Spring Hill	Maury	1986	916	141 4/8	Taylor T Emery	Cross Plains	Cumberland	1968
856	142 4/8	Tim Ross	Michie	Mcnairy	1995	917	141 4/8	David Morrow	Hendersonville	Dickson	1989
857	142 4/8	Larry W Olinger	Dayton	Rhea	1999	918	141 4/8	Bill Cunningham	Fayetteville	Lincoln	1986
858	142 4/8	Bob Crittenden	Spencer	Van Buren	1998	919	141 4/8	Mark Flowers	Petersburg	Lincoln	1989
859	142 3/8	Kevin Yarbrough	Greenbrier	Davidson	1997	920	141 4/8	William S Smiley	Nashville	Montgomery	1984
860	142 3/8	David Smith	Savannah	Hardin	1980	921	141 4/8	Nathan Thomas	Williston	Shelby	1998
861	142 3/8	Woodrow Wilson	Oldfort	LBL WMA	1977	922	141 3/8	Sammie Heard	Daisy	Bedford	1984
862	142 3/8	Thomas Lott	Bethel Springs	Madison	2000	923	141 3/8	Cecil N. Smith	Rockwood	Catoosa WMA	1982
863	142 3/8	James L Robinson	Jackson	Madison	2001	924	141 3/8	Billy Hill	Newport	Cocke	1984
864	142 3/8	Ron Seaton	Dyersburg	Obion	1982	925	141 3/8	Earl Bowling	Rockwood	Cumberland	1978
865	142 3/8	Greg Poole	Martin	Stewart	2001	926	141 3/8	Carl King	Toone	Hardeman	2000
866	142 2/8	Rick Acosta	Memphis	Benton	1982	927	141 3/8	Johnny Ford	Kingsport	Hawkins	1987
867	142 2/8	Ricky Smith	Crab Orchard	Cumberland	1997	928	141 3/8	Richard Chunn	Munford	Haywood	1981
868	142 2/8	Dan Hicks	Charlotte	Dickson	1994	929	141 3/8	Lloyd Lemaster	Murfreesboro	Humphreys	1989
869	142 2/8	Paul Blankenship	Rossville	Fayette	1990	930	141 3/8	Polly Williams	Springhill	Maury	1992
870	142 2/8	Ronnie Pyle	Jamestown	Fentress	1992	931	141 3/8	Danny Perkins	Ramer	Mcnairy	1990
871	142 2/8	Bobby Bue	Ardmore	Giles	1985	932	141 3/8	Richard Chaffin	Cookville	Putnam	1999
872	142 2/8	Ricky Simons	Mcminnville	Grundy	1991	933	141 3/8	Larry Hancock	Oneida	Scott	1981
873	142 2/8	Bill West	Nunnelly	Hickman	1981	934	141 3/8	Jeff Quinn	Dover	Stewart	1989
874	142 2/8	Mark Collins	Smithville	Montgomery	1999	935	141 3/8	Stoney Lynn	Waynesboro	Wayne	2000
875	142 2/8	Bobby Thomas	Memphis	Wayne	1984	936	141 2/8	Dennis Cotton	Helenwood	Campbell	2001
876	142 1/8	Tommy Scott	Scotts Hill	Decatur	1989	937	141 2/8	Anthony Anderson	Grimsley	Fentress	1989
877	142 1/8	Paul Gerringer	Smithville	Dekalb	1987	938	141 2/8	James R Mayers Jr.	Saulsbury	Franklin	1984
878	142 1/8	Jerry Williams	Bon Aqua	Dickson	1993	939	141 2/8	Johnny Baggett	Belvidere	Franklin	1975
879	142 1/8	Gary Mealer	Lenoir City	Hickman	1991	940	141 2/8	Bud Stang	Savannah	Hardin	1984
880	142 1/8	Tim Polk	West Point	Lawrence	1991	941	141 2/8	Ronnie Howard	Springville	Henry	1986
881	142 1/8	Michael Staggs	Union City	Obion	1988	942	141 2/8	Ronald K. Harris	Columbia	Humphreys	2000
882	142 1/8	Roy Payne	Jonesboro	Washington	1979	943	141 2/8	John Work	Waverly	Humphreys	1985
883	142 0/8	Steve Monroe	Celina	Clay	1987	944	141 2/8	Johnny Kilburn	Waverly	Humphreys	1990
884	142 0/8	Randy Lucas	Mason	Fayette	1989	945	141 2/8	Caleb Smith Jr.	Elizabethton	Johnson	1967
885	142 0/8	Johnny Henderson	Cottage Grove	LBL WMA	1979	946	141 2/8	Paul B Searcy	Guys	Mcnairy	1990
886	142 0/8	Ronald Hatmaker	Andersonville	Morgan	1974	947	141 2/8	Steve Sublett	Morristown	Morgan	1972
887	142 0/8	John Hensley, Jr.	Chattanooga	Oak Ridge WMA	1985	948	141 2/8	Gary Bowman	Ocoee	Polk	1994
888	142 0/8	Kevin High	College Grove	Williamson	1991	949	141 2/8	James Strunk Jr.	Helenwood	Scott	1992
889	141 7/8	Larry Frady	Pikeville	Bledsoe	1994	950	141 2/8	Jackie Davis	Ooltewah	White	1979
890	141 7/8	David Mcbride	Jackson	Chester	1997	951	141 2/8	Tom Crawford	Sparta	White	1982
891	141 7/8	Ike Warner	Crossville	Cumberland	1988	952	141 1/8	Joe Ted Lynch	Camden	Benton	1998
892	141 7/8	Tony Creasy	Waynesboro	Eagle Ck WMA	1989	953	141 1/8	Franklin Tapp	Somerville	Fayette	1996
893	141 7/8	Lawrence Toone	Pulaski	Giles	1981	954	141 1/8	Keith Marcum	Bolivar	Hardeman	1994
894	141 7/8	Robert H. Wunner	Lawrenceburg	Lawrence	1986	955	141 1/8	Ricky Layne	Tracy City	Marion	1978
895	141 7/8	Jeffery Sisk	Johnson City	Oak Ridge WMA	1986	956	141 1/8	Anna Brady	Livingston	Overton	1982
896	141 7/8	Henry Reno	Harrison	Stewart	1991	957	141 1/8	Yancey Carlton	Lobeville	Perry	1992
897	141 7/8	Tim Costello	Franklin	Williamson	1990	958	141 1/8	Chester Bush	Crossville	Putnam	1989
898	141 6/8	Steve Hughes	Erin	Dickson	1982	959	141 1/8	Michael Burns	Greenbrier	Robertson	1998
899	141 6/8	Jewell Loggins	Burns	Dickson	1993	960	141 1/8	Nicholas Duncan	Clinton	Scott	1995
900	141 6/8	Jeff Slayton	Prostect	Giles	1985	961	141 1/8	Ronald Measles	Spencer	Van Buren	1993
901	141 6/8	Homer O Johnson	Sneedville	Hancock	1987	962	141 1/8	Hartford Daniels	Sparta	White	1986
902	141 6/8	James Deakins	Kingsport	Humphreys	1982	963	141 0/8	Dwayne Walker	Pikeville	Bledsoe	1986
903	141 6/8	Max Oliver	Shelbyville	Marshall	1995	964	141 0/8	Jackie Southerland	Morristown	Claiborne	2001
904	141 6/8	Kevin Harrison	Adams	Montgomery	1985	965	141 0/8	Bryan Biggers	Joelton	Davidson	2000
905	141 6/8	David Parsons	Wartburg	Morgan	1997	966	141 0/8	Wilbur Mangrum	Fairview	Dickson	1981

Rank	Score	Name	Hometown	Area Killed	Year
967	141 0/8	Bjorn Robinson	Sevierville	Fentress	1998
968	141 0/8	Tommy Reagan	Louisville	Ft Campbell	1997
969	141 0/8	Stephen Fuller	Milan	Gibson	1997
970	141 0/8	Billy Tummis	Mcewen	Humphreys	1990
971	141 0/8	Dennis Turner	Waverly	Humphreys	1995
972	141 0/8	Tom Minnis	Athens	Mcminn	1986
973	141 0/8	Tim Isbell	Michie	Mcnairy	1997
974	141 0/8	Ted Cook	Knoxville	Scott	1987
975	141 0/8	Kenny Hedrick	Helenwood	Scott	1988
976	141 0/8	Thomas Vaughan	Indian Mound	Stewart	1991
977	141 0/8	Clarence Bonner	Mcminnville	Warren	1984
978	141 0/8	Larry Fults	Morrison	Warren	1994
979	141 0/8	Ronnie Burks	Waynesboro	Wayne	1996
980	141 0/8	James A. Dunn	Brentwood	Williamson	1992
981	140 7/8	Wallace Cole	Camden	Benton	1998
982	140 7/8	Colby Gilliam	Lexington	Decatur	2000
983	140 7/8	John C Castellaw	Dyersburg	Dyer	1999
984	140 7/8	Anthony Anderson	Jarnestown	Fentress	1989
985	140 7/8	William Rogers	Dyersburg	Ft Campbell	1977
986	140 7/8	Steve Clark	Pulaski	Giles	1986
987	140 7/8	Jack Crowley	Bolivar	Hardeman	1967
988	140 7/8	Sandra Whitt	Toney	Lincoln	1984
989	140 7/8	Rodney E Ivy	Medina	Madison	1990
990	140 6/8	Curtis Marshall	Camden	Benton	1982
991	140 6/8	Garry E. Songer	Dunlap	Bledsoe	1967
992	140 6/8	Joe M Smith	Bruceton	Carroll	1974
993	140 6/8	Robert Frost		Hardeman	1975
994	140 6/8	Scott Melton	New Johnsonvill	Humphreys	1992
995	140 6/8	Travis Tidwell	Bon Aqua	Lawrence	2001
996	140 6/8	Billy Long	Lawrenceburg	Lawrence	1979
997	140 6/8	Michael Phillips	Clinton	Loudon	1987
998	140 6/8	Greg Lamberson	Mt Juliet	Montgomery	1991
999	140 6/8	Douglas Howell Jr	Dyersburg	Nb Forrest Wm	1990
1000	140 6/8	Brian Burgess	Crossville	Overton	1993
1001	140 6/8	Jeff Betcher Jr	Mcminnville	Putnam	1994
1002	140 6/8	Steven Marler	Dayton	Rhea	1962
1003	140 6/8	Taylor T Emery	Cross Plains	Robertson	1982
1004	140 6/8	Darrel Burke	Oneida	Scott	1972
1005	140 6/8	Mike Babb	Oneida	Scott	1984
1006	140 5/8	J.P. Johnson, Jr	Maryville	Catoosa WMA	1987
1007	140 5/8	Ralph Barnett	Decaturville	Decatur	1995
1008	140 5/8	Terry Hooper	Brownsville	Haywood	1995
1009	140 5/8	Jeffery Lindsey	Big Sandy	Henry	1995
1010	140 5/8	Joe Vaughn	Centerville	Hickman	1979
1011	140 5/8	John Warden Jr	Waverly	Humphreys	1989
1012	140 5/8	Junior Smith	Waverly	Humphreys	1990
1013	140 5/8	Ricky Booth	Dover	LBL WMA	1986
1014	140 5/8	Roy P. Holt	Clarksville	Montgomery	1994
1015	140 5/8	Robert Brown	Baxter	Putnam	1985
1016	140 5/8	Joel Jernigan	Murfreesboro	Rutherford	1988
1017	140 5/8	Timmy Keatts	Indian Mound	Stewart	1990
1018	140 5/8	David M. Arms	Dover	Stewart	1990
1019	140 5/8	Tommy Hutson	Whitehouse	Sumner	1998
1020	140 5/8	Dwayne Finger	Mcminnville	Warren	2000
1021	140 5/8	Andy Long	Waynesboro	Wayne	1989
1022	140 5/8	Gerald Caldwell	Sharon	Weakley	1987
1023	140 4/8	Ronnie Campbell	Dyersburg	Dyer	1990
1024	140 4/8	Jerry York	Hermitage	Ft Campbell	1966
1025	140 4/8	Larry Ross	Bartlett	Hardeman	1989
1026	140 4/8	Steve Anzini	Drummonds	Haywood	1997
1027	140 4/8	Stephen Pulley		Henderson	2000
1028	140 4/8	Jim Napier, Sr	Springville	Henry	1991
1029	140 4/8	Ricky Jones	Iron City	Lawrence	1973
1030	140 4/8	Wayne Whitt	Springhill	Maury	1997
1031	140 4/8	Sam Davis	Livingston	Overton	1988
1032	140 4/8	Kyle Gentry	Maynardville	Union	1963
1033	140 3/8	Mark Stout	Decaturville	Decatur	1986
1034	140 3/8	Robert A. Dixon	Lawrenceburg	Eagle Ck WMA	1986
1035	140 3/8	Johnny Key	Williston	Fayette	2000
1036	140 3/8	Douglas	Jamestown	Fentress	1994
1037	140 3/8	David Baker	Belvidere	Franklin	1981
1038	140 3/8	W.S. Ragland Jr	Livingston	Jackson	1962
1039	140 3/8	Micky Maynor	Knoxville	Rhea	1987
1040	140 3/8	Jim Tippitt	Goodlettsville	Stewart	1994
1041	140 3/8	Bennie Briley	Savannah	Wayne	1990
1042	140 2/8	Virgil L.Andrews, Jr.	Clinton	Anderson	1985
1043	140 2/8	J. R. Mcknight	Union City	Benton	1975
1044	140 2/8	Darrell Young	Mcminnville	Cannon	1983
1045	140 2/8	Jackie Tollett	Crab Orchard	Cumberland	1985
1046	140 2/8	James Gamel	Cum'land Furnace	Dickson	1995
1047	140 2/8	Bob Wade Curtis	Ardmore	Giles	1982
1048	140 2/8	Don Hinkle	Pulaski	Giles	1985
1049	140 2/8	David Wooten	Whiteville	Hardeman	1989
1050	140 2/8	Jim Forrest	Puryear	Henry	1982
1051	140 2/8	Alden Poyner	New Johnsonvill	Humphreys	1988
1052	140 2/8	Jeff Smithson	Culleoka	Maury	1995
1053	140 2/8	Molton Sanders	Holladay	Montgomery	1980
1054	140 2/8	Thomas R Hughes	Hernado	Shelby	1999
1055	140 2/8	Tim Wanamaker	Mcminnville	Warren	1991
1056	140 2/8	Buford Fisher	Fairview	Williamson	1998
1057	140 2/8	Tommy Payne	Lebanon	Wilson	1984
1058	140 1/8	Dennis Beecham	Lexington	Carroll	1985
1059	140 1/8	Kevin Garrett	Clarkrange	Fentress	1995
1060	140 1/8	James L. Syler	Huntland	Franklin	1978
1061	140 1/8	Tony Young	Talbot	Ft Campbell	1996
1062	140 1/8	Marvin Mathews	Rogersville	Hawkins	1989
1063	140 1/8	Dale Moser	Jackson	Henderson	1999
1064	140 1/8	Ernie Crick	Unionville	Marshall	1980
1065	140 1/8	Alan Perryman	Chapel Hill	Marshall	1980
1066	140 1/8	Vam Carter	Walnut	Mcnairy	1966
1067	140 1/8	Walter W. Carlen	Cookeville	Putnam	2000
1068	140 1/8	Sammy Terry	Helenwood	Scott	1983
1069	140 1/8	Chris Diehl	Knoxville	Stewart	1995
1070	140 1/8	Mark Smith	Decaturville	Tennessee Nwr	1999
1071	140 1/8	Frank Perritt	Nashville	Williamson	1999
1072	140 1/8	Rich Scott	Franklin	Williamson	1995
1073	140 0/8	Bobby Hollingswrth	Bruceton	Benton	1988
1074	140 0/8	Randy Lessenberry	Mckenzie	Carroll	1985
1075	140 0/8	Keith Frazier	Crossville	Cumberland	1988
1076	140 0/8	David Clendenin	Paris	Henry	2000
1077	140 0/8	Eddie Lane		Jackson	1993
1078	140 0/8	Lynn K. Frye	Culleoka	Marshall	1977
1079	140 0/8	Troy Gibson	Franklin	Marshall	1984
1080	140 0/8	Ray Whitaker	Lavergne	Marshall	1991
1081	140 0/8	Ronnie Mulder	Selmer	Mcnairy	1995
1082	140 0/8	Kenny Louden	Springville	Montgomery	1996
1083	140 0/8	Jason Roberts	Dayton	Rhea	1984
1084	140 0/8	David Irby	West Memphis	Shelby	1994
1085	140 0/8	Patrick Woodside	Smithville	Stewart	1995
1086	140 0/8	Wayne Kress	Doyle	Van Buren	1965
1087	140 0/8	Floyd T Cunningham	Sparta	White	1994

Tennessee Whitetails

NON-TYPICAL BOW ENTRIES

Rank	Score	Name	Hometown	Area Killed	Year		Rank	Score	Name	Hometown	Area Killed	Year
1	191 2/8	Skip Coppinger	Rockford	Blount	1994		13	153 6/8	Terry Bowles	Woodlawn	Stewart	1990
2	186 6/8	Mark Phillips	Kingsport	Holston Aap	1983		12	153 2/8	Adrien Boudoin	Clarksville	Montgomery	1990
3	176 6/8	Charles Brewster Sr	Madisonville	Loudon	2001		14	149 7/8	Vernon Jr Spicer	Nashville	Williamson	1998
4	176 6/8	Charles Brewster Sr	Madisonville	Loudon	2001		15	148 6/8	Marlin Perry	Ashland City	Dickson	2000
6	171 6/8	Dennis Morris	Heidrick	Montgomery	1991		16	147 1/8	Jeffrey Hightower	Harrison	Dickson	1999
5	171 0/8	Steven Layne	Manchester	Franklin	1981		18	145 4/8	Terry Miller	Jacksboro	Oak Ridge WMA	1986
7	170 6/8	Michael R Castle II	Whitwell	Bledsoe	1995		17	145 3/8	Mark Sircy	Madisonville	Anderson	1989
8	160 7/8	Rodney Maynard	Mcminnville	Oak Ridge WMA	1986		19	144 7/8	Timothy Calhoun	Kingsport	Holston Aap	1987
9	156 0/8	Will Jones	Franklin	Davidson	1999		20	144 4/8	Christy Wilson	Cum'land Furnace	Montgomery	1999
11	154 6/8	Marvin Stewart	Madison	Williamson	1998		21	142 4/8	Darryl Chapman	Jacksboro	Oak Ridge WMA	1990
10	154 2/8	Ron Widner	Knoxville	Stewart	1974							

NON-TYPICAL GUN ENTRIES

Rank	Score	Name	Hometown	Area Killed	Year		Rank	Score	Name	Hometown	Area Killed	Year
1	244 3/8	David K. Wachtel	Nashville	Sumner	2000		44	181 1/8	Kim Hall	Maury City	Haywood	1991
2	232 7/8	Justin Samples	Jackson	Haywood	2001		42	181 1/8	Bobby Grishom	Mt. Juliet	Ft Campbell	1976
3	223 0/8	Luther Fuller	Kingsport	Hawkins	1984		45	180 4/8	Melvin L. Nichols	Holladay	Ft Campbell	1978
4	214 2/8	Ronnie Jr Perry	Brydstown	Pickett	2001		46	180 4/8	Donald Ragland	Livingston	Lbl WMA	1974
5	208 2/8	Duane Hodges	Spencer	Van Buren	1994		48	179 7/8	Mark Hulse	Castallian Spgs	Ft Campbell	1994
7	207 3/8	Todd James	Clarksville	Montgomery	1997		49	179 6/8	Jason Delph	Sneedville	Hancock	1995
6	207 1/8	Mike Davis	Adams	Montgomery	2000		47	179 5/8	Jim Bale	Goodlettesville	Ft Campbell	2000
8	204 5/8	Terry Crosby	Kingston	Catoosa WMA	1956		50	179 4/8	Stanley Redmon	Rockwood	Morgan	1973
9	203 2/8	James Cobb	Jackson	Reelfoot Nwr	1988		53	178 5/8	Stephen Umhoefer	Jackson	Madison	1995
10	198 3/8	Clarence Mcelhaney	Crossville	Ft Campbell	1978		55	178 5/8	Mark Mosley	Leoma	Wayne	1997
12	197 6/8	Elmer Payne	Jonesboro	Washington	1972		54	178 4/8	Gregg Mitchell	Memphis	Obion	1998
11	197 0/8	Charles A. Ford	Seymour	Catoosa WMA	1956		52	178 2/8	Jimmy Patterson	Waverly	Humphreys	1980
13	196 0/8	Bradley S. Koeppel	Germantown	Mcnairy	1993		56	178 2/8	J P Jones	College Grove	Williamson	1977
14	195 1/8	Chris Hagan	Lawrenceburg	Maury	2002		51	178 1/8	Bobby Mc Earl	Henderson	Chester	1999
15	192 6/8	Mickey Bush	Murfreesboro	Grundy	1988		57	177 3/8	Bruce Fox	Knoxville	Anderson	1996
16	192 2/8	John Teeter	Clarksville	Montgomery	1998		59	177 2/8	Jamie Cantrell	Nolensville	Williamson	1983
17	190 4/8	James Metcalf	Eagan	Campbell	1992		58	177 1/8	John Markle	Arlington	Fayette	1978
18	190 1/8	Ted Harvey	Jamestown	Fentress	2000		63	176 7/8	Kenny Ambrose	Clinton	Hickman	1987
21	189 7/8	Bobby Sullins, Jr	Millington	Hardin	1995		64	176 7/8	Harrison Walling	Pikeville	Van Buren	2001
19	189 6/8	Eddie Medlin	Camden	Benton	1989		60	176 5/8	Sam Ward	Jacksboro	Campbell	1989
22	189 5/8	Eddie Dean Smith	Lynchburg	Moore	1986		61	176 3/8	J. C. Bradford	Winchester	Fall Ck Falls	1955
20	189 0/8	Boyd Arthur	Germantown	Fayette	2000		62	176 3/8	Thomas T. Smith	Jamestown	Fentress	1997
23	188 6/8	William Crawford	Ripley	Shelby	1997		65	175 7/8	Tim Underwood	Woodbury	Cannon	1991
24	187 1/8	Patrick Anderson	Gallatin	Rutherford	1983		67	175 6/8	Rick Grabe	Dyersburg	Dyer	1992
25	186 7/8	William Powers	Sumerville	Fayette	1999		71	175 6/8	Danny Phillips	Clinton	Henderson	1998
27	186 6/8	Barry Toomey	Athens	Meigs	1994		72	175 6/8	H. Earl Mealer Jr.	Puryear	Henry	1978
28	186 2/8	A. T. Bayless	Morristown	Morgan	1958		68	175 4/8	Mark Stephens	Jamestown	Fentress	1996
26	186 1/8	Earl Haynes	Chapel Hill	Marshall	1975		69	175 4/8	William Shelby	Collierville	Hardeman	1998
32	185 5/8	Frank Jr Hutchison	Hornbeak	Obion	1979		70	175 3/8	David Willis	Saltillo	Hardin	1994
35	185 4/8	Joe Sullivan	Spencer	Van Buren	1998		73	175 2/8	Danny Whitt	Toney	Lincoln	1977
33	185 4/8	Gregory Smith	Union City	Obion	1999		66	175 0/8	Daniel Conatser	Ashland City	Cheatham	1991
29	185 4/8	Crook Jeffrey	Arlington	Fayette	2000		74	173 3/8	Ray Herrell	Southside	Montgomery	1986
31	185 2/8	Bobby Baggett	Humbolt	Haywood	1980		75	173 0/8	Jason English	Crossville	White	1995
34	185 1/8	Galyn Cross	Clarksville	Stewart	1991		76	172 0/8	Steve Cook	Brighton	Tipton	2000
30	185 1/8	Bill Thompson	Oneida	Fentress	1999		77	171 4/8	Gene DeFoor	Mason	Fayette	2000
36	184 6/8	Willie D Hallum	Goodlettsville	Davidson	2001		79	171 3/8	Mickey Bush	Christiana	Rutherford	1990
37	183 2/8	Tommy Willcuti	Michie	Hardin	1999		78	171 0/8	Charles Mathis	Erin	Houston	1987
40	182 7/8	Rodney Edwards	Lobelville	Perry	2001		81	170 5/8	Nathan Mccarter	Mc Donald	Lbl WMA	1994
38	182 5/8	Robert K. Mcpeake	Parsons	Benton	1996		82	170 4/8	Mike Reed	Martin	Obion	2000
39	182 3/8	Ronnie West	Decaturville	Decatur	1996		80	170 1/8	Ronnie Frederick	Corinth	Hardeman	1985
43	181 4/8	Terry Burns	Rogersville	Hawkins	1983		83	170 0/8	Chad Brewer	Hohenwals	Perry	2001
41	181 3/8	O. B. Jr. Sorrell	Sparta	Catoosa WMA	1959		89	169 7/8	Michael Moss	Gallatin	Sumner	1990

Rank	Score	Name	Hometown	Area Killed	Year	Rank	Score	Name	Hometown	Area Killed	Year
86	169 6/8	Roger Callahan	Saulsbury	Hardeman	1999	96	167 0/8	Danny Bishop	Whitevile	Fayette	1998
85	169 4/8	David Byard	Clarksville	Ft Campbell	1987	102	166 7/8	Curtis D. Neal	Mansfeild	Henry	1995
88	169 4/8	Dewey Potts	Clarksville	Montgomery	1982	106	166 7/8	Philip Evenett	Dayton	Rhea	1995
84	169 3/8	Calvin Hillin	Memphis	Fayette	1994	99	166 6/8	William Faulkner	Humbolt	Ft Campbell	1981
87	169 0/8	Mark Rhodes	Cordova	Lauderdale	1990	103	166 4/8	Jeffery Lindsey	Big Sandy	Henry	1994
94	168 6/8	Hal Adcock	Nashville	Williamson	1995	107	166 4/8	Ricky Johnson	Cederhill	Stewart	2001
91	168 4/8	Kenny Bivens	Bells	Crockett	1999	105	166 2/8	Scott Duggan	Englewood	Mcminn	2001
90	168 3/8	Wayne Moore	Humboldt	Carroll	1994	100	166 1/8	Darren Holt	Ashland City	Ft Campbell	1986
92	168 3/8	Jackie Davis	Ooltewah	Cumberland	1972	101	166 1/8	Aaron Daniels	Woodlawn	Ft Campbell	1996
93	168 3/8	Greg Mc Askill	Cumberland City	Houston	2001	104	166 1/8	Chuck Lair	Erin	Houston	1989
98	167 6/8	Anthony Martin	Madisonville	Rhea	1991	108	165 5/8	Rodney Austin	Savannah	Hardin	1998
95	167 3/8	Hilda Bracey	Ashland City	Cheatham	2000	109	165 2/8	Jeff Stapleton	Sneedville	Stewart	1998
97	167 1/8	Jimmy Fowler	Loretta	Lawrence	1989						

Notes

CHAPTER 5

1. E.T. Seton, *Lives of Game Animals.* Vol. III, Part 1 (Garden City, NY: Doubleday, Doran and Co., Inc., 1929) 244.

2. Lowell K. Halls, *White-tailed Deer: Ecology and Management.* (Harrisburg, PA: Stackpole Books, 1984) 29

3. E.G. Bourne, ed. *Narratives of the Career of Hernando de Soto,* 2 Vols. (New York: A.S. Barnes and Co., 1904)

4. Burd S. McGinnes and John H. Reeves, Jr. "Conner's Midden," *Quarterly Bulletin: Archeological Society of Virginia* 12, (1957)

5. McGinnes and Reeves

6. Halls,

7. Halls, 42-47.

8. V.W. Crane, *The Southern Frontier, 1670-1732.* (Durham, NC: Duke University Press, 1928).

9. J.B. Trefethen, "The Return of the White-tailed Deer" *American Heritage* 21(2) (1970), 97-103.

CHAPTER 6

1. S.N. Rhoades, "Contributions to the Zoology of Tennessee," In *Proceedings of the Academy of Natural Sciences* 48 (1896), 178-205

2. A.F. Ganier, "Wildlife of Tennessee," *Journal of the Tennessee Academy of Sciences,* 3(3) (1948), 10-22.

3. E.V. Komarek and Roy Komarek, "Mammals of the Great Smoky Mountains," Bulletin, Chicago Academy of Science 5(6) (1938), 137-162.

4. T. Henry, Joe Farrar and Jack Murrey, Tennessee Wildlife Restoration Agency Unpublished report (Nashville: 1973)

5. J.D. Newsom, "History of Deer and Their Habitat in the South," In *White-tailed Deer in Southern Forest Habitat,* Proceedings of a Symposium (Nacogdoches, Texas: 1969), 1-4.

6. Jack Murrey, Personal correspondence, 1993.

7. A.J. Marsh, Tennessee Wildlife Restoration Agency unpublished report, Nashville, 1971.

8. Joe Farrar, Tennessee Wildlife Restoration Agency unpublished report, 1971.

9. A.R. Cahn, "Tennessee's White-tailed Deer," *Tennessee Wildlife Magazine,* Nashville, Vol. 1(5) (1937) 5; 25.

10. Vincent Schultz, "Status of White-Tailed Deer in Tennessee," *Journal of Tennessee Academy of Sciences* 30(1) (1955) 66-75.

11. F.J. Ruff, "The White-Tailed Deer on the Pisgah National Game Preserve" *North Carolina.* (USDA, Forest Service, Southern Region:1938).

CHAPTER 7

1. Henry P. Bridges, *The Woodmont Story* (New York: A.S. Barnes and Company, 1953) 73

2. Bridges, 85

CHAPTER 8

1. Robert G. Nichols and Clifton J. Whitehead, *Investigations Into the Effects of Dog Harassment on Relocated White-Tailed Deer*, Tennessee Wildlife Restoration Agency Report (Nashville: 1977).

2. Joe Farrar, Personal Correspondence, 1993.

3. Tennessee Wildlife Restoration Agency, *A Strategic Plan for Wildlife Management for the 1990s* (Nashville: 1989)

4. Farrar,

CHAPTER 9

1. James M. Wentworth, *Deer Habitat Relationships in the Southern Appalachians*, Tennessee Wildlife Restoration Agency Wildlife Research Report (Nashville: 1992)

CHAPTER 10

1. Phyllis K. Kennedy, Diana A. Garland and Michael L. Kennedy, *Spatial Variation in the Diet of White-Tailed Deer in Tennessee*, Tennessee Wildlife Restoration Agency Technical Report No. 91-6 (Nashville: 1991).

2. Wentworth, 62.

CHAPTER 11

1. Bruce R. Hastings and Michael R. Pelton. *Perceptions of Hunters About Deer Management in Tennessee with Emphasis on Potential Trophy Deer Programs*, Tennessee Wildlife Restoration Agency Wildlife Research Report No. 88-9 (Nashville: 1988).

CHAPTER 13

1. Tim A Snyder, *Ohio Department of Natural Resources Newsletter*, (1992), 1.

2. Halls, 249.

Bibliography

Bourne, E.G., ed. *Narratives of the Career of Hernando de Soto.* 2 Vols. New York: A.S. Barnes and Co., 1904.

Bridges, Henry P. *The Woodmont Story,* New York: A.S. Barnes and Company, 1953.

Cahn, A.R. "Tennessee's White-tailed Deer." *Tennessee Wildlife Magazine.* 1(5) (1937): 5-25.

Crane, V.W. *The Southern Frontier, 1670-1732.* Durham, NC: Duke University Press, 1928.

Farrar, Joe. Personal correspondence, 1993.

Farrar, Joe, TWRA unpublished report. 1971.

Ganier, A.F. "Wildlife of Tennessee." *Journal of the Tennessee Academy of Sciences* 3(3) (1948):10-22.

Halls, L.K. *White-tailed Deer: Ecology and Management.* Harrisburg, PA: Stackpole Books, 1984.

Hastings, Bruce R. and Michael R. Pelton. *Perceptions of Hunters About Deer Management in Tennessee with Emphasis on Potential Trophy Deer Programs.* TWRA Wildlife Research Report No. 88. Nashville, 1988.

Henry, T., Joe Farrar and Jack Murrey. TWRA unpublished report. Nashville, 1973.

Kennedy, Phyllis K., Diana A. Garland and Michael L. Kennedy. *Spatial Variation in the diet of White-Tailed Deer in Tennessee.* TWRA Technical Report No. 91. Nashville, 1991.

Komarek, E.V. and Roy Komarek. "Mammals of the Great Smoky Mountains." *Bulletin of the Chicago Academy of Science* 5(6) (1938):137-162.

Marsh, A.J. TWRA Unpublished report, Nashville, 1971.

McGinnes, Burd S. and John H. Reeves Jr. "Conner's Midden." *Quarterly Bulletin: Archeological Society of Virginia* 12(1) (1957).

Murrey, Jack, personal correspondence, 1993.

Newsom, J.D. "History of Deer and Their Habitat in the South," In *White-tailed Deer in Southern Forest Habitat,* Proceedings of a Symposium. Nacogdoches, Texas: 1969, 1-4.

Nichols, Robert G. and Clifton J.Whitehead. *Investigations Into the Effects of Dog Harassment on Relocated White-Tailed Deer.* TWRA Report, Nashville, 1977.

Rhoads, S.N., "Contributions to the Zoology of Tennessee." *Proceedings of the Academy of Natural Sciences.* 48 (1896): 178-205.

Ruff, F.J. "The White-Tailed Deer on the Pisgah National Game Preserve." In *North Carolina.* USDA, Forest Service, Southern Region. (1938)
Schultz, Vincent. "Status of White-Tailed Deer in Tennessee." Journal of Tennesse Academy of Sciences 30(1) (1955): 66-75.

Seton, E.T. *Lives of Game Animals.* Vol. III, Part 1. Garden City, NY: Doubleday, Doran & Co., Inc., 1929.

Snyder, Tim A. *Ohio Department of Natural Resources Newsletter* (1992).

TWRA, *A Strategic Plan for Wildlife Management for the 1990s.* Nashville: 1989.

Trefethen, J.B. "The Return of the White-tailed Deer." *American Heritage* 21(2) (1970): 97-103.

Wentworth, James M. *Deer Habitat Relationships in the Southern Appalachians.* TWRA Wildlife Research Report. Nashville: 1992.

Photography Credits

Paul T. Brown: *Cover;*
Stewart "Bear" Dunn: *7;*
Jay T. Langston: *13, 17, 18, 20, 27, 35, 37, 43, 45, 46, 47, 49, 50, 55, 57, 61, 63, 75, 83, 151, 160, 164, 184, 185, 186, 191, 193, 194, 196, 217, 220, 224, 229, 230, 241, 243, 259, 260, 264, 267;*
Tom Evans: *10-11, 70-71, 146-147, 155, 156, 157, 158, 183, 244, 256-257;*
TWRA: *39, 67, 73, 76, 79, 88, 91, 93, 96, 98, 107, 115, 116, 117, 118, 119, 120, 122, 127, 165, 167, 168, 188, 203, 206, 212, 214, 223, 226, 235, 253, 255;*
Duncan Dobie: *53;*
Elmer J. Schowalter: *100, 101, 103, 104;*
Dodd Clifton: *210*